Table of Contents

A Requiem For Arturo Gatti

July 16, 2007

These are the closing credits of "the Human Highlight Reel."

Forty-nine fights. Forty wins. Thirty-one knockouts. Titles in two weight classes. Nearly two dozen appearances on HBO. Four fights-of-the-year.

Countless excitement.

Arturo Gatti built his reputation on giving everything he had and never giving up, on taking punishment and then digging into his huge reservoir of heart to return fire in an attempt to pull out a miracle.

There was Gatti, twice convincing the ringside physician that he could see well enough for the fight to continue, then rising from the stool to drop Wilson Rodriguez with a body shot in the fifth and finally putting him down for the count in the sixth. There was Gatti, his head bobbing up and down from Gabe Ruelas' uppercuts, blood coming from below his left eye, ending the fight with a left hook that seemed to come out of left field. Fans flocked to his fights, where they became accustomed to seeing Gatti take far too many shots, to seeing his face swollen and the odds lengthened.

But not like this.

Not like how Gatti looked wobbling drunkenly toward his corner after six rounds of being surgically dismantled by Floyd Mayweather Jr.

When then-trainer Buddy McGirt told Gatti that he was stopping the fight, Gatti protested out of pride, asking for one more round, but he ultimately stayed on his stool, his head cradled within McGirt's arms.

1

Not like how Gatti looked in the ninth round against Carlos Baldomir, a left hook sending Gatti crumbling forward onto the canvas, from where he needed the ropes to lift himself up. The second knockdown saw Gatti fall flat on his back, and that was where he stayed, tired, trounced.

And not like how Gatti looked Saturday against Alfonso Gomez, when Gatti's feet worked but not his fists, when there would be few of those desperate bombs thrown in hopes of a comeback, when New Jersey State Athletic Control Board chief Larry Hazzard Sr. had to step up into the ring to stop the bloodletting himself. Hazzard's actions also ended the career of a local favorite, a fighter who had appeared nine straight times at Atlantic City's Boardwalk Hall and 30 times in the state.

This is the opening scene of "the Human Highlight Reel."

May 18, 2002. The Mohegan Sun casino in Uncasville, Conn. It is the ninth round of Arturo Gatti's first war with Micky Ward. The momentum has repeatedly shifted over the course of the previous eight stanzas. This round would prove no different.

Ward came out fast, dropping Gatti in the opening seconds with his trademark combination of a left hook upstairs followed by a left hook to the liver. Gatti, wincing, rose from his right knee at the count of nine, only to get chased around the ring by a Ward looking to close things out.

Ward punched himself out, however, and Gatti came back with thudding body shots, vicious left hooks and stiff right crosses. This time, it was Gatti who expended too much energy, and Ward had recovered enough to leave Gatti reeling and essentially defenseless on the

2

ropes.

HBO blow-by-blow announcer Jim Lampley called for referee Frank Cappuccino to step in and stop things, but the third man in the ring let the other two continue. Gatti, arms at his sides, stayed on his feet to finish off one of the sport's best rounds in one of the sport's best fights.

Flash back to previous years. Gatti's career is a mix of highs and lows. A rise toward junior lightweight contention and a two-year title run. Three straight losses, one to Angel Manfredy and two to Ivan Robinson. Four straight wins that led him into a fight with Oscar De La Hoya, who made Gatti's corner throw in the towel. Ten months off, followed by a stoppage of Terron Millett that began Gatti's rebirth.

The great trilogy of fights with Ward not only cemented Gatti as a true entertainer, but it also launched the final phase of his career in which he would seek to show the boxing world that he could be a legitimate contender, too.

Gatti captured a vacant belt at junior welterweight, successfully defending it twice before losing to Mayweather, a defeat that marked the beginning of the end.

For years, Gatti had struggled to make weight, ballooning in size by fight night but simultaneously increasing his tendency to swell up when punched in the face. The Mayweather loss was the last that Gatti would see of 140, a jump to welterweight giving him seven pounds of relief.

Gatti's first bout in his new division came against Thomas Damgaard, an undefeated 34-year-old who had probably squandered his prime fighting pastries in front of a faithful Danish crowd. Gatti stopped Damgaard, and he still had enough drawing power that Carlos Baldomir chose him for the first defense of the Argentine's welterweight championship.

Gatti would never win again.

At 140 and below, Gatti was often able to use advantages, either in speed or in size and strength, to overcome his other limitations. Moving up one division, though, brought him to a weight class populated by natural welterweights whose unimpressive knockout ratios didn't necessarily indicate that they would have heavier hands than expected and chins battle-tested against bigger fighters.

Gatti was too small against Baldomir, and against Gomez he would again be too small — and too scarred by a lifetime of wars inside and out of the squared circle.

With 356 days off since the Baldomir loss, Gatti's mind may have felt rejuvenated, but his body failed to agree.

Gomez countered with right hands over Gatti's jab, led with left hooks and limited Gatti's offense to 74 total punches landed out of 358 thrown, including a pitiful power punch output of 113 launched and 29 on target. In the final minute of the seventh round, Gomez sent his right paw crashing into Gatti's maw, knocking him down, splitting his lip and tearing out his heart.

Referee Randy Neumann, who had probably shown far too much respect for the battered warrior while Gomez beat Gatti from pillar to post, issued a count, but New Jersey's Hazzard stepped in, doing what so many fans and observers would unfortunately admit was far too necessary.

Gatti's long and storied career was over, the end for a fighter who was, through the years, a cult figure, a rock star, a blood-and-guts warrior, a man who represented so much of what people adore about the Sweet Science. He was neither a virtuoso boxer nor a menacing bruiser, but he was nonetheless deservingly on television screens, in feature articles, in the spotlight. He was a Rocky, an Italian Stallion, an everyman who had achieved his full potential and thereby received our approval.

This, then, is the scene leading into the closing credits of "the Human Highlight Reel."

July 14, 2007. Boardwalk Hall in Atlantic City. Gatti, bleeding through a bandage over his lip, gives one last post-fight interview to HBO.

"He was just stronger than I was," Gatti told interviewer Max Kellerman. "He's a hungry fighter, a young fighter. I did my best. I came in thinking I could outbox him, but, you know, the ring was getting smaller and smaller with a bigger man. And it just sucks that from '40 to '47, it's just a different me. I wish I could make 140 but it's impossible. So, I don't see myself continuing at 147. I want to retire. And I can't be taking this abuse no more."

Earlier in the night, Kellerman had compared Gatti to Bruce Willis' John McClane, the protagonist of the Die Hard movies. In the post-fight interview, Gatti turned to the camera and waved, clearly with another action hero in mind.

"Hasta la vista, baby."

De La Hoya-Forbes:
The Inconsequential Infomercial
May 5, 2008

Introducing the new and improved Oscar De La Hoya. Faster. More powerful. And he doesn't run out of energy at inopportune moments.

You've seen past versions of Oscar De La Hoya. You remember the undefeated junior lightweight and lightweight titlist who went on to capture championships at 140 and 147. You remember that when Oscar De La Hoya came up short against Felix Trinidad and Shane Mosley, he came back bigger and badder. He captured titles at 154 and 160, and though he didn't seem to work as well as when he first came on the market, nostalgia kept him in high demand.

Sure, there are faster, younger boxers that are closer to their primes. But watch this — put Oscar De La Hoya in with someone smaller or slower and he can look just as sharp as ever.

Jim Lampley, Larry Merchant and Emanuel Steward all agree: the new and improved Oscar De La Hoya is a praiseworthy product that belongs in every home this September, when he takes on Floyd Mayweather Jr. Just a one-time payment of $50 to $55, depending on how much we want to siphon from your wallets.

But wait, there's more! Mayweather-De La Hoya 2 includes two or three undercard bouts that will probably suffer in quality due to the expenses and attention directed toward the main event. But who cares? More than one million people will tune in. The arena will sell out. And few will take their seats until the national anthems anyway. Forget supply and demand. We make the product. You buy it.

Click.

Like most late-night infomercial offerings, Saturday's bout between Oscar De La Hoya and Steve Forbes was full of hype and hyperbole, the modus operandi of advertising, a sales job predicated on a limited perspective. The product? The Ronco Showtime Platinum Rotisserie of the Sweet Science, a colossal, lavish promotion that seems at first like a good purchase but inevitably leaves a bad taste lingering in one's mouth.

This hour-long advertising vehicle was for Mayweather-De La Hoya 2, a reminder to those 2.4 million souls that forked over $55 to see a fight that did more for the principals' savings accounts than for the unnecessary advertised principle of saving boxing. From the beginning, and despite the best intentions of one-half of the bout to make "the Golden Boy" look like fool's gold, De La Hoya-Forbes was less about De La Hoya and Forbes and more about both Mayweather and the overly appropriate nickname now used by the former "Pretty Boy Floyd" — Money.

Forbes was handpicked to be De La Hoya's opponent because he was smaller than De La Hoya, because he is a crafty boxer who had been trained by Roger Mayweather, the longtime chief second to Floyd Junior. That Forbes was undersized, that Roger Mayweather had been replaced by another Mayweather uncle, Jeff, well, none of that held any pull in the push toward September's super-fight. Forbes was there to make De La Hoya look good. He was there to help De La Hoya shake off the rust. He was there to make De La Hoya seem like less of an underdog against the man viewed by many as, pound for pound, the best in the sport.

That he even got a few minutes of face time on HBO's "Countdown to De La Hoya-Forbes" could be seen as an upset. The fight posters that initially had no mention of the former 130-pound beltholder were insulting enough. But the 30-minute infomercial in advance of the hour-long in-ring infomercial focused as much on the Mayweathers as on the May 3 match. Post-fight interviews rarely go toward the man on the losing end, but such a status quo only cemented the idea of Forbes as inconsequential, a cog in the marketing machine.

The infomercial, for all its inevitable benefit to the bottom line, can be seen as ineffective in preparing De La Hoya for Mayweather.

For all the recognition that Forbes was the B-side and a stepping-stone, he came without the sparring partner mentality, but rather as a crafty veteran looking to give his career an even bigger boost than that had come following his stint on "The Contender." In doing so, Forbes made sure De La Hoya ditched some of his ring rust, but he also erased any expectations that fighting Forbes would ready De La Hoya for what he will see in the squared circle come September.

Forbes began his career as a junior lightweight — like De La Hoya and like Mayweather. But Forbes is far more suited these days to junior welterweight. De La Hoya's height and build allow him to compete comfortably between 147 and 154. Mayweather, meanwhile, remains fast at welterweight, and he has retained enough power to keep foes honest.

Whereas Mayweather used footwork and crisp counters and leads in his first bout with De La Hoya, Forbes often opted to stand in front, allowing De La Hoya to pepper his jab and pound away with power punches to Forbes' head and body. With just nine knockouts in 33 victories, Forbes didn't have enough pop to keep De La Hoya at bay. And the extra weight on Forbes' frame slowed his punches enough that De La Hoya could more easily pick them off with his gloves.

Still, when Forbes put his punches together, his combinations landed cleanly — and with emphasis. Fighting Forbes was intended to groom De La Hoya for Mayweather, but watching De La Hoya take on Forbes may have actually done more to help Mayweather.

Mayweather knows what De La Hoya plans to do: work behind the jab, the same weapon that helped give the Golden Boy the early lead against Floyd last year, and then remain relaxed and keep consistent down the stretch. But whatever confidence De La Hoya built against Forbes can slip away once he sees that, with Mayweather, his strategy isn't working as advertised.

De La Hoya is buying that lightning will strike twice. De La Hoya, Mayweather, Golden Boy Promotions and HBO are buying that fans will once again buy in, especially with this year being the one in which De La Hoya will say goodbye. They're right. But it doesn't take a Forbes to realize that this De La Hoya is sub-prime. Buyers beware.

The Prices They Pay:
Of Warriors and Tragedies
May 12, 2008

Police chases, celebrity overdoses and reality television. We are a society fascinated with both glamour and the unvarnished truth, with outsized personalities and individual failings. We favor human drama, and we are often compelled by tragedy while largely forgetting about the underlying humanity.

At its core, the Sweet Science is neither sweet nor scientific. It is thudding jabs, cracking crosses, hooks and uppercuts intent on disorienting an opponent and delivering him into unconsciousness. It is swollen tissue, gaping cuts, welts, bruising and bleeding supplied and taken the same whether the payday is eight digits or $100 a round, whether the prize is a championship belt and a roaring ovation or an arm raised in the air in front of the few faithful gathered for preliminary action.

It is what it must be: two men, for one hour or less. The impact of all that impact stretches longer.

The most visible example is Muhammad Ali, whose Parkinson's disease is attributed to the punishment he took through decades of prizefights and sparring. His lighting of the Olympic torch in Atlanta in 1996 touched many as recognition of a personality that transcended the sport, but the attention it brought to his condition is the proverbial exception to the rule. Most other fighters are remembered solely for who they were in the ring.

Theirs are lives chronicled in scrap-books, each fight a chapter with a protagonist and his foil, rising and falling action. The canon compiles the greatest of epic warriors, men armed for battle and prepared to go out on their shields. They speak of being willing to die in the ring and fight as if that is true. Sometimes it is.

At least 1,465 boxers have died due to injuries suffered between the ropes, according to the Journal of Combative Sport, which last updated its figures in November. Those numbers include 38 since 2001, beginning with the death of Beethavean Scottland in New York and continuing through to Anis Dwi Mulya in Indonesia.

Scottland's was one of six tragedies in which veteran boxing writer and broadcaster Steve Farhood was ringside.

"The first time it happened, I was 21 or 22, and it seemed almost inconceivable that it would happen," Farhood said. "As I gained some experience, the shock value went away and a different kind of reaction began to take place, which is, I believe, a human one. Is this justifiable, watching this happen? These are lives. This is not a pitcher getting knocked out of a game in the second inning. This is not a running back spraining his knee. This is a human being — being punched to his death."

The names remain in Farhood's mind: Scottland, against George Jones; Stephan Johnson, against Paul Vaden; Willie Classen, against Wilford Scypion; Cleveland Denny, against Gaetan Hart; Fred Bowman, against Isidro Perez; and then Perez, two and a half years later, against Juan Ramon Cruz.

The images are vivid, too.

"They leave snapshots in your mind," he said. "Willie Classen was on a stretcher in the Felt Forum [in New York City]. In those days it was not state law that you had to have an ambulance on site. Because of that fight, the law was changed. They literally hailed an ambulance off

11

the street. There was Willie Classen spitting blood into the air. You don't forget a sight like that. The snapshots remain. And in a way, that's a good thing. It serves as a reminder, at least in the back of your mind."

Farhood has never watched any of those fights again: "Seeing them live is enough," he said.

Yet some watch tragedies play out again and again, be it through archival video or the expanding library of bouts available on the Internet. There are documentaries centered around Benny "Kid" Paret and his dying after a pounding at the hands of Emile Griffith, around Duk Koo Kim and the role his death played in the career of Ray Mancini. For some, there is a morbid fascination in returning to a fighter's final footsteps, footage as ingrained in the collective consciousness as the fictional finales to the stories of Sonny Corleone and Tony Montana.

Though some tragedies have led to various steps toward making the sport safer, the potential for death or permanent injury remains part of pugilism.

"There are people who are boxing apologists. I like to consider myself realistic about this subject," Farhood said. "For me, it makes the sport not only more entertaining, but it makes it a lot more beautiful because of what's at stake, because of what the fighters are risking. It's what separates boxing from the other sports. The stakes are ultimate."

It is the unfortunate truth with Kim, who took a beating and kept coming. It is the tragedy behind Leavander Johnson, who won a lightweight title on his fourth attempt and then died from his first chance defending it. It is why Diego Corrales, who died one year ago in a motorcycle accident, remains beloved: because he took the pain in order to return it. For those who lost their lives in the ring, it is heart that defines them — and heart that did them in.

Many are men who came from hardscrabble lives, who fought their ways out and went on to fight to better the realities for themselves and their families. To get paid. To get respect. And, tied into both, to get adoration and adulation from the crowd.

"Nothing turns fans on more than two guys freewheeling, punching each other back and forth," Farhood said. "The audience is living vicariously through what they're watching, and the human element is forgotten. The human element needs to be forgotten."

It needs to be forgotten for that one hour or less. Too often it remains forgotten afterward.

Thirteen years have passed since Gerald McClellan last fought. On that night in London, he sent Nigel Benn crashing through the ropes in the opening minute, and to some the fight could've been called off at that point. Yet it wasn't, and the two proceeded to brutalize each other for 10 rounds, until McClellan took a knee, dazed, feeling the effects of brain damage that would leave him unable to see, barely able to hear or walk, a shell of the man who captured two middleweight titles.

"It's been the same condition since," said Teddy Blackburn, the longtime fight photographer who has played a major role since then in making sure that people know who and how McClellan is.

"After that tragedy in England, people forgot about him," Blackburn said. "They don't even want to remember. Think of Derek Jeter. Let's say Derek Jeter got a bean ball, and he couldn't play baseball anymore and ended up in a wheelchair. Do you think Steinbrenner would just let him sit in a wheelchair in a home and not hold a benefit? Think of how many fighters give their lives and soul to the sport for 10, 12 years. Five percent make good money."

There are some who have helped McClellan and his sisters, who have cared for their brother in the years following.

"Some people have a good heart. People like Roy Jones; he's helped out Gerald more than any other boxer that I know of," Blackburn said. "But Roy won't go see him."

For virtually everyone else, McClellan and others are out of sight, out of mind. The cliché is too true in this case. But for every Leavander Johnson and Diego Corrales, whose deaths prompted outpourings of charity, there are those who wither and pass away quietly because their conditions are too painful to confront. They are prizefighters who have paid prices, who gave and took until they could no longer do either, whose sacrifices are more troubling now that the punishment has taken its toll.

Tapping Out, Giving Up or Going On
August 4, 2008

Their cuts gape and gush. Their flesh swells and bruises. Their faces become misshapen, their hands tender, their organs mashed by each successive blow. With their bodies exposed under glaring lights and high-definition cameras, boxers' injuries are made apparent from the moment they are inflicted. And while football players line up hurt and feel the consequences of each collision long after their careers have ended, the men who go to work on the gridiron are able to limp to the sideline, tape up sprains, ice down aches, inject cortisone and lay down as athletic trainers tend to their wounds.

Not so for those who go to battle in the squared circle.

Rest comes in one-minute intervals, brief breaks from three-minutes of battle. A fighter sits down on a stool, where he listens to directions that must be put into action just moments later. There are no time outs. An enswell can be applied to puffed-up skin. Gauze and pharmaceuticals can stem bleeding. But any treatment is temporary. The boxer will be hit again. Wounds can and will worsen.

The courage to stand a short distance from another man who is seeking to render one unconscious is undeniable. The commitment to continue doing so when every landed punch further breaks one's body down is questioned far too often.

Boxers face the stigma whereby quitting is equated with cowardice. Mixed-martial artists confront no such conundrum. They can tap out, a sign of submission wholly acceptable when airways are squeezed shut or bones are about to break. If escape is impossible and the end is inevitable, then injury is seen as unnecessary. Similarly, if blows rain down upon a fighter so dominated that defeat is guaranteed, there is little shame in turning one's back and giving up his neck.

Not so for those who go to battle in the squared circle. They are to fight through broken hands and dislocated shoulders, with compromised vision and while bleeding crimson, even when their opponents outclass them. Anything less is an affront to a sport where fans, promoters and those who control the money can be unforgiving.

Vitali Klitschko was derided, dubbed "Chicken Kiev" when he chose to remain on his stool with a torn rotator cuff despite being comfortably ahead against Chris Byrd with three rounds to go. Danny Williams was lauded, applauded when he dislocated his right shoulder against Mark Potter but went on to score a knockout with his left.

Arturo Gatti often battled through eyes that swelled shut, preventing him from seeing punches that were already permeating a porous defense. He still had the kind of power that could — and did — end fights dramatically. Gatti refused to call it a night in his third bout with Micky Ward after his right hand collided with Ward's hip and shattered. Instead, he sent out jabs and hooks with his left, and he soldiered through the pain when he needed a right to keep Ward honest. And when Gatti remained on his stool after six rounds of surgical dismantling from Floyd Mayweather Jr., he did so only because trainer Buddy McGirt kept him there. Gatti always would go on, never giving up.

He need not be the standard.

Israel Vazquez felt his broken nose had left him at far

too large a disadvantage against Rafael Marquez in March 2007, and he chose to stay in his corner and fight another day. Fight they did, and Vazquez would go on to beat Marquez in their two stellar sequels.

Vazquez's decision paid off. He would be remembered for the way he won rather than why he lost. Some of the unforgiving masses have refused to afford other fighters the same luxury.

Miguel Cotto's stoppage loss last month against Antonio Margarito was, in essence, a submission in a battle of attrition. He had taken the early rounds against Margarito, but he had also taken punishment along the way. Margarito's well-placed punches and constant pressure wore Cotto down, each sledgehammer shot breaking away his resistance until Cotto took a knee for a momentary respite.

Cotto got up, but he had nothing left that could change the course of the fight. He attempted to buy himself some time by spinning away from Margarito and backing up, but he was a beaten man. He kneeled down to the canvas again, and his trainer threw in the proverbial towel.

The bout need not have gone the full 12 rounds for it to be clear that Margarito had won. Cotto didn't need to take unnecessary punishment until the referee stepped in out of mercy. This fight was done. Another one will come.

Boxers cannot always rely on referees, their corners or athletic commissions to protect their health. But they can also be too honest.

Hasim Rahman told a ringside physician he could not see after clashing heads with James Toney when the two fought last month. The butt came in the third round, which saw Toney dominate the action with crisp, clean punches. Whether Rahman was looking for a way out is up for debate — tapping out based on what might happen rather than what had happened. If so, the decision nearly came back to haunt him, with ringside officials initially awarding Toney the technical knockout victory.

Zab Judah, too, told a doctor he could not see following what had been ruled a clash of heads in his welterweight title bout this past weekend against Joshua Clottey. The gash over Judah's right eyelid had actually been opened up by a Clottey uppercut. But Judah's situation differed from that of Rahman. Whereas Rahman had a wound from a head butt that came at a point in the fight where the result should have come down as a "No decision," Judah was in the ninth round of a close bout. It would go to the scorecards, and Judah was far from guaranteed the victory.

The doctor tested Judah: "How many fingers am I holding up?"

"Three," Judah said.

The physician had two fingers in the air.

With that came the end, and speculation that Judah — who had a history of losing focus as fights entered the later rounds, and who had once blatantly resorted to punching Floyd Mayweather Jr. in the groin and behind the head in the face of a clear Mayweather win — had given up.

Judah was indeed fading. He was throwing far fewer punches than in the opening stanzas, and Clottey was controlling the action. But Judah was in a fight that he needed to win, having gone years without beating a ranked welterweight.

A year before, Judah had fought through pain and pressure against Miguel Cotto in the same fashion that

Cotto would a last month against Margarito. For Judah, that loss revived a flagging career. Another one, however, would place him on the perilous edge of never contending again.

Even if the fight were done, another one wouldn't necessarily come.

If there's one thing a boxer fears, it is the end of his career. What starts as sport becomes lifestyle and livelihood, a defining routine that reaches beyond those nights under glaring lights and high-definition cameras. The stigma of failure, then, sticks with him. But to be dismissed unjustly as a quitter can leave a wound unseen on the body that will remain within, unforgiving, unforgettable.

Joe The Composer
(Roy The Challenger)
November 10, 2008

His father was a jazz musician turned boxing trainer. The son became a virtuoso who plucked from two philosophies, tuning them until they were in harmony. One is an art form, groundbreaking and soul shaking, based on fundamentals of improvisation, originality and change. The other is a sweet science, flesh thudding and bone rattling, rooted in strategy, predictability and adjustment.

Joe Calzaghe found comfort in each, crafting a style all his own, one of rhapsody, rhythm and beatings, a symphony when on key. His latest masterpiece may have been his last, a high note for a composer on the grandest stage of all.

In the boxing mecca of Madison Square Garden, Calzaghe took what could end up as his final bow, raising his gloved hands toward the rafters after landing those same fists 344 times on the face and frame of Roy Jones Jr.

Less than an hour earlier, those gloves rested on the canvas, Calzaghe hunched over and hurt just two minutes into the fight. For so long Calzaghe had been criticized for slapping with his shots rather than turning his punches over. Yet in this first round it was Jones who had landed a damaging blow with his right forearm.

That brought blood from the bridge of Calzaghe's nose and fire from his veins. Against Bernard Hopkins seven months prior, Calzaghe had recovered from a flash knockdown in the opening stanza and rallied back en route to a split-decision victory. There would be no controversy this time. Calzaghe never lost another round. Jones, emboldened by his early success, began to showboat, dipping his head forward, dropping his gloves and unleashing unorthodox flurries and counters from unexpected angles. Calzaghe, himself no stranger to grandstanding, brought his hands to his waist and rested his face within tempting proximity, occasionally keeping his forehead mere inches away from Jones' arms, pulling away only when his opponent took the bait.

Each pot-shotted. Each shoe-shined. Each danced. Jones had raised roosters at his Florida panhandle ranch. Now these two were cockfighting, heads forward, strutting, spurring each other on.

Jones was winging it for old time's sake. There he was, in the ring with the best light heavyweight in the world. Five years ago that had been him. Five years ago to the day, Jones had earned his last win over a top 175-pound fighter. On that night he had been tested in a give-and-take affair against Antonio Tarver, Jones' first fight since he'd challenged John Ruiz and became the first former middleweight to capture a heavyweight title in more than 100 years.

Six months after outpointing Tarver, Jones found himself in a rematch and in an unfamiliar position — on his back. The one-punch knockout would be the first of three straight losses, the end of an era that dated back to the previous decade.

Jones could have retired in 2004, when Glen Johnson left him unconscious. Jones could have retired in 2005, when he celebrated the moral victory of lasting the distance in a rubber match with Tarver. He continued on, though, fighting once in 2006 and once again in 2007, a fading superstar facing lesser names on smaller shows.

He won, and he won again in January when the spotlight finally returned, when the smaller, slower, rustier Felix Trinidad came back to boxing and allowed Jones to show off what remained of the speed and skills that once made him stand out.

Jones could have continued on the senior tour on which so many of his fellow aging contemporaries have embarked, the rich seeking to stay relevant. His best no longer made him better than the rest, but instead he chose to step into the role of challenger, one final test of what he had left.

In the opening rounds, Jones, 39, was competent and competitive but far from comparable to Calzaghe, who at 36 and undefeated through 45 fights was still outclassing all comers. Calzaghe dug right hooks into Jones' side, sent straight left hands into Jones' mug, brought blood flowing from over Jones' left eye and showed himself, against a man who was a legend in his own time, to be a cut above.

"I'm trying to get him," Jones said in his corner before the ninth round began. "I can't get him."

Jones couldn't get him 316 times. Of the 475 punches Jones threw, he landed just one-third, an average of just 13 a round. That output just about matched the work rate of Jones' last three fights, in which he landed 14 of 37 shots for every three minutes. In his prime years, between 1998 and 2002, Jones still threw only 39 punches per round, but he would land an average of 20, a connect percentage of better than 50 percent.

Forty-five percent of Jones' power punches landed against Calzaghe. But Calzaghe, as he has done in the past, adjusted early in the fight, ducking to his right to make many of Jones' crosses, which had landed before, miss their target. And when he wasn't elusive, he was active, hitting Jones with more punches than anyone else ever had before — 344. Calzaghe more than doubled Jones in number of shots landed, hitting him nearly 29 times a round. What Jones could still do, Calzaghe could do better. So as Jones followed Calzaghe around the ring, attempting to land, Calzaghe had little difficulty strafing the person in front of him. And when Jones went to the ropes, Calzaghe was there with a flurry, never letting him rest.

All three judges at ringside saw Calzaghe the easy victor, 118-109, each scoring the first three minutes 10-8 to Jones and then giving Calzaghe every round after.

It was a fitting coda to Calzaghe's career.

The final movements to his symphony included victories over previously undefeated titlists in Jeff Lacy and Mikkel Kessler and experienced future Hall of Fame inductees in Hopkins and Jones. He cleared out the super-middleweight division and then inserted himself into the top echelon of light heavyweights. Calzaghe mentioned retirement before this latest bout. Though he has not yet made a decision, this last win would prove a suitable swan song.

Manny Pacquiao Slays
The Golden Calf
December 8, 2008

Oscar De La Hoya's friends, those boxers and businessmen, those promoters and professionals, sat in the few ringside rows, hushed, stunned, certain that he who was once Golden would soon only be gone.

Manny Pacquiao's fans in the stands rose from their seats to their feet, aware, from a distance, that the moment was close. Expectation begot exhilaration, exclamation, a collective roar for he who would continue to be their conquering hero.

Thirty minutes of emotion gave way to 60 seconds of catharsis.

There sat De La Hoya, framed by a red corner and red ropes to match the markings on his cheeks. Above those, his eyes wandered from person to person, like a newborn in unfamiliar surroundings, glancing toward the anticipatory murmurs coming from the crowd, looking at the physician, the referee and his trainer, all speaking of that which was to be the end.

Beyond the heaving of his chest as he caught his breath, De La Hoya was motionless. Between, beyond the one-word responses, he was speechless.

He was overwhelmed. He was over.

What would have been a bell to restart the action was instead clanging that signaled the conclusion. De La Hoya rose from his stool and trudged, gloves at his side, toward the man who walked on clouds, whose hands were now raised in the air.

"You're still my idol, whatever happens," Pacquiao

said before De La Hoya left the ring, ceding the stage, the spotlight.

"No, now you're my idol," De La Hoya responded, passing the torch.

Seven-and-a-half years before, Pacquiao had traveled from the Philippines to this very arena, the MGM Grand in Las Vegas, where he made his American debut, capturing a junior-featherweight belt on the same card that De La Hoya won a junior-middleweight title by beating Javier Castillejo.

So much had changed since.

Pacquiao quickly graduated from undercards to main events, challenging and defeating the best fighters in the 126- and 130-pound divisions. He grew from a one-dimensional slugger into a well-rounded boxer-puncher. He promised excitement and was still in his prime.

De La Hoya had decelerated, no longer fighting full-time but rather presiding, between headline bouts, over his own promotional company. He would often hold out for the biggest events, hand-selecting his foes but falling short against top-flight opponents.

His diminishing abilities mattered little, for he could still parlay his past into paychecks, drawing tens of thousands of fans and hundreds of thousands of pay-per-view buys. There would always be others who deserved attention, but none who had the same box-office appeal. De La Hoya remained a revered figure. The revenue he produced left him worshipped.

Absent his replacement, the Golden Boy became a Golden Calf.

Every subsequent fight added another eight digits to his bank account. The spirit of competition may have kept De La Hoya from retirement; the money didn't hurt either.

But he was a part-time fighter whose reflexes, skills and stamina were no longer close to world class. Against those who could capitalize on his flaws, this Golden Calf was but an idle threat; he would be dead meat.

Size matters, but speed kills. Bernard Hopkins had faster hands and faster feet than Kelly Pavlik. Joe Calzaghe had quicker hands and quicker reflexes than Roy Jones. Chad Dawson had faster hands and more stamina than Antonio Tarver. All won easily.

Manny Pacquiao began his career in 1995 at 106 pounds. He was 16 at the time, and as he grew older, he grew into the 112-, 122- and 126-pound decisions. He carried enough pop in his fists at 130 to do damage to others the same size. And in his lightweight debut in June, he held a distinct advantage in speed over David Diaz.

The De La Hoya fight was to be at welterweight. Pacquiao would be bigger than ever, but he still would be faster than De La Hoya. And though the Golden Boy was of a higher class and at a higher weight class than Diaz, Pacquiao would still be able to do the same at 147 as he had at 135.

Pacquiao's movement left De La Hoya offensively impotent, kept him from getting off. Pacquiao would circle to his left, away from De La Hoya's jab and his best punch, the left hook. He darted in and out of range, pot-shotting De La Hoya with lead left hands from his southpaw stance, making him miss and then responding with effective combinations.

De La Hoya landed 32 jabs over eight rounds. As for landed power punches, he never hit double digits in a single round, going 51 of 164 for a 31 percent connect rate. On the night, De La Hoya threw a total of 402 shots, only 83 of which hit their target.

Pacquiao, meanwhile, saw that De La Hoya couldn't handle his speed, couldn't block his shots, couldn't adjust. Pacquiao's worst round was the first, when he threw 47 punches and landed 11. Even then, he went 9 for 18 with his power punches, a 50 percent connect rate that would wind up as his lowest of the night.

Pacquiao sent out jabs but rarely landed them. He didn't need to, not when he was hitting De La Hoya with 59 percent of his 333 thrown power punches, including an astonishing 32 of 47 in the fourth round and 45 of 76 in the seventh stanza.

By the end of that round, the Golden Calf resembled another hoofed animal — De La Hoya was a deer that had been caught in the headlights and was now wounded, waiting to be put out of his misery.

In the eighth, Pacquiao trapped De La Hoya on the ropes, digging into his body and then following upstairs. De La Hoya made it back to the center of the ring, but his jabs, like nearly everything else from him that night, seemed tentative. Pacquiao remained aggressive, forcing De La Hoya back to ring's edge before easing up, retreating to the middle as if he was taking pity on him.

De La Hoya threw a wide, slow shoeshine combination to Pacquiao's sides, and then tossed in a few punches up higher, few of which landed, none of which did any damage. Pacquiao clapped his gloves above his head to show he wasn't hurt, pressured De La Hoya into the blue corner and then wailed away until the bell rang.

Those who had come in support of De La Hoya sat as the Golden Boy now did, hushed, stunned, accepting that this was the end. Those there for Pacquiao stood, rising for the idol who had risen out of the Philippines, the idol who carried a country on his shoulders.

For one evening these two stars, one glowing, one now just glimmering, shared the squared circle. By the night's end only one belonged.

Klitschko vs. Rahman: Steelhammer Hits Rock, Rock Hits Bottom
December 15, 2008

The belts he wears make him king of the heavyweight division. The men he beats seem far more suited for the heavy-bag division.

With his sharp skills and pounding power, Wladimir Klitschko ascended to the throne of boxing's marquee weight class, what was once the standard-bearer of the Sweet Science.

He who vies to be king does so to rule over splendor and prosperity, to be the crown jewel, the cream of the crop, the best of the best. Alas, by no fault of his own, this king of the hill is atop a heap.

Klitschko, like his older brother and many others from former Soviet countries, came from a strong amateur system. He is 32, still close enough to his prime not to show signs of slipping. He has won 10 straight, many against the best his division has to offer, capturing two alphabet titles and recognition as the number one big man.

Many of his counterparts are aging former champions and contenders, men who have fooled themselves, thinking they still belong in a weight class that is without the depth to move on. Others are converts to combat, athletes who started in other sports, started boxing late and sought to make up with size while they still developed skill.

Not every Klitschko opponent fits into these categories. Not that it matters. All have gone down.

The latest was far from the greatest, though Hasim

29

Rahman had arguably achieved more than any who had come before.

While other Klitschko foes had captured belts and defended them successfully, Rahman, with one punch, had knocked out Lennox Lewis to become the true heavyweight champion. Of course, in an immediate rematch, Lewis, with one punch, knocked out Rahman to take said distinction back.

That jolt of reality came seven years ago.

Since then, Rahman had seesawed from winless streak to rebuilding phase to holding a title to losing it and then starting the process once again. But he tended to be heavier than he'd been at his best, and his reflexes indicated that, at best, he belonged on the fringe.

He came to this title shot as a late replacement. Klitschko's original opponent, Alexander Povetkin, suffered an injury during a training run. Rahman, now 36, wasn't expected to bring much to the match. No one imagined he'd show up with even less.

In the beginning, Rahman teetered between tentative and ineffective, confronted by the imposing presence of the man in front of him and confounded by the ability of that man in front of him to move quickly out of range. Like so many of Klitschko's recent foes, the large gap in talent was quite apparent. Rahman no longer had the ability to put pressure on Klitschko.

Instead, Rahman was in for a beating from the outset.

Klitschko thudded Rahman early with a quick and heavy jab and the occasional one-two combination. That remained Klitschko's strategy for the first five rounds, when his landed jabs totaled 17, 17, 28, 27 and 24. Each round brought connect rates of more than 50 percent.

Rahman, meanwhile, landed 2, 2, 2, 5 and 3, with his

highest connect rate coming in the fourth round, when he threw 32, of which 27 missed. His power punch statistics were no better — he sent out 56 on the night, only 15 of which hit their target. None were crisp or clean enough to test Klitschko's chin.

Rahman's fate appeared inevitable from the third round forward, if not earlier. In that round, he retreated to the ropes, covering up in what was either a futile attempt to rope-a-dope or a foolhardy attempt to rest. Klitschko stood within range, jabbing at what amounted to a heavy bag with unsteady legs. Rahman's defense throughout the night had consisted of gloves on his temples, the proverbial earmuffs, unmoving arms that never parried a punch. Klitschko split that so-called guard with ease, landing a fight-high 28 jabs, never needing to kick into a higher gear.

While Klitschko pounded down what little resistance Rahman brought, he found himself safe to open up his offensive arsenal. Jabs were followed with left hooks and right crosses, combinations that brought about a knockdown and would soon bring the bout to an end.

In the sixth stanza, Klitschko put out more power punches than jabs, landing 14 of 41. He also tagged Rahman with 14 of 27 jabs. In contrast, Rahman threw 16 punches, 15 of which were jabs. Only one was credited as a scoring blow.

Rahman never threw another power shot. In the seventh and final round, all five jabs either whiffed or were blocked. Klitschko needed just nine jabs and nine power punches, landing more than half of each, shaking Rahman with many and forcing referee Tony Weeks to end the bludgeoning.

Dr. Steelhammer hit the Rock for some 19 minutes, and

he couldn't help but to look sharp while doing so. The only thing the Rock hit was the bottom.

Klitschko's beatings have earned him belts and made him king. If only he didn't have to share a ring with jokers.

What UFC Fighters Have Learned From Boxing

February 9, 2009

They are different sports with different fan bases, different histories and different strategies. But boxing is a part of mixed martial arts, or MMA. The skills used within the squared circle are incorporated into the arsenals of those who step into the cage. The ability to punch is as essential as the ability to wrestle, to kick, to fight on the ground and to defend against all of the above.

Fighters may excel in one aspect, but they cannot specialize and merely expect to get by. From the very first Ultimate Fighting Championship (or UFC) pay-per-view, Royce Gracie turned conventional beliefs upside-down, using Brazilian Jiu-Jitsu to take out experts in various fighting forms. More than a dozen years later, Gracie would be dominated by a modern MMA fighter, Matt Hughes.

Every so often a boxer spouts off with the naïve belief that he could step into the Octagon against the best the UFC has to offer and win based solely on his superior boxing skills. But while some boxers seem to underestimate what it takes to succeed in mixed martial arts, many mixed martial artists appreciate — and incorporate — the skills of the Sweet Science.

Marcus Davis is a mixed martial artist with five-and-a-half years in the sport and 20 fights on his record. He's fought nine times in the UFC, winning all but one. Before he ever tried out MMA, however, Davis was a boxer, and somewhat successful, fighting 20 times around New

England, winning 17 times, losing once and drawing twice.

"I always wanted to fight. That's it," Davis said in an interview last month. "That's all I ever wanted to do. I didn't want to punch a clock. I didn't want to sit behind a desk. I didn't have aspirations of being anything but a fighter."

Both of Davis' grandfathers had boxed, as had his uncles. But there were no boxing gyms in the area. He took up karate at 8 and didn't start boxing until five years later. He soon entered the amateur ranks, going 32-2. He turned pro at 19, only to leave the sport seven years later after his only defeat.

"At the time, I saw what the potential was, what I thought was going to happen with MMA," Davis said. "I just knew that it was going to get big, that it was going to explode like it did, so I wanted to jump in."

His first pro MMA fight came three years later. The transition, Davis said, was difficult.

"There's probably a lot of boxers that watch it and just think they can get into MMA and box and get away with it, that their hands would be so fast that they'd be able to hit guys when they're trying to take them down," he said. "You watch it from the outside. You're like, "If a guy shot in on me I'd throw an uppercut and just catch him and it'd be over. It doesn't work that way. They think it does, but it doesn't. The first time you go in there, you try to hit something, they shoot and take you down. If you don't know anything about the ground, you won't get back up. They'll keep you there and finish the fight there."

Davis said he had to get rid of bad habits that were part and parcel of being a boxer.

"One is the way you stand," Davis said. "The way

everyone stands so upright and staggered. You need to square your hips to defend a takedown. Also, to check a kick, you can't do that from a staggered stance. You have to center up a little bit, hips pointed forward, in order to check a kick correctly.

"That right there takes away a lot of your boxing stuff," he said. "And then the way you throw punches, the way you move your head. The defense is different. In boxing you lean back and do, like, the fading out of a punch. You can't do that in MMA. If you lean back, you leave your legs forward. That leg will either be kicked or it leaves the leg open for a takedown."

Davis said one cannot bob and weave because of the danger of being kneed, or of the chance of being caught in a Muay Thai clinch that leaves one vulnerable to knees and elbows.

But once he made the transition, Davis said, there were elements of boxing he continued — and continues — to use.

"The timing of punches, being able to get into the pocket, throw punches and not get hit, I was still able to carry that over into my MMA," he said. "Defensively, I figured out what works in MMA and what does not work in MMA. The big thing is head movement. You have to be able to move your head, and you still have a lot of MMA fighters who don't know that. A lot of MMA fighters do what I call framing up, where they just put both their hands up and keep them nice and tight around their head."

Watching Davis in action, one sees his ability to control timing and distance, to make an opponent miss by inches, to move his body and head at just the right time and in just the right place.

Davis was a boxer who got into MMA. Jens Pulver is a mixed martial artist who got into boxing.

"I was a wrestler. I wrestled all the way through college, but I'd always been a big fan of boxing," Pulver said in an interview last month. "I wanted to be a boxer because I wanted to continue fighting in a legal sense. I wanted to continue to train. Then MMA started coming around. It's like, 'Oh, dear God, this gives me a chance to work on my boxing, but it's kind of like boxing with training wheels. Worst-case scenario, I shoot in and take somebody down.' "

Pulver entered the pro MMA ranks in 1999, becoming the 155-pound champion in the UFC two years later.

He left the company, competed in other organizations, and lost twice via punches.

"I got beat twice on my feet. I'm like, 'I really gotta work on my hands,' " Pulver said. I went into a boxing gym. The trainer said, 'Well, let's go pro.' I can't go amateur because I've been fighting already."

Pulver spent a brief time as a boxer — five fights and five victories by his count, four fights and four victories according to BoxRec.com — but it was time well spent once he returned to MMA, he said.

"It helped me from the beginning. I was a combo throwing machine," Pulver said. "It made a big difference, even to this day, with my defense, my hands, my throwing. It's just a lot better."

Pulver, like Davis, says there's much from boxing that just won't translate into MMA.

"I've seen [boxer] Verno Phillips, he tried to go into a Muay Thai bout. It's still stand-up the whole time, and he got destroyed," Pulver said. "If you don't try to learn the other stuff, you're going to get wrecked standing up, too.

People throwing knees in your gut, tying up your head, tying up your hands, kicking the inside of your leg. There's a lot to it."

But MMA fighters continue to improve on their boxing. UFC welterweight champion Georges St. Pierre has former boxer Howard Grant helping him with his hands. Former UFC heavyweight champion Andrei Arlovski has Freddie Roach as his boxing trainer.

"It's still a good thing to work on," Pulver said. "Learning how to roll with punches, throwing straight shots. It still helps a lot. You take what you can from every sport."

A Farewell to Harms

February 23, 2009

In his dressing room he sits, a fighter alone in his thoughts, an artist deliberating over an empty canvas, a writer whose story is still being told.

He has a setting: 400 square feet, more or less, an elevated stage in a coliseum where the masses gather, seeking either his triumph or his demise. That desire — victory or defeat, success or failure — is the driving force, the conflict, internal and external. There is a man who will punch him hundreds of times that night, sending forth hundreds of pounds of force cushioned only by eight or 10 ounces of leather and padding.

He sits, alone in his thoughts. What is to come soon. What has come before.

Each fight, at most, may last 47 minutes a night. Many fighters, at most, will have but four of those nights a year. In-between, their finely sculpted forms balloon, their bodies heal, their minds find distractions and their lives continue. But each punch is absorbed forever.

Miguel Cotto has taken 267 punches with him for the past seven months, 267 bruising uppercuts, thudding hooks and pounding crosses that left his lips swollen and his mouth agape, that brought crimson streaming from his nose and spattered about his face.

Kelly Pavlik has carried 148 shots with him for four months, 148 blows that came accurately and efficiently, that came faster and harder than expected from an old man not quite too old to give a young man a beating, a humbling.

Cotto and Pavlik had been hit before. But with those

415 punches, Antonio Margarito and Bernard Hopkins gave them something neither had experienced before: a loss.

That first blemish on their professional ledgers took away their momentum, their confidence, their auras of invulnerability. For months, each carried one night with him. Their bodies healed. Their minds went elsewhere. Their lives continued. But their losses are forever.

Eventually, they returned. Back to their dressing rooms, alone in thought. Another chapter for stories still being told. This chapter about redemption, about beginning again, about a farewell, as best as is possible, to harm.

Cotto came to Madison Square Garden in New York City, to an arena in which he had fought four times before, to assembled masses numbering more than 11,000, nearly all of whom had come to see him triumph.

Pavlik came to the Chevrolet Centre in Youngstown, Ohio, to his hometown, where 7,200 of his friends and neighbors gathered in support of a man who, physically and spiritually, was one of them. They came from an industrial city that in recent years had seen hard times. He, like them, would fight back when that proverbial going got tough.

They were in comfortable places, against safe opponents. Cotto faced Michael Jennings, a welterweight who had never met another top name in what is a talented division. Pavlik met Marco Antonio Rubio, a no-nonsense fighter who had spent much of his career in the 154-pound weight class and now was competing at middleweight.

Jennings was mobile from the outset, focusing more on moving his feet than moving his hands. Jennings landed just four punches in the opening round. Cotto tracked Jennings down enough to land 12.

Ultimately, Cotto closed in, putting Jennings on the mat in the final minute of the fourth round, then doing so again 30 seconds later. Jennings made it to the bell, but his time left in this fight was ticking away. The third and final knockdown came as the fifth stanza came to a close. The referee had seen enough. It was over.

Rubio would be there for Pavlik to hit throughout the night, far less elusive than Hopkins had been. Pavlik punished Rubio with hard shots, turning the fight into a glorified sparring session. In one corner, the middleweight champion. In the other, a heavy bag. After nine rounds, Rubio sat on his stool, done taking punches, unable to offer enough in return. It was over.

Cotto and Pavlik returned to their dressing rooms, returned to their thoughts. Their stories are still being told

Cotto earned a vacant welterweight title, putting him back toward the top of a division in which Antonio Margarito is now absent. Margarito had been caught with tampered hand wraps just before his fight last month with Shane Mosley. That bout would end with Mosley stopping Margarito, ending his aura of invulnerability just as Margarito had done to Cotto.

Many have speculated that this was not the first night Margarito had hardened wraps. They wonder whether he had done the same against Cotto, a question Cotto has likely tried to answer even though he may never know the truth. But Cotto cannot rewrite history. Those punches, that punishment, is still within.

Pavlik is still the top name at 160 pounds, having returned to that weight class after moving 10 pounds north to challenge Hopkins. Pavlik looked sluggish that night, and afterward stories came out that he was sick. Pavlik said little, making no excuses for why he had taken those lumps. He could console himself with knowledge that he had lost to one of the best fighters in history. That loss, however, would now be part of his own history.

Losing to Margarito and Hopkins had been steps back. Beating Jennings and Rubio was movement forward. Those bouts were their first exercises in exorcism — fitting for Pavlik, really, that "The Ghost" would be haunted himself by "The Executioner." Cotto, meanwhile, was picking up from wreckage left behind by "The Tijuana Tornado."

Whether either will rebuild, renewed, is not yet known. There will be more nights, more chapters, more punches, more pain — conflict, internal and external, until they can no longer turn the page on the past, for their stories will have reached the end.

Marco Antonio Barrera: The Final Cut
March 16, 2009

We open in a faraway arena, a distance from the casinos, stadiums and venues to which the faded hero had long ago become accustomed.

The camera cuts to Marco Antonio Barrera, 35 years old, 5-foot-6, adorned in a blue, hooded robe. He walks forward, expressionless, his movement a steady gait until the moment just after he ducks between the second and third ropes of the ring. His gloved hands pull his hood back, and he bounces into a trot. Those in this faraway arena welcome him with cheers. Some have donned sombreros, tokens of affection for a fighter who has come from Mexico City to Manchester, England.

Their applause is more for who he once was than what he is now.

Barrera traversed the Atlantic Ocean, crossing through six time zones to confront his past, to compete against the future. He traveled to this British city to face Amir Khan, a 22-year-old, 5-foot-10, from nearby Bolton, the homegrown favorite, an Olympic medalist who captured silver in 2004.

The lights dim. Khan, clad in red, steps out of the darkness, away from the specter of disappointment. Six months before, he took to this very ring, only to be pounded into defeat within a minute. He wastes little time entering the squared circle. This is his second fight since then. With a second straight victory, he can pick up his career from where it was — before he had to pick himself up off the canvas.

Khan had until then been undefeated as a professional,

a prospect being groomed for prominence. Now he would enter the proverbial crossroads fight. A win over an established, accomplished opponent such as Barrera would put him back on track. A loss, and he'd wind up derailed.

Barrera was a boxer back when Khan was but a toddler. In the two decades since, he had fought 469 rounds. He had won 65 of those 72 fights, with a world title on the line 25 times. Khan entered the pro ranks in 2005, going 70 rounds in 20 bouts.

The scene is set. The bell is rung. We have lights. We have cameras. We have action.

*   *   *

We cut to the first round, one minute and 53 seconds in.

Barrera is cut.

He and Khan have just butted heads, each dipping forward and to the left as they begin to throw right hands. The collision opens up a large, vertical gash high on the left side of Barrera's forehead, just below his hairline. The impact, combined with a right hand from Khan, leaves Barrera momentarily reeling. Khan sees blood, and he smells it, too, closing in and trying to end the bout early. Barrera throws out hard hooks in an attempt to keep Khan at bay, then weaves around the ring to escape the onslaught.

Barrera's "Baby-Faced Assassin" moniker stuck with him even as he aged. To call him poker-faced always seemed more apt. He maintained the same expression no matter the direction of the action. That's not to say he showed little in the way of emotion. This was the consummate professional who once put Prince Naseem

Hamed in a full nelson and, like a pro wrestler, bashed his head into the corner. This was the consummate professional who twice had points deducted for intentional fouls during his bouts with Manny Pacquiao.

We cut to the end of the second round.

Barrera is walking back to his corner, having gone to work despite the blood pouring down his forehead into his left eye. The cut is so bad that it seems to spurt, a crimson river streaming south.

This poker-faced assassin was playing against a stacked deck.

Barrera's best years had come in lighter weight classes, in the 122-, 126- and 130-pound divisions. Those years had long since passed. Though his last two losses came in 2007 against the two best fighters in the sport — Pacquiao and Juan Manuel Marquez — Barrera, most agreed, was not what he had once been.

Against Pacquiao in their rematch, Barrera should have been motivated to make up for the beating he'd received four years earlier. Instead, he was a warier warrior, staying at a distance, rarely committing, barely putting punches together in combination, going the distance but doing little more.

Barrera retired after that fight. Thirteen months later, he came back.

He had left Golden Boy Promotions, a company for which he, like other aging fighters Oscar De La Hoya, Bernard Hopkins and Shane Mosley, acted as an executive. His new contract called for five years under Don King. Those terms seemed an eternity, but Barrera's competitive fire still burned, and perhaps that necessitated a deal with a man some in the sport see as the devil.

44

Three fights into the deal, Barrera had a bout with Khan that would land him a shot at the lightweight title if he won.

He had to win first.

* * *

Cut to a montage.

Khan shows himself to be a full-fledged lightweight, a natural 135-pounder, bigger, faster and stronger than his undersized opponent. Though Barrera has advantages in experience and wile, the unceasing flow of blood places the underdog against overwhelming odds.

We see Khan strafing Barrera with speedy flurries. We see Barrera looking to trap Khan with a counter. We see Barrera looking to trap Khan in a corner. We see Barrera unable to do either.

A ringside physician checks on Barrera's wound halfway through the fourth round but sends him back into battle. The doctor does the same in the waning moments of round five, though this time the fight is called off.

The judges issue a technical decision, scoring the bout 50-45 (twice) and 50-44 in favor of Khan. Cut to the post-fight interviews.

"They didn't stop the fight in the first round," Barrera says. "I think they should've stopped it before because [the cut] was a big as it is now. I couldn't see the guy since the first round. The blood was on my eye."

Had the fight been stopped before the fourth round was over, the bout would have ended as a "No Contest." Once the bell rang to begin round five, the rules called for the bout to go to the scorecards.

"I didn't really even feel his punches," Barrera said.

"He's got fast hands, but his punches did nothing to me. I really didn't feel them. I just went a little crazy, because I wanted to try to fight before they stopped the fight."

* * *

We close on a career filled with thrills, with blood feuds and fights of the year, with back-and-forth brawls and scientific clinics.

Between his first bout, in Mexico City, and this latest one, in Manchester, Barrera became a fixture in the United States. He fought 17 times in Las Vegas, 15 times in Southern California, and on at least 19 occasions he appeared on HBO or HBO Pay-Per-View.

Barrera's last three fights have come against a 25-19 opponent in China, with a 1-7-1 fall guy in Mexico and against Khan in Manchester. He is far from the venues to which he had long ago become accustomed. He is a boxer hanging on to his name, his past accomplishments, seeking to turn them into one last run at the top.

Not every story has a heartwarming conclusion.

In the canon of the Sweet Science, a fading hero is thought to have one last great performance left. History tells of George Foreman knocking out Michael Moorer, of Bernard Hopkins defying his age and the odds against Antonio Tarver and Kelly Pavlik.

Less storied are the accomplished veterans, long past their primes, served up as fodder to contenders and prospects.

For the moment, we remember Barrera for who he once was, not what he is now.

He will get older and slower. His opponents will remain young, fast and strong, capable at doing in the ring what he cannot, despite his experience, which with every year accumulates as wear and tear.

We close on a night in Manchester when this faded hero was offered one last shot at glory, only to have this story cut short. Fate can be a cruel mistress.

May the wound heal, and may the credits roll after what those watching their screens would hope was the final cut.

Punishing Antonio Margarito: A Year or a Career?

March 30, 2009

Does the crime dictate the punishment? Or do the consequences of the crime dictate the consequences for the criminal?

Those are the questions that those in boxing must ultimately contemplate when it comes time to decide whether Antonio Margarito should be allowed to fight again.

Two months ago, Margarito was caught with a foreign substance in his hand wraps prior to his fight with Shane Mosley. The California State Athletic Commission official charged with supervising Margarito's dressing room never noticed the tampering. Only when Mosley's trainer, Naazim Richardson, entered was the foul play discovered.

Here is the rundown of what happened Jan. 24, 2009, according to Lance Pugmire of the Los Angeles Times:

Richardson objected to the way in which Margarito's hands were wrapped, telling officials the tape was too thick. As Margarito's hands were unwrapped, Richardson noticed two pads that had been inserted inside the hand wraps. Those pads looked as if they were wet and had a substance on them that looked like Plaster of Paris.

The substance was removed. Margarito's hands were rewrapped. Nine rounds later, Margarito was knocked out.

Margarito could be out much longer.

In February, the CSAC revoked Margarito's license and

that of his trainer, Javier Capetillo, a ruling that would prevent either from working in the state for a year. Last week we found out just what was on those pads.

Calcium and sulfur. Combine those two with oxygen and you have Plaster of Paris.

A boxer's fists are dangerous weapons. Coat the wraps around them with something harder than the normal tape and gauze and those fists become deadly weapons.

By revoking Margarito's license, the CSAC effectively kept him from fighting throughout the United States. Margarito could apply for a license elsewhere, but other states would likely respect California officials' ruling.

Margarito could fight outside of the United States. Doing so, however, would probably raise the ire of commission officials in America should he choose to fight in the States again.

All that may be moot.

Margarito can apply for reinstatement in 2010. When he does, those who hear his case must decide whether the crime alone dictates the punishment, or if what consequences became of the crime dictate what consequences there should be for the criminal.

The difference between the latter and the former will decide what Margarito's punishment will be: a year or a career.

In 1983, Luis Resto was caught cheating after giving a 10-round beating to Billy Collins Jr. Resto and his trainer, Panama Lewis, would spend time behind bars after being convicted of removing padding from Resto's gloves. Collins, partially blinded, struggled with depression and died in a car accident less than a year later. Earlier last year, 25 years after that fight, Resto admitted that, in addition to having unpadded gloves, he had soaked his hand wraps in plaster of Paris before the bout.

Resto and Lewis were banned from boxing forever. In criminal law, there is a difference between actually assaulting a person and conspiring to commit an assault. Boxing is not bound by such a line.

Those in power need not be forced to wait for a fighter to move beyond the conspiracy stage. The intent was there. Illegal, hardened pads were in Margarito's wraps. Those hands would soon be in gloves. Those hands would soon hit another man. Had Margarito fought with those wraps and given Shane Mosley a career-ending beating, there would be no need for debate.

There are those who defend Margarito. Capetillo, his trainer, took the blame at a CSAC hearing, saying he was fully responsible for the illegal hand wraps. Capetillo offered a dubious reason for why it happened, saying he mistakenly picked up wraps another fighter had previously used in the gym.

Right.

Capetillo fell on his sword for the sake of his fighter, doing so in a manner in which he tried to deflect the brunt of any backlash away from Margarito while still salvaging his own career.

Margarito is the boss of his team. Though he entrusts his trainer and his cornermen with the responsibility of getting him through everything from training camp until the final bell, elite athletes should not be able to plead ignorance and blame others when caught breaking the rules.

A baseball player should know what substance is being injected into his body. A boxer should know what his trainer is putting on his hands — the tools of his trade.

True, Margarito didn't wear those illegal, hardened

pads into the ring. He did not give a career-ending beating. But the same could be said of Edward Mpofu and his bout with Thanduxolo Dyani.

Mpofu, a featherweight from South Africa, was allegedly caught with Plaster of Paris in his gloves following a fight this past September. Mpofu would lose a six-round decision to Dyani, and Dyani reportedly escaped with little injury beyond a swollen left eye.

Mpofu is the middle ground between Antonio Margarito and Luis Resto. Unlike Margarito, he didn't get caught with the Plaster of Paris until after the fight. Unlike Resto, the cheating didn't do him any good.

Mpofu will never be allowed to fight again. Margarito shouldn't either.

Margarito has more backing because he has a name and a following. Before he lost to Mosley, he was the welterweight champion, a longtime veteran who many had avoided and few had respected. When Margarito stopped Miguel Cotto last year to become the top welterweight in the world, he also became a Mexican hero, a guaranteed ticket seller.

In this sport, money often wins out over integrity.

After the CSAC revoked Margarito's license, the fighter's promoter, Bob Arum, decried the commission's decision and spoke of bringing Margarito to Mexico.

What will he say now? What would he have said had another fighter tried this against someone from his own stable?

Arum would probably say he'd want what many of us are now calling for. For a cheater not to prosper. For the punishment to match the intent of the crime. For the commissions and sanctioning bodies to ban Margarito, hitting him as hard as he could have and would have hit someone else had he gotten away with it.

The Drive, The Dead-End, The Delay
April 20, 2009

There is no plateau, no stagnation. We either rise or decline, improve or decay. Whether one's level is known dictates just where one goes — to drive toward a destination; to head into a dead-end and not return; or to delay, to stay in neutral until the gas tank hits empty. It is an eventual truth for superstars, next big things and never-will-bes, reality from which no multimillionaire, no coddled prospect and no local-show regular is immune. To be an athlete is to compete. To fight is to face another man one-on-one. For nearly all, someone, someday, will be better.

Oscar De La Hoya reached that moment years ago. He finally realized it last week, when he retired at 36 years old, with 39 wins and 6 losses, a future entrant into the Hall of Fame who will be worthy of induction but who falls short of recognition as an all-time great. No matter. He was on top of the fight game, and he was long handsomely rewarded for being so.

"I thought it was only fair to my self," De La Hoya told media members following his retirement. "I thought it was only fair to my fans that I make this decision. because it hurts me that I cannot compete at the highest level anymore. It kills me inside that every time I step inside the ring now, it's not me. It's not the person, the fighter, that people grew up watching."

De La Hoya was undefeated in his first 31 fights. In his final 14 appearances he went 8-6, all six defeats coming against opponents seen as among the best in the sport: Felix Trinidad, Shane Mosley (twice), Bernard Hopkins,

Floyd Mayweather Jr. and Manny Pacquiao.

His final two wins came against hand-selected opponents: a knockout of Ricardo Mayorga, a decision over Steve Forbes. In-between those victories came the loss to Mayweather, a night De La Hoya said was the first sign he was nearing the latter stages of his career, the dead-end after a long journey.

"I felt that that was the beginning of me not having it anymore," he said. "At the time you don't want to accept it. You want to continue to lie to yourself and say, 'You know, maybe something went wrong.' "

Mayweather was considered the best boxer, pound-for-pound. There was no shame in defeat. Forbes, meanwhile, was a capable veteran but an undersized opponent with little power. De La Hoya cleaned up on the scorecards but wound up marked up — "Even though I won, I got hit like there's no tomorrow," De La Hoya said. "That obviously was a clear sign to me."

And then in training camp for the Manny Pacquiao fight came more signs of his decline, more evidence of deterioration.

"I did start getting beat up during sparring, which in all of my boxing career ... never happened," he said. "I've never got beat up by sparring partners. And I was getting beat up by sparring partners in that training camp. But I didn't want to accept it. I didn't want to realize it. I was lying to myself."

Stories of De La Hoya's training camp woes leaked out. Pacquiao would be at least as fast as De La Hoya's sparring partners. In December he exploited the same weaknesses, punishing De La Hoya, embarrassing him and giving him exactly the kind of stinging beating he needed.

"It actually made it much easier for me to decide that it's over," De La Hoya said. "I needed that perfect excuse. I was searching for that perfect exit strategy. How do I retire? How does it happen? What is it going to take? Because we athletes are very stubborn and we never know when enough is enough. And when I got beat by Pacquiao, it obviously makes it easier for me to say, 'That's it. You don't have it anymore.' "

It is the same conclusion Arturo Gatti reached two years ago, when he was sent to the canvas for his second straight knockout loss. Against Floyd Mayweather Jr. in 2005 he had been on the receiving end of an extended, one-sided beating, a loss cementing that Gatti did not belong in the ring with a certain caliber of opponent. His final two defeats came against Carlos Baldomir and Alfonso Gomez, two fighters on much lower tiers than Mayweather, and those knockouts made it clear that Gatti needed to call it a career.

But for other fighters, such a conclusion is not as easily accepted.

Like Gatti, Roy Jones Jr. suffered two consecutive brutal knockouts, the first against Antonio Tarver, the second at the hands of Glen Johnson. Jones would follow those losses with another bout against Tarver, a decision defeat in which Jones seemed content to last the distance.

He would not retire, however. Instead, Jones has delayed such a decision. Four of his last five fights came against opponents who, even though Jones is no longer the transcendent talent he once was, didn't exactly pose a threat to him. Against Prince Badi Ajamu, Anthony Hanshaw, an inactive past-his prime Felix Trinidad, and Omar Sheika, Jones was fighting for the sake of fighting. He is winning for as long as he could win and seems revitalized, enjoying himself like a retired basketball player taking part in high-level pickup games.

His loss last year to Joe Calzaghe could have signaled his end. Instead, Jones continues on, seeking another challenge, another test of where his level is.

Too often we write off boxers if they do not belong in the highest echelons, forgetting that the primary nature of the Sweet Science is to enjoy the story unfolding within the ring. Gatti packed arenas even though he was never the best in his division. Julio Cesar Chavez Jr. and John Duddy sell tickets because their fights are entertaining. They do not need to be hyped as anything but what they are. The fans still get their money's worth.

And though they do not need to step up their competition, fighters like them eventually do. They have the drive, a strong urge to see, at some point, how they compare, whether they belong. For some, such knowledge can bring a harsh reality. For others it is an eventual truth that is easier to swallow.

De La Hoya can look back at his career and see that he belonged, that he packed arenas and often gave the fans what they wanted.

"I've had the opportunity to face many world champions, and a lot of them I won. Some I lost," De La Hoya said. "But my satisfaction comes, my satisfaction is because at least I tried. I tried to accomplish the impossible, and not too many do that. And so if people want to remember me as an attraction, then I'm glad I gave a lot of people a lot of entertainment."

Froch-Taylor: The Last Moment, A Lasting Moment
April 27, 2009

MASHANTUCKET, Conn. — Count down from 14. Count down from 14 to zero at a deliberate pace and it will take you twice as many seconds as it took you to reach the end of this sentence.

Those moments were all that remained before Carl Froch, the super-middleweight titlist from Nottingham, England, would become a former world champ who lost his title in his first defense.

It is less than one quarter of a minute, less than one-twelfth of a round in a boxing match, time that passes by unnoticed when a round begins but turns into a deadline as those three minutes approach their end

Froch met that deadline and made way for the headlines. His 12th-round knockout of Jermain Taylor was a last-moment Hail Mary, bombs away, all-or-nothing, now or never.

Through 11 rounds, Froch was the low man on two of the three judges' scorecards, whose tallies totaled an insurmountable deficit. Froch needed to do more than simply win the round. He could not win the fight with one knockdown, or two, or even three. He needed the fight to end before the round did.

Froch threw, and Taylor caught.

"My shots got through his guard," Froch said afterward. "I punched very hard and very solid. I broke his spirit, I broke his will, and I near broke his jaw."

Froch went for broke when Taylor was spent, fatigued from 33 minutes in which the former middleweight champion took an early lead, only to lag late.

Some great fights are action films featuring two fighters too alike, warriors willing to battle for victory without ever taking a backward step.

Other great fights are classic dramas featuring contrasting characters, men who are proficient in areas in which their opponents are deficient and weak where their opponents are strong.

Froch and Taylor matched up well as the latter.

Taylor was named middleweight heir apparent before he had ever defeated a top opponent in that division. He captured the 160-pound crown with two controversial victories over Bernard Hopkins, wins that many felt came more due to what Hopkins failed to do rather than because of what Taylor did.

Taylor fought high-quality opposition for the duration of his middleweight stay, though he never could do enough to win over his skeptics, not when he fought to a draw with Winky Wright, not when he was backing down during his victory over the much smaller Kassim Ouma, and not when he took a split-decision nod against Cory Spinks.

The best Taylor looked was on the night he first lost, when he knocked Kelly Pavlik down hard and was moments away from a second-round victory. Pavlik made it to the bell, recovered, knocked Taylor out and then outpointed him in their rematch.

Froch had not yet lost in his campaign to replace the retired Joe Calzaghe atop the super-middleweight throne. But he was a claimant without acclaim. This fight with Taylor would not be aired live in the United Kingdom.

Froch was a slower puncher with a porous defense who called upon his determination, stamina, strength and sturdy chin to win. Taylor seemed to be an athlete who took up boxing rather than a boxer who is athletic, but he had quicker reflexes and faster hands.

That speed advantage showed early. The opening round saw Taylor countering Froch with a few good right hands. Froch tempted fate further by continuing to hold his left glove low.

That defensive liability came back to hurt Froch in round three. At one point he had both of his hands down. When he punched, those hands returned toward his hips instead of his head. Taylor's counters had a clear path.

One right hand from Taylor landed atop Froch's head, putting him on the seat of his pants. Froch had never been on the canvas before, not as an amateur and not as a pro.

"I'm guilty of starting too slow, opening up too wide, keeping my chin up to dry, pulling back," Froch said afterward. "I was a little bit nervous, a little bit deer in the headlights."

But Froch was clear-eyed. He rose before the referee's count reached eight with his legs stable beneath him. Taylor either recognized that Froch wasn't badly hurt, or he simply never pressed for the finish. Taylor then slowed down his work rate in the fourth. He may have taken the round off to conserve himself. Or he may have expended too much energy while swinging for the fences.

As with the loss to Pavlik, that failure to end the fight would come back to haunt him.

Taylor's activity dwindled. Froch, meanwhile, kicked into a higher gear and adjusted to keep himself from getting caught again. Though his left hand remained low, Froch would duck to his right or pull back after his jab, attempting to dodge the anticipated right-hand counter from Taylor.

By the end of the eighth round, Froch was down 78-73 on two of the judges' scorecards, up 77-74 on the third. Entering the 12th, Froch was behind 106-102 on two scorecards, ahead 106-102 on the third.

Taylor had the lead, but he hadn't done anything to deter Froch, who found his rhythm and took back the momentum.

This time it was Taylor's low left hand that left him vulnerable. Froch hurt him with a right hand one minute into that last stanza, then followed him around the ring, landing more big shots along the way. Another right hand put Taylor down, his head resting on the lowest of the ring's four ropes. Taylor looked up, clearly weary, barely beating the count.

Taylor still had the lead. If he could hold on to Froch, he could hold on to win.

Thirty seconds remained.

They met in the center of the ring.

Twenty-five.

Froch threw a jab and a right hand. Taylor retreated to a corner. Froch closed in, sending out one-two after one-two as the clock wound down from 22.

Taylor's high guard did nothing to stop the shots. Froch easily laced his punches through.

Eighteen.

Another left and a right left Taylor dazed, defenseless. He leaned forward involuntarily, his arms in front of him. The referee jumped in, pulling Froch away with 16 seconds left, waving his arms to signal the fight's end two seconds later.

Time is relative. Count down from 14, the number of seconds between when Jermain Taylor got up from the mat and when Carl Froch threw his final punch. It is twice as many seconds as it took you to reach the end of this sentence.

Those last moments flew by for Froch and dragged on for Taylor. Those last moments are lasting moments, a dramatic victory and an indelible memory.

Pacquiao-Hatton: The Shots Heard Round The World

May 4, 2009

The first right hook rumbled through Ricky Hatton, continued on to nearby cameras, beamed through satellites miles into space and traveled across the globe to countries captivated by the images on their screens.

Each subsequent shot brought tremors, reverberations in faraway nations, punches seen and heard around the world.

The entire fight lasted six minutes — seven, if you count the 60 seconds of respite Hatton had from Manny Pacquiao between the bout's two rounds. A casual observer would ponder the length of the fight and note that it was over before it began. A student of this sweet science would have already taken his measure of the fighters before coming to the same conclusion.

Pacquiao's speed is such that he hits before he can be hit. He is gone in a split second, his head, body, feet and hands in perpetual motion. Forget floating like a butterfly. He buzzes about like a fly that cannot be swatted. And his sting? It hurts far worse than that of a bee.

Hatton's strength had been his willingness to take hits in order to hit. He is there at all times, punching and mauling for three minutes a round. But for all of his perpetual motion, his head is stationary, his chin is up and his approach is one of straight lines.

The entire fight lasted six minutes, ending shortly before 8:45 p.m. in Vegas when Pacquiao put Hatton to sleep early. In Manchester, England, those who had stayed up to 4:45 a.m. to watch their local hero fight found themselves caught in a waking nightmare. In Pacquiao's native Philippines, dreams came true at 11:45 a.m. Their native son rose to the occasion, shining brighter than ever before.

Each man had long carried the weight of being a hero. Pacquiao is a national icon. Crime stops when he fights. He has acted in movies, sang on albums and run for office. His gym, the Wild Card Boxing Club in Los Angeles, closes to the public when he trains because of the flood of fans who would otherwise show up.

Hatton is the third franchise in Manchester, joining the city's two soccer teams as the object of raucous support. His countrymen flock in droves, filling arenas near and far, bringing planeloads to the United States, even when many of those crossing the pond will not be able to get tickets to his fights. Their singing of "Hatton Wonderland" is the sort of rhythmic tribute that has taken the place of epic poems.

Their fight was billed as "The Battle of East and West." Pacquiao rolled through Hatton like an invading army, obliterating any and all resistance.

In those six minutes, Hatton threw only 78 punches, landing just 18. Not a single shot stands out.

Pacquiao hit Hatton with 73 of his 127 punches thrown, an astonishing 57 percent connect rate.

All but eight of those landed punches were power shots, the right hooks from Pacquiao that started Hatton's downfall and the final left hook that had Hatton falling down.

Pacquiao was ready to start before the fight even began. He was at the center of the ring seconds before the opening bell rang; the referee, Kenny Bayless, had to order him back to his corner.

Pacquiao was once a one-dimensional power-puncher overly reliant on two southpaw jabs followed by a left hand. As he grew into higher weight classes, though, he developed into a multifaceted boxer-puncher. He fought Hatton as he had Oscar De La Hoya in December and David Diaz the preceding June, moving in and out of range and relying on his superior hand speed. The punches that a fighter doesn't see coming are the punches that do the most damage.

Hatton, meanwhile, stuck to his bread and butter, attempting to close the distance on Pacquiao without throwing punches, trying to keep the faster man in one spot, be it trapped against the ropes or stuck in a clinch.

Most of the time Pacquiao had little difficulty evading Hatton. Any clinches were broken quickly, with Pacquiao taking but a few rabbit punches and body shots lacking leverage behind them.

Hatton held his left hand at his chest, leaving his already vulnerable head all the more wide open. Pacquiao capitalized. When Hatton jabbed or cocked his arm back for a left hook, Pacquiao would counter with a right hook.

The first right hook that rumbled through Hatton came half a minute into the opening round. Hatton took that one. He wouldn't take many more.

With a minute remaining, Hatton started to throw a left hook. Pacquiao's counter right hook landed first. Hatton fell forward to the canvas, landing on all fours. He rose at the count of eight.

Pacquiao, eager to close the show, couldn't contain himself in a neutral corner. Bayless held Pacquiao back once again, buying Hatton about five extra seconds to recover.

It wouldn't matter.

Hatton couldn't handle the speed at which the shots were coming. He was soon hurt again, and a series of left and right hands sent him falling backwards for the second knockdown of the round. Hatton once more got up as the count reached eight, a look of dazed disbelief on his face. His bell had been rung.

The bell rang.

Hatton had a minute to rest and adjust. Those 60 seconds passed. He would be flat on his back in three minutes.

Pacquiao set up the eventual knockout by letting Hatton come toward him. He drew Hatton in with a jab that fell short, seemingly intentionally, then took a step back and planted his feet for the final left hook.

The punch connected low on the right side of Hatton's jaw. On the button.

Hatton fell down and left, the side of his head crashing to the mat. His body turned involuntarily, his arms above his head, his eyes unfocused and glaring at the lights. Bayless stopped his count. There was no need.

When Muhammad Ali declared, 45 years ago, that he shook up the world, capturing the heavyweight crown by forcing Sonny Liston to quit after seven rounds in Miami, there was no Internet. There were no live global broadcasts. There was no ability for the world to watch a world champion in real time.

When Manny Pacquiao knocked out Ricky Hatton after two rounds in Las Vegas, capturing the junior-welterweight throne and giving him a title claim in a record-tying sixth weight class, he did so in front of cameras that sent his victory through satellites to television screens thousands of miles from where the technology first captured his technique.

He did so with speed and power, several fast right hooks and one strong left hook, punches seen and heard around the world.

Belting It Out (A Satire)
June 1, 2009

My prizefighting career started in places where the prizes were small and the crowds smaller. I had no amateur acclaim to speak of. No illustrious tournaments. No national championships.

The smoke wafted inward from those who nevertheless showed to watch us pugs trade punches, a stench that mixed with my sweat and soaked into my clothes. It came with me on the long drives home, almost always overnight, when the only landmarks were state lines and the only company was whatever came through the radio on my beater of a car.

It was worth it.

I captured the West Virginia state title first. I never fought there again. Instead, I moved east and won the Pennsylvania state title. If I had kept going to all 50 states, I guess that would have made up for never winning a national championship.

I found my name in rankings of organizations that sounded more like they should be lobbying the federal government rather than sanctioning a fight between two semi-anonymous pros. The NABA. The NABF. The NABO. Who knew boxing in North America was governed by an association, a federation and an organization?

I was a former ham-and-egger now dealing in alphabet soup.

I got even better. And it got even better.

I went overseas next, brought across the pond to pad the record of the British champion.

I challenged the British champion and won.

That didn't make me the British champion. Not yet, at least. First I had to capture the British Boxing Board of Control title. Or maybe it was the Commonwealth title.

I moved east, from country to country, like a college graduate backpacking through the Old World.

There was the European Boxing Association. And the European Boxing Union. It never mattered whether or not I was European.

One night, I, a Polish transplant out of Chicago, took on an American of Italian heritage who hailed from the Chicago suburb of Oak Lawn, Ill. We fought over something called the World Boxing Association Fedelatin heavyweight title (1). That's Fedelatin, as in Federacion Latinoamericana.

Eventually, I tired of the travel. So I returned to America and took the globe with me, finding more sanctioning bodies that said they were international and proffered world titles.

I won a title from the International Boxing Council, or IBC, which I always thought was a root beer. I took custody of a belt from the International Boxing Association, or IBA. And then I found myself in line for a championship sanctioned by the International Boxing Organization, or IBO.

It didn't matter to the IBO that their own computerized rankings had me all the way down at 27th among welterweights while my opponent was in the 57th slot down at junior welterweight. On the undercard, that same sanctioning body had a bantamweight title fight between guys ranked 26th and 45th (2).

I didn't think about whether it made sense. This was an organization vying for legitimacy, one that claimed transparency and quality.

I know, I know.

Ultimately, I realized it was better to dance with the devil I knew rather than the devil I didn't.

Some people pick the cream of the crop. Between the IBF, WBA, WBC and WBO, I had to settle for the best of the worst.

That meant signing my soul over to the WBC.

For all my experience, I was still young. That qualified me for the WBC Youth Championship. And I could even get away with defending it against a 34-year-old man who was 12 years older than me (3).

But then my career stalled.

My manager and promoter didn't have enough pull to grease the skids and move me up in the rankings, so the sanctioning bodies had little use for me. They could get their percentage cut in sanctioning fees from a fighter with more star power and bigger paychecks.

I decided to enter "The Contender" boxing reality series. We filmed, and we fought. But we waited, too, sitting on the sidelines until the show aired. Can't exactly ruin the results. That would take money from the billionaire network executives and millionaire producers. Doing so, however, kept money from those of us who actually got in the ring for a living.

I was fortunate. I won the "Contender Championship," which once was worth $1 million but now earned me $150,000. That wasn't too bad, and it meant Tournament of Contenders could fight me just once or twice a year until it found me a name opponent for whom I would be the designated fall guy.

I'm still thankful I got out of that contract.

The one thing "The Contender" did do was raise my

marketability. After I was able to regain my momentum by fighting more often, the World Boxing Association, or WBA, took notice.

I fought for their cruiserweight title and won. Except I didn't — that was just their interim title. There was still their "regular" world title. And their "super" world title (4). The WBA heavyweight titlist, meanwhile, had to look over his shoulder for the injured "champion in recess."

I didn't need that. I'd prefer an organization that's open about screwing fighters.

I went back to the WBC.

I went down to junior middleweight and beat Carlos Baldomir for the title. Meanwhile, Sergio Martinez became my mandatory challenger. But then I made a voluntary defense against Sergio Mora and lost my title. Thankfully, I had a rematch clause within our contract. I faced Mora again and won.

Meanwhile, Martinez became the WBC interim titlist. I lobbied the WBC to let me make a voluntary defense against Charles Whittaker, who was not ranked and had no reason to be ranked, not even in the WBC's poor rankings for the 154-pound division.

The WBC, showing rare wisdom, said no. And then I suffered an injury. The WBC said I had to face Martinez, and soon. I wasn't physically able, so I lost my title. Martinez ditched the "interim" distinction and now holds the belt.

But I've got nothing to worry about. The WBC named me its "Ambassador of Peace and Good Will in the World Through Sports." I can come back when I'm healed up, get an immediate shot at Martinez and even have the money split in my favor (5).

That's not too bad. I could always retire, too, and the

WBC would name me "Champion Emeritus" like it did for Vitali Klitschko. Between that and the ambassadorship, would that give me one mandatory shot and one more to spare in case I lose?

*   *   *

1. No, wait, that was Andrew Golota against Mike Mollo in January 2008.

2. No, wait, that will be Lovemore N'dou and Phillip N'dou, on July 11, with an undercard featuring Eric Barcelona and Simpiwe Vetyeka.

3. That was Chad Dawson, then a 22-year-old middleweight, facing 34-year-old Carl Daniels in December 2004.

4. That was Firat Arslan, who became the WBA interim cruiserweight titlist by beating Valery Brudov in June 2007. The "regular" titlist was the injured Virgil Hill, while the "super" world titlist was unified belt holder David Haye.

5. And that is Vernon Forrest.

*   *   *

Like the sanctioning bodies themselves, this story shouldn't be taken seriously.

Mayweather-Marquez: A Squash Match and a Post-Fight Angle
September 21, 2009

Floyd Mayweather Jr. flashed a smile, his top row of ivories glistening in the spotlight. His face, the face that had made the nickname "Pretty Boy Floyd" more than just a nod to the storied killer, was unmarked. His record, now 40 wins in 40 fights, remained unblemished.

And then Shane Mosley crashed the moment, succeeding in taking away Mayweather's smile, striving to do the same to his face and his record.

Mayweather, his hands still wrapped after 12 rounds with Juan Manuel Marquez, after 290 punches to Marquez's head and body, waved Mosley toward him, into the camera frame and the post-fight interview. That interview had spent just two minutes on the fight that just ended before turning the conversation to making the next fight begin.

A limp handshake led to a tense confrontation, fingers pointed, voices raised, bodies jostled. There was no need to linger on Mayweather-Marquez. It was a squash match with the sole intention of driving the storyline to the next encounter, the next opponent. Mosley inserted himself, thickening the plot, creating a post-fight angle and turning talk away from Mayweather-Marquez and toward Mayweather-Mosley.

It was a page straight out of the wrestling handbook. It was fitting. Mayweather has an outsized personality that landed him appearances on World Wrestling Entertainment programming. And Mayweather's appearances in WWE led to him being accompanied to the ring Saturday by one of wrestling's outsized personas, the muscular mound of machismo known as Triple H.

At times within WWE storylines, Triple H has been called the "Cerebral Assassin," a wrestler who combined mental acuity with physical ability.

Against Marquez, as against so many who had come before, Mayweather used his smarts to pick his opponent apart.

One judge gave Mayweather all 12 rounds. A second judge gave Mayweather all but one round. The third gave Mayweather all but two.

The first judge was right; Marquez was never in the fight.

Marquez, despite his skills and pedigree, was the underdog for good reason. He was a great smaller man not only challenging a great bigger man, but challenging a great bigger man who was stronger and, most importantly, quicker.

At featherweight, where Marquez held a world title, at junior lightweight, where Marquez was a world titlist again, and at lightweight, where Marquez became a champion, he had been both hittable and victorious. Earlier this year, he had been rocked in the early rounds by Juan Diaz before coming back to score the technical knockout. That he had done so was a testament to his toughness and his craft. He could withstand the onslaught and adjust, throwing the right shots at the right time.

Diaz has never been a fighter known for his power. Mayweather would have heavier hands, thrown faster and placed better. And his defense is as good as his offense.

After stopping Diaz, Marquez called out Mayweather,

who at the time was still claiming to be retired. Marquez either truly believed he could beat Mayweather, or he wanted to test his pound-for-pound talent against the man who had long been atop the pound-for-pound list. Marquez and Mayweather agreed on a weight limit of 144 pounds, a catch-weight that fell within the welterweight limit. Marquez would be rising two divisions; Mayweather, always in shape, would need to cut a few pounds.

One presumed.

Mayweather's camp contacted Marquez's a few days before the fight, asking for the contract to be changed. Mayweather was going to come in above 144 pounds. Under the original contract, if he were to be at 146, he would owe 10 percent, or $1 million, of his guaranteed $10 million payday. If he were to weigh in at 147, that amount would jump to 20 percent, or $2 million.

Much of that money would go to the Nevada State Athletic Commission. Marquez agreed to a change in contract, and in exchange, he would get $300,000 for every pound over 144 at which Mayweather came in.

Mayweather tipped the scales at 146 pounds, meaning Marquez got $600,000. Marquez weighed 142 pounds.

Their fight was a day away. On fight night, Marquez had unofficially gained six pounds. Mayweather did not allow himself to be weighed again. He looked more muscular, more natural for the weight.

From the outset of the fight, Mayweather looked confident, comfortable and in control.

Marquez, meanwhile, was wary at times, wild at others.

Mayweather stood in front of Marquez. Sometimes he would jab to the body to keep him at a distance.

Sometimes he would jab to the head to tempt Marquez to return fire with right-hand counters. And sometimes he would step forward with a left hook. Marquez would drop his right hand just slightly, ready to counter, leaving himself open for the shot.

It was such a left hook that scored the fight's only knockdown, putting Marquez on his back halfway into the second round. Marquez got up at four, his eyes wide, catching his breath and recapturing his wits. Mayweather came back in. He stepped in. A left hook landed. He stepped back. He stepped in. A left hook was blocked. He stepped back. He jabbed to the body, then stepped in. A left hook landed.

Marquez was never close enough to Mayweather. Mayweather could take a step back before returning, simple but effective footwork. Marquez either had to lunge forward or force awkward, ineffective punches in the rare moments when Mayweather was within range

Marquez landed just 69 of 583 punches, a paltry 12 percent connect rate. He never landed more than eight shots in a round. He averaged fewer than six landed punches per three minutes. Of those, just four power punches landed per round. Those in the crowd who came to support Marquez were so desperate to find something to cheer for that they did so even when Mayweather blocked shots or made Marquez miss.

Any solid connects didn't provide much cause for optimism; Mayweather laughed them off, and for once a fighter truly seemed to be laughing a punch off rather than indicating that he was hurt.

Mayweather was expertly effective, hitting Marquez with 59 percent of what he threw, be it a jab or a power punch. His connect rate only dipped below 50 percent twice; he was 15 of 31, or 48 percent, in round three, and 16 of 39, or 41 percent, in round eight.

It was a whitewash.

In wrestling, it would have been a squash match, but the type of squash match in which the heel has a pin but picks up his opponent's shoulders before the count of three so as to prolong the punishment.

One got the feeling that Mayweather could have disposed of Marquez at any time but chose not to do so.

Perhaps he carried Marquez out of respect for the one opponent in years that Mayweather had not constantly torn down and taunted in the pre-fight promotion. Or perhaps he carried Marquez because a 12-round decision victory could actually look better than an early knockout.

Most saw Marquez as too small, as not having a chance. Mayweather putting Marquez away promptly would only prove them right, giving fuel to those who argue that Mayweather chooses his opponents carefully so as to ensure that his undefeated record remains intact.

But Marquez went the distance, and Mayweather could compliment his opponent, an attempt to head off the criticism that he couldn't stop someone who appeared to be so obviously outmatched.

"He's tough as nails," Mayweather said of Marquez. "He's one hell of a fighter."

And then the post-fight interview moved in a different direction.

"There is another truly great fighter here tonight who's your size," said HBO analyst Max Kellerman. " 'Sugar' Shane Mosley. What [is] the possibility that we see that fight in the near future?"

Like a wrestling storyline general manager introducing a champion's next challenger, Kellerman spoke Mosley's name, and, just like that, Mosley was in the ring.

"Shane Mosley is one hell of a fighter," Mayweather said, looking toward Kellerman. "I don't take that away from Shane. ... I'm not scared of Shane Mosley. I'm not scared of no fighter."

Mosley leaned toward the microphone, leaning in mere inches away from Mayweather. Their first staredown. "We just want to get it on, that's all," Mosley said. "The fans want to see a great fight. Me and 'Money' Mayweather. Let's get this on. Let's do it."

Mosley has not fought since January, when he knocked out Antonio Margarito to become the top welterweight fighter. Since then, he has repeatedly called out other fighters, to no avail. Words from a distance weren't doing him any good. He turned to actions, up close and personal.

Antonio Tarver had once crashed a Roy Jones Jr. press conference, goading that got him a fight. Mosley tried to do the same, and the normally reserved fighter had back-up from one of boxing's biggest talkers, former middleweight and light heavyweight champion Bernard Hopkins.

Hopkins disrupted. Mayweather ended up agitated.

"I don't come up here and interrupt you when you're doing your interviews," Mayweather said. "Don't disrespect me. Respect me as a man."

A line in the sand. A face-off. The introduction of a conflict producing the need for a resolution.

Mayweather-Marquez was the first of two major welterweight pay-per-views scheduled for the final half of 2009, the second being the November bout between Miguel Cotto and Manny Pacquiao. Mayweather-Marquez and Cotto-Pacquiao are seen as an unofficial tournament, with the winners potentially facing each other, receiving riches at the expense of Mosley.

But Mayweather does not want to deal with his former promoter, Bob Arum, who also promotes Cotto and Pacquiao. And Pacquiao has driven a hard bargain in negotiations for his previous two fights, nearly canceling bouts with Oscar De La Hoya and Ricky Hatton. Could both Mayweather and Pacquiao ever have their egos placated when deciding who would get paid what?

The post-fight angle is in place. Now the angle need only come full circle, with Mayweather and Mosley sharing the ring once again.

Chris Arreola: All Guts, No Glory

September 28, 2009

There are two types of tears: those for triumph, and those for tragedy.

Witness the contrast between two fighters on one night. Floyd Mayweather Jr., the victor, dropping to his knees, crying out, "God is great." Arturo Gatti, the vanquished, remaining on his stool, his eyes swollen shut, his head cradled by his trainer, just crying.

There are two types of tears shed from tragedy: those that come from an outside force leaving one broken, and those that come from internal flaws rendering one brokenhearted.

Witness Chris Arreola, brokenhearted and broken, his internal flaws making him all the more vulnerable to external blows

The winner, Vitali Klitschko, stood tall, a statuesque 6-foot-7 figure raising his right glove high. The wounded, Arreola, hunched over, his right glove covering his eyes.

For 10 rounds, Klitschko was better from head to toe, with a strategy that played to his strengths and exploited his opponent's weaknesses, with fists that found flesh 300 times in 30 minutes, with footwork that helped both to deliver harm and to deliver himself from it.

For 10 rounds, Arreola was all guts. After, there was no glory.

"I'm so sorry," Arreola said afterward, attempting to hold back tears. "I worked my ass off. Fuck."

Arreola is blue-collar, beer-drinking, belly bulging, brawling over boxing. He can be nothing beyond what he is. It is his character. It is his curse.

"Sometimes I don't think he gives us the best chance to win," Arreola's trainer, Henry Ramirez, said during the build-up to the fight. "Sometimes he comes in a little too far out of shape."

"Michael Phelps smokes weed. Why can't I drink a beer?" Arreola said in the weeks before the fight. "That guy's still setting records. Why can't I have a beer?

"It's a problem, but at the same time it's not," Arreola said of his lifestyle. "I work hard. I'm going to play hard."

His character. His curse.

Arreola had last fought in April, tipping the scales at 255 pounds for his knockout victory over Jameel McCline. Since then, his weight had risen in the vicinity of 290 pounds, held heavily on his 6-foot-3 frame.

For the Klitschko fight, Arreola's trainer brought in conditioning coach Darryl Hudson.

"A lot of people use weight as a barometer for saying they're in a certain shape," Hudson said. "You can't go by weight. We're not training to lose weight. We're training to be in the best condition. So if the weight falls, it falls."

As is customary for heavyweights, Arreola stepped on the scale two days before his fight. Other divisions have to make a certain weight and must do so the day before they step in the ring.

Arreola weighed 272 pounds. But he was smiling. He was wearing a weighted vest beneath his T-shirt. He took off both and got back on the scale. He was 251 pounds.

By no means was he svelte. He weighed more than the 229 pounds he'd been about three years ago, when he made his HBO debut with a technical knockout of Damian Wills. He weighed more than the 239 pounds he'd been 15 months year ago, when he returned to HBO for a win over Chazz Witherspoon and the network began to market him as a potential challenger for the heavyweight championship.

Still, he was noticeably less tubby than in his previous three fights, when he weighed 255, 254 and 258.5.

"He'll feel the strength," Hudson said. "He'll feel that his breathing is under control. He'll be able to do the things he did in the first round in the ninth round."

It wouldn't be enough.

Arreola is a pressure fighter, coming forward behind combinations, roughing up his opponents into defenselessness or submission. The problem is that while his conditioning would allow him to continue to pressure, his weight would still inhibit his ability to land punches.

It is a mistake so many have made when facing Vitali or Wladimir Klitschko. To compensate for the brothers' height, weight and proportional strength, they pack on the pounds, believing that doing so will help. Rather, they become slower targets in the ring with surprisingly agile men.

Vitali Klitschko had harpooned several of these beached whales: Kirk Johnson, Corrie Sanders, Danny Williams and Samuel Peter. Against Arreola, however, he treated the match like a bullfight. Arreola would move in, but Klitschko would stab away, keeping him off with jabs, hooks and body shots, none with one-punch knockout power, all with enough force that Arreola rarely got within range. Klitschko would also pivot, jog a few steps away, and make Arreola, like a drugged, slowed bull, reset for his next charge.

Klitschko kept his hands at his sides, knowing that Arreola could neither catch him nor catch up with him.

Klitschko was far more active than the typical

heavyweight, throwing 802 punches, or 80 per round, and landing 301, or 30 per round. Half of his landed shots were jabs, half of them were power punches.

Arreola, who of the two of them was the one who usually overwhelmed opponents with activity, threw only 332 punches in the whole fight, landing 86. That was an average of less than nine landed punches and 33 thrown per three minutes. He landed only 24 power punches over the entire fight, staying in the single digits each stanza: one, two, one, two, three, five, two, four, four, and zero.

"He was fighting the fight he was supposed to fight. He ran when he was supposed to," Arreola said afterward. "He's just a smarter fighter. Whatever I did, he found a way to counteract that. He just found a way to win. I found a way to lose."

After that 10th round, when it became clear that all Arreola had left to offer was his willingness to get off his stool and take more punishment, the fight was stopped. Two of the three judges had given Klitschko all but one round, scoring the eighth round for Arreola. The third judge had it a shutout and had scored the 10th stanza 10-8 for Klitschko in a round without a knockdown, seeing the action one-sided enough to warrant such a tally.

"I never wanted to quit," Arreola said afterward. "I wanted to go the full 12 rounds. I knew he was fucking me up."

It is tempting to give Arreola credit for courage, for staying upright. At least he had gotten in the ring with Klitschko. That is more than could be said for David Haye, the former cruiserweight champion who called out both Wladimir and Vitali upon his rise to the heavyweight division but then bailed on fights with each.

Arreola had been guided toward an eventual title shot, but despite his undefeated record, his professional experience was still that of a prospect, not a contender. His best wins had come against Chazz Witherspoon and Travis Walker, two heavyweights who had never beaten an upper-tier opponent, and against Jameel McCline, a longtime contender who had since grown long in the tooth.

Arreola took the title shot that was offered to him. In an era when beltholders fight only two or three times a year, it was better to fight now rather than to get more experience and hope another shot would come.

But Arreola didn't help his chances at winning.

"These are 365-day-a-year guys," HBO blow-by-blow announcer Jim Lampley said of the Klitschko brothers following the fight. "Somebody who thinks they can take 10 days off, have a party, drink and then come back to the gym and be on the same page is not going to beat a Klitschko."

Michael Phelps can smoke marijuana because he already has the gold medals. Chris Arreola must now understand that in the deep waters of the heavyweight division, the more one weighs, the quicker one sinks. If he wants to down a pint, he's going to need to drop some pounds.

Cotto-Pacquiao: The Mercenary and the Mercy Rule

November 16, 2009

Manny Pacquiao, basking in admiration, savoring the moment, pulled himself up on the ropes. The slow-motion camera captured him, two raised fists, a bare-chested hero looking out, the clarity of the camera shot presenting a 147-pound man as the larger-than-life figure he'd become.

Behind him and below, Miguel Cotto peered through distorted features: swelling above his right eye, bruising below, a cut over his left eye. His mouth remained agape as someone dabbed at the blood, wiped off the sweat. Someone else grabbed his right arm, and his puffed lips pursed shut. "I'm fine," he said, an insistence, an answer to a question normally reserved for his opponents.

Pacquiao, a mercenary unmatched, had disposed of yet another who stood against him. With that: his 50th win, his 10th current or former titlist vanquished, his seventh world title captured, his third "Fighter of the Year" award cemented.

Cotto had been saved by mercy, the referee stepping in 55 seconds into the 12th round, stopping the bout after the 336th punch to hit him, the 276th power punch landing solidly but being no worse, no more damaging than many that preceded it. The technical knockout as much saved him from further punishment as it did acknowledge that the fight, in reality, had long been over.

Cotto's father had asked his son's trainer to stop the bout before the 12th round even began. Cotto's wife and son had left the arena after the ninth round ended.

Pacquiao, neck-and-neck with Cotto at the beginning, took the lead early and, as he has done again and again, used his speed to pull away.

Pacquiao has three types of speed: lightning-fast punches, darting footwork, and elusive head and body movement. Individually, they can pose a difficult challenge. In concert, they present a dangerous combination.

Pacquiao stood in front of Cotto in the beginning of the fight, a seemingly hittable target. Cotto, emboldened by what was before him, threw out jabs, sent out hooks to the body, and, with Pacquiao often standing still while punching, was able to block or dodge some of the incoming fire.

But Pacquiao has more than one gear.

In. Out. Up. Down. Jabs. Crosses. Hooks. Uppercuts. He is an electron, never in one place, rotating between positions and punches with atomic energy.

The first round seemed even enough. Both fighters landed 12 shots. Then Pacquiao unleashed himself in the second half of the second round. He threw 81 punches, twice what he'd thrown three minutes before. He landed half of those, with 33 of those 40 being power punches.

Years ago, Pacquiao would use his speed as a method of delivering one-punch power. Now, his speed was part of his power; the shots that aren't seen are the ones that do the most damage.

Cotto got an example of that one round later: Less than a minute into the third, Pacquiao burst forward with a southpaw jab, a left hook to the body and a right hook to Cotto's left temple, all within the span of a second. Cotto, caught, and caught by surprise, fell to his right, touching the canvas with both gloves to keep himself from going down.

Pacquiao's most recent victories were a result of him being too fast for his opponents to hit, too fast for his opponents to keep from getting hit.

Cotto, the natural welterweight, was considered the bigger man, the harder puncher. But against such speed, Cotto deciding to use his own speed instead of his power, opting against loading up on the big shots and leaving himself more open to counters.

They traded flurries in the fourth, and then the momentum swung in a single sequence. Pacquiao, with a minute to go, had his back on the ropes, his gloves at his head, inviting Cotto to wail away at his body before following upstairs. Cotto obliged. Pacquiao clapped his gloves together and returned to the same position, asking for more.

He was Muhammad Ali to Cotto's George Foreman, resting in a Rope-a-Dope. Cotto missed a left hook, Pacquiao ducking under and escaping to the center of the ring.

Soon he had Cotto backed to the ropes. Cotto attempted to retaliate, landing a left, missing a right hook to the body, then throwing another left. Pacquiao threw a right hook upstairs, and as Cotto came in with a right cross, Pacquiao laced through a left uppercut that turned Cotto's head. Cotto toppled down. As with the first knockdown, he rose quickly, though this time he wasn't just surprised, but stunned, too.

Pacquiao could hit him. Pacquiao could hurt him. Pacquiao would continue to do both.

It became target practice. Between the sixth and ninth rounds, Pacquiao hit Cotto with 140 of 317 punches, a 44 percent connect rate, with 121 of those landing punches being power shots. Cotto, in contrast, hit Pacquiao with just 57 of 187 punches, less than half what Pacquiao landed, a 30 percent connect rate. Only 26 of those landed punches were power shots.

After the seventh round, a Nevada State Athletic Commission member checked on Cotto in his corner. After the ninth round, Cotto's wife took one of their sons from ringside, unable to watch any longer.

A Pacquiao punch cut Cotto above his left eye in the eighth. Not only would Cotto have to deal with blinding speed, but he'd have to do it half-blind.

By the 10th round, Cotto was doing what he could to survive, engaging with Pacquiao intermittently but mostly moving around the ring. With his opponent on his bicycle, Pacquiao took his foot off the gas. In that round, he threw only 57 punches, his lowest total since the early rounds, landing 20, half of what he'd landed in the ninth.

On more than one occasion in the 10th, 11th and 12th rounds, Pacquiao would stand his ground in the middle of the ring, displeased with Cotto's retreating. The audience booed as the 11th round drew to a close.

"There's one left?" Cotto asked his trainer as he returned to his corner.

"Yes," the trainer, Joe Santiago, responded. "Let's go."

Cotto, mentally and physically, was already gone.

In the 55 seconds that was the 12th round, Cotto threw just seven punches, six of them jabs. He landed nothing. Pacquiao threw 26 punches, landing 13, 11 of them power shots. The final left hand drove Cotto to the ropes.

He was not hurt by it, but he didn't need to be hurt any more than he already was. Referee Kenny Bayless jumped in, his left arm curling around Cotto's neck, embracing the wounded warrior, his right arm waving in the air, signaling his mercy.

After 34 minutes, Pacquiao had nearly doubled Cotto in landed punches, 336 to 172. He had nearly tripled Cotto in landed power shots, 276 to 93.

He had taken on his biggest test and made it look easy.

Tough Love: Jermain Taylor and Lou DiBella

December 14, 2009

Promoters can be parents, nurturing their fighters from the early years, recognizing their potential, providing them with opportunities, celebrating with them when they succeed and mourning with them when they fail.

Promoters can be pimps, sizing up fighters and signing them for what they can do — and what the fighters can do for them. They ply the fighters with play and pay, giving them attention so long as the investment is beneficial to both.

Some fighters remain worthwhile, their name value carrying forth long after their talent has faded. Others wind up treated like a flavor-of-the-month girlfriend. If they cannot sell tickets, or if they lose their titles, promoters lose interest. They become ignored, inactive.

Most promoters are a mix of both.

That is why the latest chapter in the story of Jermain Taylor and Lou DiBella is so different than the norm.

Taylor is 31 years old. Four years ago, he was the new middleweight champion, an undefeated talent with the backing of HBO marketing him a star. He was the heir apparent made heir actual. The future looked bright.

Today, everything about Taylor is former. He is the former champion, formerly undefeated, formerly on HBO, formerly a star. The future looked dark the moment his lights got turned out for the third time in his career.

That loss was in October, in the opening round of the round-robin "Super Six" super middleweight tournament. It was the 12th round when a straight right hand from Arthur Abraham sent Jermain Taylor falling backwards. Taylor's head slammed onto the canvas. He was unconscious, his right arm angled stiffly above.

There were six seconds on the clock, just six seconds left in the fight, when the referee stopped counting.

Six months before, that number was 14. Just 14 seconds remained when Jermain Taylor was knocked out for the second time in his career.

That loss came in April against Carl Froch. Taylor was ahead on two of the three scorecards, 106-102. He had knocked Froch down in the third round, but Froch got up and battled back. In the final round, Froch hurt Taylor, knocked him down and then finished him soon thereafter against the ropes.

Ahead early. Knocked out later. That was the same story as when Jermain Taylor was knocked out for the first time in his career.

That loss came in September 2007 against Kelly Pavlik. Taylor put Pavlik down in the second round but could not seal the deal. Five rounds later, Pavlik hurt Taylor with a right hand that sent him staggering to the ropes, following with a fusillade that left Taylor unconscious in a limp heap.

Lou DiBella was there with Taylor in January 2001, the night the Olympic bronze medalist made his professional debut. While other DiBella prospects eventually fell short of expectations, Taylor succeeded on the path so many promoters use for their fighters, a path DiBella has also used for Andre Berto and Paulie Malignaggi — build up their record, get them experience, get them on television, get them in the rankings, get them to challenge for a world title.

DiBella was there in July 2005, eyes closed, hands on

Taylor's shoulders, when Michael Buffer announced that Taylor had outpointed middleweight king Bernard Hopkins. DiBella jumped in the air and then cried as he embraced his fighter. He was there when Taylor retained the title in a rematch with Hopkins and for every subsequent defense of his championship.

DiBella was there with Taylor after the knockout loss to Pavlik, after the decision loss to Pavlik in their rematch, after the technical knockout loss to Froch, and after the knockout loss to Abraham.

DiBella can't be there anymore. It's hard to blame him.

"I have just been informed through numerous press reports that Jermain Taylor has elected to continue with his participation in the Super Six: World Boxing Classic tournament and will face Andre Ward in April," DiBella said Friday, Dec. 11, in a press release. "It is with a heavy heart, but strong conviction, that I will recuse myself and DiBella Entertainment as Jermain's promoter.

"Jermain's career has been outstanding, and it has been a pleasure and honor to promote him," DiBella said. "His victories against Bernard Hopkins remain the highlights of my career as a promoter. Jermain is not only a great fighter, but a good and decent man with a wonderful family. It is out of genuine concern for him and his family that I am compelled to make this decision.

"I informed him, as I do all my contracted fighters, that my goal was to help him secure financial stability for his family, maximize his potential, and leave our unforgiving sport with his health intact," DiBella said. "It is my belief that the continuation of Jermain's career as an active fighter places him at unnecessary risk. While he is undoubtedly capable of prevailing in future bouts, I cannot, in good conscience, remain involved given my assessment of such risk."

Few would have batted an eyelash had DiBella instead played the part of the pimp, profiting while Taylor continued for a minimum two more bouts in the Super Six tournament.

Rather, DiBella is acting like a parent, worried about Taylor's wellbeing, resorting to tough love.

The consensus following the knockout loss to Abraham was that Taylor should withdraw from the tournament and consider retirement. Reports were that Taylor had suffered a concussion and short-term memory loss. He had fought five times in the past 25 months, losing four of those fights, three by knockout.

Taylor could try to convince himself that he wasn't done as a fighter, that he had gassed out in the first fight with Pavlik and done better despite coming up short in the rematch, that he was beating Froch and was just 14 seconds from victory when he lost, that Abraham is favored to win the tournament and there should be no shame in being beaten by a world-class opponent.

But to many, Taylor has a pattern of getting knocked out against the upper tier of competition. In a time when there is more awareness of head injuries and how every concussion makes a person more vulnerable for suffering another, continuing in the tournament would be akin to playing Russian roulette.

That was the decision Taylor had to make: Was it worth it to bet his health, to say the knockouts were not part of a pattern, but a fluke, and to assume he could come back and redeem himself? And if he were to drop out of the tournament, would it be worth it to no longer compete at the highest level, to swallow his pride and face lesser opposition for smaller paychecks?

Taylor made his choice. And so DiBella made a choice of his own.

Parents nurture their children, recognizing their potential, providing them with opportunities, celebrating with them when they succeed and mourning with them when they fail. They give their children second and third chances, hold their hand when they struggle and hold them upright when they are unsteady.

Sometimes, however, there is nothing more that can be done.

Their love never dies. But the best choice left is to walk away and hope their children will understand why before it is too late.

Ask Not What Boxing
Can Do For You
February 1, 2010

Ask not what boxing can do for you. Because it won't. Why would it? Boxing is a business. The top priority is the bottom line.

"I know what people want, and they can go fuck themselves," promoter Bob Arum was quoted as saying after a January doubleheader on which Juan Manuel Lopez and Yuriorkis Gamboa both came out victorious. What people wanted, of course, was to see Lopez and Gamboa face each other sooner rather than later. Arum wants to make people wait.

In this case, Arum is right. Delaying Lopez-Gamboa is the best choice, not just for sales, but also for suspense. Promoters do so much less actual promoting these days, getting subsidized by networks and casinos instead of figuring out how to sell a fight to the fans. More will watch Lopez-Gamboa if it is built up over time instead of rushed before it ripens.

It's rare that anyone from within the boxing industry thinks about the good of the many rather than the good of the few. It's the exception. Whether it is the networks, the promoters (including Arum), or the athletic commissions, the prevailing attitude tends to be "Take it our leave it."

Take three nights of boxing scheduled on HBO for the first three months of 2010.

Take three pay-per-views scheduled for the first half of 2010 that will either be broadcast or distributed by HBO — Manny Pacquiao vs. Joshua Clottey, Bernard Hopkins vs. Roy Jones Jr., and Shane Mosley vs. Floyd

Mayweather Jr. — when in 2009 HBO finally seemed to grasp the idea, broadcasting three pay-per-views and distributing one other.

Take poor undercards either lacking in star power or lacking in competitive action, devoid of emotional investment in the voices of the broadcast commentators and devoid of noise from the sparse arena crowds. The overall product suffers, but the only thing that matters is the main event. Undercards don't contribute to sales; they only diminish profits.

Take promoters and networks either failing or refusing to harness the Internet for the benefit of the fans and, through that, the benefit of themselves. The UFC sells past fights on its Web site. Television channels have used Web sites such as Hulu to provide another outlet for people to view their programming, and the online advertising provides supplemental income. If Showtime could get a handle on all the various parties' rights to their broadcasts so past bouts can be shown on ESPN Classic, then why can't HBO wrangle all the selfish parties together to get the Gatti-Ward trilogy put on DVD? Illicit vendors have found a market for past fights on DVD. The demand is there.

Take the number of sanctioning bodies watering down the competition to the point that the best boxers rarely face the best boxers. This will never change — even if one sanctioning body were to go out of business, it's easy to imagine it being bought out by another sanctioning body and kept afloat just to bring in the additional sanctioning fees.

Take promoters refusing to do business with other promoters, other managers or other fighters because of grudges, greed, or a combination of each.

Take the biggest fights being inaccessible to regular fans. Take exorbitant ticket prices. Take most tickets going to high rollers, sponsors, and brokers who buy and then scalp.

Take the lack of stars being local attractions first. Take the fighters to Las Vegas instead. No wonder so many fighters complain about being avoided — they've not been promoted enough to bring any money to the table without relying on someone else to finance the match, and so there is little incentive to face them. They become high risk, low reward. Take Chad Dawson, for example. He came of age in a light heavyweight division with Antonio Tarver, Bernard Hopkins, Roy Jones Jr. and Joe Calzaghe. Only Tarver faced Dawson, and only after Showtime (and then HBO) came up with the money. Their two bouts had a combined attendance of 2,337.

Take promoters taking advantage of television license fees and putting on putrid cards. It has happened on ESPN2. It has happened on Versus. It has happened on Fox Sports Net. It has happened on HBO. And it has happened on Showtime.

Take bad decisions and talk of corruption or incompetence. Take talk of reform with a grain of salt. It doesn't matter that credibility is lost and fans lose confidence. Athletic commissions get their money from the promoters bringing cards to their states. So long as the promoters earn money, so do the commissions. There is no obligation to the paying customer.

And that is because we do take it instead of leaving it.

Boxing is a niche sport. The casual fans occasionally pay attention and occasionally pay for fights. But the rest of us are the hardcore, those so hungry for boxing that we are willing to subscribe to HBO and Showtime just for the boxing, willing to buy the pay-per-views no matter how many there are and no matter how bad the undercard, willing to dole out the dollars for the excitement of being at an event, willing to return again and again no matter how many times the bad decisions and other disappointments break out hearts.

We don't speak with our wallets. We do what we do because we enjoy the sport, and because the boxers deserve every dollar, every moment of attention. Floyd Mayweather Jr. earning eight figures for less than an hour of action is more palatable than Alex Rodriguez earning more than $170,000 per game, more than $40,000 per at-bat.

Sports arenas and concert venues can sell $5 hot dogs and $8 beers because we will pay for them. Movie theaters will charge $10 for tickets and $7 for popcorn because we will pay for them. Those in the boxing business will not do anything for the boxing fans unless their bottom line is threatened.

Ask not, then, what boxing can do for you. Ask what you are willing to put up with for the boxers.

Sudden Dearth:
Heartbreak, Emptiness
February 22, 2010

There would be no heartbreak if not for the closeness that precedes it and the distance felt following its abrupt arrival.

It is a shock to the system, unfortunately unforeseen, unsettlingly unstoppable. Happiness drains. Emptiness reigns.

We have hobbies, and those hobbies produce heroes, people whose fame, talents and perceived personalities produce such emotional connections despite the division between celebrities and commoners.

It is why large crowds showed to mourn Michael Jackson, whose death one man was quoted as comparing to the assassination of President Kennedy — "I will always remember being in Times Square when Michael Jackson died," the man told the Associated Press.

With actors, with singers and with dignitaries, grief results from death, from the person no longer being. With individual athletes, heartbreak comes from the person no longer being what we remember them being.

In no sport is that decline more immediate and more evident than boxing. We who are boxing fans all derive pleasure from the sport as a whole. But we all then become fans of certain boxers, investing extra emotion and attention, at first living vicariously through their victories, then later suffering sympathetically after their losses.

It can happen as quickly as a knockout, shattering the aura of invincibility. It can be painfully prolonged, with deteriorating skills leaving them shells of themselves. A fighter can recover much more easily from the setback of getting beat than he can from getting beat up and shellacked.

It begins as an eye-opener, the realization that the flame is flickering and the torch is being passed. Witness Roy Jones Jr. knocked off his perch and his feet with a single left hand from Antonio Tarver. See a fighter once known for his awesome speed rendered unable to move by Glen Johnson.

Watch Felix Trinidad get out-boxed and then stopped by Bernard Hopkins. See the mythical Mike Tyson proven mortal against Buster Douglas. Look on as Kostya Tszyu remained in his corner against Ricky Hatton and then never fights again.

Your world is turned upside-down watching world champions suddenly on the downslide. You must recognize the new reality, even as you struggle to accept it. And then you must wait for rock bottom before the worst is over.

What began as an eye-opener becomes something for which you wish you could close your eyes.

Like Muhammad Ali, nearly 39, long past his best years, taking far too much punishment against Larry Holmes.

Like Roy Jones, losing all but one round to Joe Calzaghe.

Like Jones, losing in less than a round to Danny Green.

Like Felix Trinidad, returning and then retiring and then returning and then retiring, out-boxed over 12 rounds by Winky Wright and then carried over 12 rounds by the aging Roy Jones.

Like Fernando Vargas, once precocious, now portly,

losing to a handpicked opponent in Ricardo Mayorga, the same handpicked opponent other returning fighters (Felix Trinidad, Oscar De La Hoya) had been able to take out.

Like Mike Tyson, once the baddest man on the planet, getting beaten into submission first by a champion in Lennox Lewis, then by a fringe contender in Danny Williams, and finally by a journeyman in Kevin McBride.

Like Jermain Taylor, vowing to continue his career despite suffering four losses, three by brutal knockout, in his last five fights.

Like Diego Corrales, unable to make lightweight anymore, unable to make junior welterweight, stepping up to the welterweight division and getting dismantled by Joshua Clottey.

Like Arturo Gatti learning that unlimited heart could not compensate for limited speed and skill against Floyd Mayweather Jr. He could earn a world title but would never be world class.

Like Gatti learning that power and guts could not overcome the size and timing of Carlos Baldomir. He had been bigger than junior welterweights but could no longer make that weight limit. He would be too small to beat welterweights.

Like Gatti learning that all the punishment he had been willing to take in order to dish it out had left him far less able to do either against Alfonso Gomez. He had lost to the pound-for-pound best in Mayweather, lost to a transitional champion in Baldomir, and then lost to Gomez, an opponent who would never belong near the top of a division.

That Gatti knew when it was time to retire saved him from becoming the sad spectacle seen with other declining fighters who never earned top dollar or never saved their keep. They are those measuring sticks seen in crossroad fights, names such as Antwun Echols and Kevin Kelley. Men like them market their remaining recognition even as they fail to recognize that the end had long come.

Heartbreak will happen. It will take away that which is comfortable and certain and do so at a time when you are least expecting it and least prepared to deal with it. What once had made you feel content is gone — a sudden dearth.

It stuns. It hurts.

And then we move on.

We move on to new prospects, only some of whom pan out.

We move on to new fascinations, some of whom we lose interest in.

We move on to new loves, giving them the kind of emotion and attention we had been scared to give for fear of being hurt again.

We live vicariously through their victories and hold them close in the hope they'll go far before they, too, go for good.

Pacquiao-Clottey:
Pride And/Or Glory
March 15, 2010

The tale of the tape listed their ages, their heights, their weights and the length of their arms. The previews and predictions included other physical attributes — Manny Pacquiao's speed, Joshua Clottey's strength.

The mind was the deciding factor.

Manny Pacquiao won his fight against Joshua Clottey before he even stepped in the ring with the Ghanaian welterweight. He won the fight in the gym, with his dedication to grueling workouts that enhanced his endurance and made strategy part of his muscle memory.

Joshua Clottey lost his fight against Manny Pacquiao in his corner between rounds, when he ignored the words of his trainer, Lenny DeJesus, words that began as advice, a call to action, and became pleas that received no reaction. Whatever work Clottey put in outside of the ring meant little if he wasn't willing to work inside of it.

Pacquiao threw 1,231 punches on the night, averaging nearly 103 punches per round, more than 34 punches a minute, one punch thrown every 1.75 seconds. His win wasn't merely the product of activity, however. He put himself in position to send out those shots, moved and angled his body to make Clottey miss, and had the fortitude to remain standing when Clottey landed.

It was another excellent performance in a streak of excellent performances. But what Pacquiao did is being overshadowed by what Clottey did not.

Clottey threw 399 punches on the night, less than one-third the output of his opponent. That averages out to about 33 punches per round, about 11 punches per minute, one punch thrown every 5.41 seconds. And though he was solid defensively, blocking nearly 1,000 of Pacquiao's punches, the fewer shots he threw himself, the less a shot he had of winning.

"He's fast," Clottey said in a post-fight interview, trying to explain his reluctance. "He's waiting for me to open, to counter me. That's why I'm taking my time."

Clottey had lost three times before: once by disqualification to Carlos Baldomir, once by unanimous decision to Antonio Margarito, once by split decision to Miguel Cotto.

"This is the first time I've lost a fight," Clottey said after the scorecards were read. Two of the judges had him winning just a single round. The third had him getting shut out.

Clottey was admitting defeat in the post-fight interview. He'd seemingly already admitted defeat while the fight was still going on.

Despite his advantages in size and strength and his ability to counter, Clottey seemed intimidated by Pacquiao's speed. He came forward behind his high guard, more often waiting for his opportunity instead of creating it.

He threw more than 40 punches in a round just once. That 11th round was also the stanza in which he landed the most — 12. He landed just 108 punches on the night, an average of nine per round. Three per minute. One landed punch every 20 seconds.

Pacquiao, by contrast, landed 246 punches total, an average of 20.5 per round, about 7 per minute. One landed shot every 9 seconds.

The pattern stuck. Clottey's trainer tried to get him

unstuck, to no avail.

"Let's take a chance," DeJesus said after the fourth round. By that point, Clottey had thrown 121 punches total, landing 36. Pacquiao had thrown 116 punches alone in the fourth round, 397 total, landing 68. Pacquiao wasn't landing much, but he was landing more and doing more.

"Baby, you gotta take a chance," DeJesus said after the fifth. "Come on, we gotta take chances."

Clottey shook his head. It might've been from the water being squirted in his face.

"What are you waiting for?" DeJesus said. "Come on. The kid's ahead. Let's throw punches. Hurt this guy."

By keeping his gloves up, Clottey wasn't getting caught with the kind of shots that knocked Ricky Hatton down and out, that floored and finished Miguel Cotto. Pacquiao instead went to where Clottey's elbows didn't reach. Through five, Pacquiao had landed 41 shots to Clottey's body, 43 to his face and head.

Pacquiao, too, held his hands high, blocking many of Clottey's shots, though his guard wasn't as impenetrable. But he also remained moving, going from just within range (and throwing punches) to just out of range (and dodging them). The southpaw Pacquiao kept pulling his head and left shoulder back, anticipating Clottey's right cross.

Clottey could land, and the crowd responded to the force of the blows on those rare occasions when he did. Sometimes he refused to follow up. Other times Pacquiao refused to let him, responding to Clottey's combination with barrage after barrage after barrage. In several rounds, Clottey would make a case for himself by landing a few solid shots, but Pacquiao would add a persuasive closing argument to punctuate his earlier statements.

Clottey put forth his defense. But that wouldn't help him win.

"Let's create openings now, okay? Let's create openings. Let's take a chance." DeJesus said after the sixth.

"Let's be creative. Let's throw punches now, okay?" DeJesus said after the seventh.

After the eighth: "We're losing every round, so let's get to it. We're losing every damn round. Come on."

Through eight, Clottey had landed 71 of 259 punches, compared to 145 of 785 for Pacquiao. Clottey had only landed 47 power shots. Pacquiao had landed 133.

Pacquiao had landed more power punches through eight rounds than Clottey would land, between jabs and power shots, on the night.

"You're taking a whipping, baby," DeJesus said after the ninth. "What's going on? Come on! We haven't won a round, baby. We've got to do something. Come on."

Clottey finally showed some fire in the final minute of the tenth, landing a left uppercut, a left hook and a right hand, followed by another left hook, another right, and another left uppercut. Pacquiao took it — perhaps testing himself as he had against Cotto last year — then clapped his gloves together, showing he was okay, the same joy of battle he displayed after getting hit cleanly by Erik Morales and Juan Manuel Marquez. Pacquiao withstood more clean hooks and uppercuts from Clottey in the 11th and 12th.

Pacquiao is a gladiator of immeasurable machismo, the owner of the fighters' version of that kind of insanity that drives a man to run a marathon, to put his body through pain just to see if he can do it.

For Pacquiao, fighting is about both pride and glory,

about winning and giving everything he has to get the victory. Clottey opted not to go for the glory, settling for survival, for whatever pride that comes with not getting run over the way Hatton and Cotto had.

Clottey didn't go down. But he didn't go down fighting either.

Kelly Pavlik vs. Sergio Martinez: The Sledgehammer and The Sword
April 19, 2010

Once, they were raw materials, malleable, forged under fire, tempered over time. They became extensions of their personalities, which in turn were extensions of the places where they had been shaped and refined into men. Fighting men.

Kelly Pavlik, child of the steel city of Youngstown, Ohio, is blue-collar, workmanlike, punching in and punching out, a man with sledgehammers in his hands. Sergio Martinez, product of the Latin America country of Argentina, is machismo in motion, fluid on his feet, confident in conquest, a swashbuckling swordsman whose fists become blades.

Power against speed.

Will against skill.

Pavlik was bigger and stronger. Martinez was smaller but sharper. He cut Pavlik, and then he cut him down to size.

Size can be an advantage and a disadvantage. Pavlik could hurt Martinez with a single shot. The problem was catching him with one.

Pavlik, nominally a middleweight, had drained his 6-foot-2 frame within the 160-pound limit but had regained more than 18 pounds between stepping on the scale and stepping in the ring. Martinez, normally a junior middleweight, had weighed the same as Pavlik on Friday afternoon but would be 11 pounds lighter than his opponent on Saturday.

Pavlik seemed sluggish and lumbering. Martinez

capitalized on their contrasting conditions.

The Argentine tangoed around the ring, taking quick steps forward and away, stabbing with his jab and thrusting forth with straight southpaw left hands. Less than two minutes into the first round he had sliced open a sliver of skin above Pavlik's left eye. Perhaps the red flowed because of the point of Martinez's paintbrush. Or maybe it was because of the canvas. Fighters who cut a lot of weight are more susceptible to cuts.

Pavlik swung his sledgehammers but failed to nail Martinez, who would duck and deke and dance away. Ten seconds into the second round, Martinez, facing a man who could end the night with one punch, had decided that Pavlik wouldn't be able to do so. Martinez dropped his gloves to his side, bent his head forward, certain of the sword despite his being outgunned.

The key was preventing Pavlik from pulling the trigger and then seeing the shots coming when Pavlik did fire. In the first two rounds, Pavlik threw just 63 punches, landing 17. Martinez was more active and more accurate, throwing 93 and landing 34.

Martinez could land first, or he could make Pavlik miss and then land in response. He had both the point and the counterpoint.

Pavlik, down two rounds, was down on himself. His trainer, Jack Loew, sought to get him back on track. "Don't get it in your head we can't get off," Loew said after the second round. "We'll get off."

Just as size isn't always an advantage, a slower fighter can compensate for his disadvantage in speed. The blue-collar Pavlik clocked back in and went back to work, stepping up his pressure and making subtle adjustments both on offense and on defense.

It would seem counterintuitive that Pavlik winding up with his power punches would increase their chances of landing. It seems logical that Martinez would have even more time to see them coming and get away from them. But Pavlik would shuffle forward and wait for Martinez to move before throwing his right hands in the direction Martinez was heading. And when Martinez threw his straight left hands, Pavlik would block or parry them with his right glove.

Martinez had out-landed Pavlik in three of the first four rounds. Through four, Martinez had landed 61 of 174 punches, or 15 of 43 per round. Pavlik had landed 38 punches out of 156 thrown, or 9 of 39 per round.

But Pavlik out-landed Martinez in rounds five through eight, landing 75 punches out of 186 thrown, or 19 out of 47, doubling the number of punches he'd landed in the first four rounds of the fight. Many of those were jabs — 36 landed in rounds five through eight, compared to the 11 he'd landed during rounds one through four. Martinez, meanwhile, landed 57 punches of 199 thrown in rounds five through eight, or 14 of 50 per round.

Pavlik sent Martinez to the canvas halfway through the seventh stanza, a right hand catching him off-balance. Though Martinez was not hurt, it cost him an additional point on the scorecards, and Pavlik had seized the momentum.

Yet Pavlik wasn't the only one for whom one punch could change a fight.

It wasn't a knockout blow, but a single left hand from Sergio Martinez early in the ninth round brought blood from above Pavlik's left eye and opened the floodgates — combination after combination from Martinez, torrents of lefts and rights. Martinez threw and landed more punches in that ninth round than he would in any other round, hitting Pavlik with 37 of 90. A majority were power shots, Martinez landing 34 of 63.

Pavlik never went down, but there would've been little argument against scoring the round a dominant 10-8 for Martinez.

Martinez had sucked the life from "The Ghost."

Before that round, Pavlik and Martinez had been close to even with their connects — Pavlik 113 of 342, Martinez 118 of 373 — and close to even on the scorecards.

The final four rounds, starting with the ninth, saw Martinez surge to victory. He landed 112 punches out of 313 thrown in rounds nine through 12, including 98 of 202 power shots. Pavlik was limited to 51 punches landed out of 191, landing less than half what Martinez did in the final four rounds. He only landed 21 of 50 power shots, less than one-fourth what Martinez did.

Those four rounds gave Martinez the unanimous decision: 116-111, 115-112 and 115-111.

Those four rounds also gave Martinez the middleweight championship, what he had referred to before the fight as "the Queen of championships" in Argentina, the same championship another Argentine, Hall of Famer Carlos Monzon, had held and defended 14 times.

It had been an extended ascent for Martinez. He is 35 years old, 49 fights and more than a dozen years into his career. Two years ago he was fighting on a non-televised undercard. In the past 18 months he has been on HBO four times.

He has been impressive, dominating Alex Bunema. He has been robbed in a draw with Kermit Cintron. He has entertained in a Fight of the Year candidate with Paul

Williams. And he has arrived with this win over Pavlik. It has been a rapid descent for Pavlik. Three years ago he went from prospect to contender to champion, scoring three straight highlight-reel knockouts over Jose Luis Zertuche, Edison Miranda and Jermain Taylor. The Taylor win made Pavlik the middleweight champion.

But his reign consisted of three wins against lesser opposition in a shallow division (Gary Lockett, Marco Antonio Rubio and Miguel Espino) and two bouts in other weight classes — a win over Jermain Taylor at super middleweight and a loss to Bernard Hopkins at light heavyweight.

He returns to Youngstown, to his steel city in what is, rather apropos, part of the rust belt. He came to the ring Saturday as a hero to a financially depressed area. Now, like his hometown, he must see if he can rebuild.

Mosley-Mayweather: The Last Word
May 3, 2010

To hear Floyd Mayweather Jr. is to listen to a man addicted to the tenor of his voice, a man who talks with a confident tone but whose caricatural hubris suggests he is compensating for some shortcoming.

His swagger inflates his standing: "I truly believe I'm the best," he says. "I know I'm the best. Someone could say, 'Oh, he said he's better than Muhammad Ali.' Yep. I'm better than Muhammad Ali. Sugar Ray Robinson? Yep. I'm better than Sugar Ray Robinson. I would never say there's another fighter better than me. Absolutely not."

He insolently insults his opponents. There were the personal barbs about Shane Mosley's hairstyle ("He got a Jheri curl, man. Come on, man, it's 2010."), his face ("Don't talk bad about Shane because he got a nose job."), his past use of performance-enhancing drugs ("Tell Shane to stop taking them steroids."). And then there were the physical taunts: "Vernon Forrest fucked you up. Winky Wright fucked you up. Miguel Cotto fucked you up. Money Mayweather, I'ma fuck you up some more."

Shane Mosley listened to Floyd Mayweather Jr. He heard sound and fury and concluded that it signified something.

"I think sometimes when people start doing a lot of barking, he kind of shows that he might be a little bit intimidated, a little bit afraid," Mosley said.

To hear Shane Mosley is to listen a man who believes bluster is bluffing, that sometimes it takes someone coolly confident to call a bully out to the schoolyard.

"He's backed into a corner," Mosley said. "He wants to believe that he's the best. He keeps saying that he's the best. He runs his mouth and says 'I'm the best. I'm the best. I'm the best in history.' At some point you have to back that up.

"I'm just as fast as he is," Mosley said. "I'm stronger than him. My arms are longer than his. I can hit him before he hits me. This is a real fight. He knows this, too.

"I don't bark," Mosley said. "I bite. My bite is very deadly."

To see Mayweather against Mosley was to watch a man whose ego wasn't compensation for what he isn't, but rather a representation of what he is — a man who can be both bombastic and fantastic, who will browbeat you and then defeat you.

To see Mosley against Mayweather was to watch a man who went from coolly confident to frozen and faltering. Just as Mosley never found the words to shut Mayweather up, he never found the way to shut Mayweather down.

Shutting down is Mayweather's game. He is quick. He is accurate. He is elusive. He makes what he does look easy. He takes what his opponent wants to do and makes it hard to get done.

Against the five men he had faced at welterweight prior to the Mosley fight, Mayweather had averaged 17 landed punches per round for every 37 thrown, nearly one in every two, an impressive 46 percent connect rate, according to CompuBox statistics. The average for welterweight fighters is 19 out of 58 per round, one in every three punches, or 33 percent.

Mayweather's five welterweight opponents averaged 6 landed punches per round for every 45 thrown, just one in every seven-and-a-half, a paltry 13 percent connect rate.

Against 13 welterweight opponents prior to the Mayweather fight, Mosley averaged 18 of 48 per round, a 38 percent connect rate. His opponents, on average, were 13 of 53 per round, a 25 percent connect rate.

It would not be the average Mosley fight. It would be the average Mayweather fight — he landed 17 of 40 per round, 208 total, a 43 percent connect rate, and he kept Mosley to 8 of 38 per round, 92 total, a 21 percent connect rate.

The scorecards: 119-109 (twice), 118-110, all for Mayweather. One round for Mosley on two scorecards, two for Mosley on the other. Fitting, for Mosley only had one big moment — as a result of two big punches.

Less than a minute into the second round, Mosley shot a jab to Mayweather's body and followed with a right hand that lifted Mayweather's left foot off the canvas. Fifty seconds later, Mosley landed a right hook that buckled Mayweather's knees.

That second round would see Mosley land 13 of 30 power shots. Mayweather survived the onslaught, however, and for the remainder of the fight he shut Mosley down — keeping him to just 29 total power punches landed in the next 10 rounds, including just 1 landed out of 7 thrown in the third, 0 of 7 in the fourth, 2 of 11 in the eighth, and 1 of 15 in the ninth. In turn, for the remainder of the fight, he shut Mosley out.

Mosley would blame his second-round success for his subsequent lack thereof. "After when I caught him with the big right hand, I might've started loading up a little bit too much," he said in a post-fight interview. "I played into his hands. I was just too tight. I couldn't throw nothing but big shots."

At first, Mosley loaded up on his punches because he knew he could hurt Mayweather. But later, he loaded up on his punches because he knew he couldn't hit him. Quick. Accurate. Elusive. Mayweather's skills didn't just cut down on the number of punches Mosley landed. His skills cut down on the number of punches Mosley threw.

Mosley's jab was mostly jittery and tentative. He was wary of the counter right hand that would come over top of it. It was a war of nerves, one man less willing to draw his gun when the other man could shoot first.

And with Mayweather's ability to slip punches, Mosley rarely had a perfect shot. The perfect shot was what he was looking for. Anything else would put him in danger of missing and getting hit hard in return. Mosley threw just 169 power punches on the night, only 14 per round, landing just 46, less than 4 per round.

As Mosley fell behind, he knew he had to do something else.

As Mayweather took over, he knew he need only do exactly what he'd been doing.

Desperation versus confidence. Mosley was a ball of nervous energy, bouncing on his feet, shuffling his hands, a speed bag shaking in motion but largely returning to the same spot, where he would be hit again and again.

"I'm as fast as he is," Mosley had said before the fight. Mayweather was faster.

"I'm stronger than him," Mosley had said. His punches lost their pop. Mayweather grinned at what his opponent had left, then landed some more crisp rights.

"I think sometimes when people start doing a lot of barking, he kind of shows that he might be a little bit intimidated, a little bit afraid," Mosley had said. In the eighth, Mosley arm-dragged Mayweather into the ropes, then started mouthing off at him. Mayweather threw a left hook and a hard right hand, and the men exchanging pleasantries, but now it was Mosley who was compensating for his shortcomings and Mayweather who was coolly confident.

To hear Shane Mosley after the fight was to listen to a man who sounded as if he had pushed his chips to the center of the table, thinking he had the winning hand, only to then learn that bluster doesn't always mean bluffing, that tough talk doesn't necessarily indicate hidden weakness.

To hear Floyd Mayweather Jr. after the fight was to listen to a man put aside the caricatural hubris that had characterized him beforehand. He didn't need it. He had done exactly what he promised he would do. For all of his talk, it was what he did — not what he said — that gave him the last word.

Amir Khan-Paulie Malignaggi: Tweet, Tweet Victory
May 17, 2010

They are called keyboard warriors.

They are those who take advantage of the impersonal nature of the Internet. They hurl insults, provoke and taunt with no fear of retribution, no potential for comeuppance. It is easy to hide behind the keyboard, be it in chat rooms, on message boards, or in newspaper comments sections.

Anonymity is empowering.

What happens when one keyboard warrior knows who the other keyboard warrior is? And what does it mean when the keyboard warriors have just as much bravado when the computers are off and the fight is on?

Rivalries become heated. Passion boils over.

In this case, the forum was Twitter, the battleground was the junior-welterweight division, and the resolution came with the first physical punches being landed more than three months after the first verbal blows were thrown.

The Internet's seemingly limitless expanses allow everyone to stake a claim. Not so in boxing. Opportunity is limited in the Sweet Science.

And so Amir Khan and Paulie Malignaggi came to a crossroads, Khan a world titleholder out of the United Kingdom searching for a foothold in the United States, Malignaggi a former titlist seeking one more chance to return to prominence.

They could've remained separate and still achieved their goals. But Malignaggi saw Khan as a threat — Khan had a world title, the backing of Golden Boy Promotions and the interest of HBO. The red carpet was being rolled out for Khan. Malignaggi, meanwhile, was close to being off the guest list.

Khan, in turn, saw Malignaggi as a stepping-stone, an established name and an accomplished fighter. Yes, Khan had the world title, the major promoter and the network money. Yet beating Malignaggi would earn him respect.

They needed each other.

In the past, one fighter might crash the other's press conference, call him out in an interview, or just say nothing publicly while privately lobbying for a match. In this case, they exchanged words megabit by megabit.

There was this Feb. 1 shot from Malignaggi: "KHAN DOESN'T WANT IT! He knows who is the man."

And this shot five minutes later: "IF U BRING UP AMIR KHAN, make sure u call him AMIR CON...or [he] will not ANSWER."

Khan — or, as Khan later claimed, a friend updating his Twitter account, fired back: "I wil fight paulie malanagi [in] may if he wants it ... let's get it on, I'll even travel 2 NYC."

And again: "I will come to paulie's city to defeat him n put up the WBA title on may 15th I have a HBO date let's get it on."

The trash talk continued. Khan's proposed fight with Juan Manuel Marquez fell through. By the middle of February, the fight with Malignaggi had been signed.

Two willing parties, each willing to motor his mouth, each wanting to shut the other up. These were no keyboard warriors. The testosterone flowed in person, too.

Rivalries became heated. Passion boils over.

They nearly brawled the day before they were scheduled to do so. At the weigh-in, Khan and Malignaggi went forehead to forehead, two rams digging in. Khan shoved Malignaggi, and suddenly Khan's supporters stormed toward the stage. All the while, the fighters' team members pulled the boxers away. If words were to be backed up, it would need to be done in the ring.

Words like: "You shouldn't throw stones if you live in a glass house and if you got a glass jaw, you should watch your mouth cuz I'll break your face."

Malignaggi's taunt spotlighted the fact that Khan had been knocked out in less than a minute by Breidis Prescott and knocked down by other opponents. But Malignaggi had only knocked out five opponents in his 27 victories, the last one being a technical knockout nearly seven years ago against an opponent of a far lesser pedigree than Khan.

Malignaggi didn't have the power to beat Khan. He didn't have the speed either.

In every sport, there are the superstars who excel at everything they do. But there are also those who become accomplished by compensating for their weaknesses and accentuating their strengths.

Paulie Malignaggi had been able to succeed despite his lack of power, calling upon fast hands and good movement. He scored victories over fighters who were slower (using his speed to avoid them) or smaller (and came forward against Malignaggi, who in turn out-boxed them).

Khan was bigger and faster. And he didn't have to worry about Malignaggi testing his chin.

Not that he gave Malignaggi many chances to hit him.

Malignaggi landed just one of every four punches he threw, 127 of 531 on the night, 57 of which were jabs, 70 of which were power punches.

Malignaggi's hand speed wasn't superior. He wasn't using foot movement either. Khan was able to target and land. Khan had a 40 percent connect rate, hitting Malignaggi with 259 of 653 shots, including 151 jabs that knocked Malignaggi's head backwards and, in turn, set up 108 landed power punches.

Malignaggi had been full of fire before the fight. Khan doused those flames. Just before referee Steve Smoger stepped in to end the bout in the 11th round, Malignaggi looked the part of a beaten man, while Khan looked prepared to issue more of a beating.

Khan beat respect into Malignaggi — "Amir just came and fought a very good fight," he said in a post-fight interview. "I give him a lot of credit."

And by taking a beating, Malignaggi earned Khan's respect. They embraced in the ring, two fighters who showed they knew how to punch more than a keyboard.

"Paulie was a tough opponent," Khan said early Sunday morning on Twitter. "He came strong and sharp.

"My eyes are a little bruised," Khan wrote. "I got a few elbows and head butts!"

You should've seen the other guy.

You sure weren't gonna hear him.

Malignaggi's Twitter stood silent, its last update coming two days before the fight. There would be no more verbal blows — not when the physical shots had given Khan the Tweet, Tweet victory.

Miguel Cotto Left Yuri Foreman Without a Leg to Stand On. As For Arthur Mercante?

June 7, 2010

BRONX, N.Y. — We talk of boxing as war, an unarmed microcosm of armed conflict. The boxers, then, are variations on themes, versions of warriors, historic and contemporary.

There were the soldiers who marched up to battle bolstered by drummers and backed by flags. And then there were the silent assassins, those samurai and sharpshooters who approached each mission with the same quiet dedication, emotionless but effective.

Yuri Foreman began his march to the ring to the sounds of the shofar, a ram's horn, the blowing of which is steeped in Jewish tradition. That gave way first to Hebrew singing, and then to heavy metal chords, the signature start to Pantera's "Walk," the aggressive anthem whose refrain demands respect.

Miguel Cotto's walk was unexceptional, briefly accompanied by music that was nothing worth noting. He would soon pick up the beat in three-minute bursts.

Every second of every minute, every minute of every round is its own little battle. Miguel Cotto did not win every battle. But he was more capable than Foreman and more confident than him. That won him the war.

Cotto was smaller but stronger. Foreman was bigger but faster. Foreman couldn't capitalize on his height advantage, nor could he handle Cotto's power. Cotto, meanwhile, offset Foreman's size and speed from the outset.

121

Cotto is naturally left-handed but fights from an orthodox stance. He worked behind a strong jab to close the distance between himself and the taller fighter. Foreman's jab lacked conviction. When it wasn't aimed at air, it hit harmlessly against Cotto's gloves.

Foreman couldn't keep Cotto away with his hands. And so he tried to keep him away with his feet.

Sometimes Foreman bounced in and out. Sometimes Foreman shuffled left and right. Rarely did he plant in one position and punch.

Whereas Cotto used his jab to get in range, Foreman advanced without covering fire. Cotto didn't need to chase after Foreman so long as Foreman put himself in the strike zone.

Cotto landed 32 punches over the first three rounds. His timing countered Foreman's movement and speed. There was the stiff jab in round one that caught Foreman as he shuffled sideways, knocking him backward to the ropes. There was the stiff jab in round two that caught Foreman as he jumped forward, and a right hand later that stanza that hit Foreman as he moved.

Before that second round ended, Foreman, with his back to the ropes, stopped moving and sent out a strong left-hook counter. Cotto barely blinked.

The trick, then, would be to blind him.

Foreman's jab, taken alone, was ineffective. When paired with a right hand, however...

Foreman started the fourth by shooting out a sharp jab and immediately followed with a hard right hand that connected flush. Later, he feinted with the left and again landed with the right. He went back to that feint-cross combination two more times.

It was the only round that Foreman won on all three

judges' scorecards (one judge also gave Foreman the third).

"I didn't use my jab much in the fourth round, and that was the point of Yuri Foreman taking advantage over me," Cotto would say after the fight. "And then I am back with [trainer Emanuel Steward's] instructions in the next rounds."

Steward told Cotto to go back to the jab. But instead it would be left hooks and a left uppercut that brought the momentum back in Cotto's favor in the fifth. Foreman, emboldened by his success in the previous round, was there to get hit by all of the above.

Foreman retreated, returning to moving around the ring. Cotto's pressure and power were breaking him.

Sometimes a fighter will land his best shot and know he can land another. But sometimes that best shot won't deter his opponent, nor will it damage him.

The song Foreman had entered the ring to unwittingly foreshadowed how the fight would go.

"Can't you see I'm easily bothered by persistence?" the song begins. And later: "Be yourself. By yourself. Stay away from me."

Foreman couldn't keep Cotto away. Foreman couldn't get away either, though he tried.

The crowd booed. They had come to a stadium, more than 20,000 strong, most of them there to see Cotto win. Like the crowd at a bullfight, they wanted blood.

The matador has the advantage because the bull has already been wounded. It has been slowed, and it is slowly bleeding out.

Forty-five seconds into round seven, Foreman, attempting to evade Cotto, shuffled to his right and had his right knee go out from beneath him. Foreman was already wearing a knee brace on that leg — the result of an injury suffered 14 years prior, an injury that had bothered him occasionally since then.

Referee Arthur Mercante Jr. gave Foreman time to try to walk the pain off, just as Mercante had done a year before when, coincidentally, Joshua Clottey hurt his leg against Cotto.

Cotto was already beating Foreman; he was up 59-55 on two scorecards, 58-56 on the other. Foreman had resorted to moving away from Cotto. The injury would keep him from doing even that.

Foreman limped forward and threw a left hook. Cotto met him in the middle of the ring and did the same. With Foreman mostly immobilized, Cotto threw and landed more punches in the seventh than he would in any other round, going 29 of 65 (27 of 44 with power punches). Foreman tried absorbing the barrage, and then he tried avoiding it. At the round's halfway point, his right leg gave out again.

Mercante called on a ringside physician to take a look at Foreman. But the physician didn't — Foreman told Mercante he wanted to fight. When Foreman could find the strength to have his legs beneath him, he fired away with flurries. The rest of the round he was hunched over, a car driving on with a flat tire when it would be wiser to pull off to the side of the road.

Foreman's leg buckled again halfway into round eight, though he remained standing. Fifteen seconds later, Foreman's trainer threw a towel into the ring.

Cotto raised his glove. Foreman walked back to his corner. The crowd roared its disapproval. And Arthur Mercante Jr. wanted none of it, ordering the ring cleared of commission members and corner-men.

Mercante asked Foreman if he wanted to continue. "You fight hard," Mercante said. "I don't want to see you lose like that."

Foreman's trainer, Joe Grier, didn't want to see Foreman lose the way he was losing.

"I recognized that it was a serious injury," Grier said later. "It wasn't something he'd be able to shake off. He was in it. It wasn't like he was out of the fight. He was fighting back. He scored very well and was very effective. But then I started noticing he was starting to get hit even more. He was no longer mobile. He was no longer Yuri Foreman.

"I wanted him to leave with some dignity."

Grier asked commission inspectors to stop the fight. They couldn't get Mercante's attention, Grier said. "I had to get this stopped," he said. "I don't know what else I was expected to do."

Two minutes after the fight was off, it was on again.

After the eighth, Mercante walked Foreman back to his corner. "Who threw in the towel?" Mercante asked. "I did," Grier said.

At the same time, ring announcer Michael Buffer tried to clarify the situation. "The towel that came into the ring came was from an outside source," Buffer announced. "Not the corner."

The fight didn't last much longer. Thirty seconds into the ninth, Cotto landed a left hook to Foreman's body. Foreman went down to one knee. Mercante waved it off.

Should he have waved it off earlier? Foreman had already been left without a leg to stand on. What about Mercante?

"The towel came in in the heat of the battle," Mercante said afterward. "There was a good exchange going at the moment. The towel came in. I didn't know where it came from. About 10 seconds prior to that, someone in the corner said stop the fight. There was no need to stop the fight.

"It was a great fight," Mercante said "That's what the fans came to see."

Referees have ignored towels being thrown into the ring — notably, Mickey Vann during the 2007 brawl between Michael Katsidis and Graham Earl. Katsidis knocked down Earl twice in the first round and again in the second. Soon thereafter, Earl's corner threw in the towel. Vann picked up the towel and tossed it out, and a little bit later Earl scored a knockdown of his own.

Referees have also let fighters continue fighting despite injuries: broken hands, broken jaws, bad cuts, eyes shut by swelling. It is up to the referee and the ringside physician — and the fighter's corner — to protect a fighter from being too brave.

From ringside, Foreman looked to be a sitting duck taking unnecessary punishment. On second viewing, he never appeared to be badly hurt, and he was fighting back when he could.

But a referee is not there to care about a fight's entertainment value. He is there to enforce the rules and protect the fighters. Whether it is a great fight, and whether the fans will be angered with a fight ending by injury, should never matter.

Foreman wanted to fight. He was willing to face Cotto despite the injury, willing to rise every time his knee failed him, willing to come out of his corner to face the onslaught.

He didn't suffer severe consequences because of this. But it is dangerous to use hindsight when evaluating decisions.

Should Mercante have waved the fight off earlier because of Foreman's injury? Perhaps not. But he shouldn't have kept it going merely because it was a good fight — a fight that most of the 20,272 in attendance wanted to see end with the bull being brought down, with Foreman being thrown to the lions.

"People came to see a good fight," Mercante said. "I felt I did the right thing."

There isn't an easy answer. We talk of boxing as a war. We cheer on action. We follow the drama.

We leave room for mercy.

They Don't Need to Be Great to Be Good
June 28, 2010

I stood in a Massachusetts concert hall. So did 1,129 others, rising from their seats in response to the action in the ring.

A regular at New England boxing shows might have recognized three of the 12 names on the card. Someone who follows boxing closely might have heard of just one, the headliner, Edwin Rodriguez, an undefeated super-middleweight prospect out of Worcester, who was fighting that night in his adopted hometown. A casual boxing fan not from the area wouldn't have known of any of the fighters.

It didn't matter.

They roared as Sonya Lamonakis, a female heavyweight making her pro debut, threw hard hooks at Kasondra Hardnette, an Ohio resident who had lost both of her two fights. They clapped at the end of a give-and-take round between Isiah Thomas, a light heavyweight from Michigan, and his opponent, Larry Pryor of Texas. And they jumped to their feet when Ryan Kielczewski, a 130-pound prospect from an hour away in Quincy, Mass., scored a knockdown against a Miami fighter named Juan Nazario.

Boxing fans are an assortment of critics, skeptics and pessimists, conditioned to evaluate speed, power, skills and smarts, to evaluate who could develop into a contender and who could someday be champion. They are logical questions to consider. The dream for fighters, after all, is to be the best.

Boxing, in a way, is like music. Most people prefer to follow a select number of performers. The talented ones stand out, get more airplay and earn more money. But there are those people who enjoy music in general. They turn on the radio and go to concerts and are moved by the notes even if the musicians aren't notable.

They don't need to be great to be good.

The natural storyline of the fight game can detract from our enjoyment. This fighter is being overhyped. That fighter has been exposed. This fighter is being protected. That fighter hasn't beaten anyone.

The biggest fights will always be those pitting the best against the best, and those fights are the ones fans should demand. We can continue to ponder fighters' places, to consider how they measure up to other combatants. We want clarity with our competition. But we also want entertainment.

The best fights, however, don't always involve the best fighters.

In 2004, the Cleveland Browns were 3-7 and the Cincinnati Bengals were 4-6 when they had a shootout that ended 58-48 for the Bengals. It was much the same in 2007, when the Bengals and Browns met in the second week of the season and combined for 96 points, 51-45 for the Browns. Neither team was terrible that year, but neither went on to make the playoffs.

Neither Micky Ward nor Emanuel Augustus ever won a world title.

They at least received respect, though. Others that have accomplished less than Ward and Augustus have still work hard even though they receive less play.

Bouts involving star boxers or main event fighters produce excited calls from ringside announcers and standing ovations from arena audiences. The action needs not be sustained so long as the suspense is intense. But fights involving preliminary fighters often are received with detached emotion and lessened interest — except, that is, for the most exceptional brawls. How many good undercard fights have been ignored while commentators discuss the coming feature attraction?

We appreciate and turn our attention to great fighters precisely because they are so rare. Still, there is boxing beyond what is shown on HBO, Showtime and ESPN2, beyond what takes place in Vegas casinos and sports arenas. Most of those boxers never make national television, never fight in the main event surrounded by several thousand. Rather, they swap leather in ballrooms and bingo halls, in bars, clubs and hotels, smaller venues with smaller audiences. Those audiences are nonetheless appreciative.

And so there are the thousands who turn up at the Carroll County Agriculture Center in Westminster, Md., to see light heavyweight Mark Tucker. There are the thousands who buy tickets to the Patriot Center in Fairfax, Va., to see junior middleweight Jimmy Lange. There are local cards where competitive matchmaking means butts in seats, and there are local cards where hometown heroes are given designated opponents so the crowd can be sent home happy.

It is about getting your money's worth. Sometimes that means a critically acclaimed movie. Sometimes that means a blockbuster popcorn flick.

That is why there were those of us who ordered the pay-per-view this past Saturday featuring Julio Cesar Chavez Jr. and John Duddy, expecting a great fight even thought it didn't involve great fighters. While they did play to a stadium audience at the Alamodome in San Antonio, they performed on an independent pay-per-view, one where the buy rate will be in the tens of thousands rather than hundreds of thousands.

Chavez Jr. has been written off as an ordinary fighter who receives attention merely because of his famous father. He lacks an amateur pedigree and has learned on the job while fighting as a pro, facing opponents who are at a disadvantage in size, power or class.

Duddy had once been touted for a title shot even though his selling point was his heavy hands, not his skills. When the unheralded Walid Smichet busted his face up in 2008, and when the ordinary Billy Lyell handed him his first loss in 2009, some saw it as only right that someone had finally deflated any Duddy hype.

Neither will ever enter the Hall of Fame. That doesn't mean they shouldn't enter a ring. Neither will headline HBO. That doesn't mean they mustn't be seen on TV. Chavez-Duddy was an entertaining brawl. They didn't need to be great to be good.

Pacquiao-Mayweather:
A PR War With No Winners
July 19, 2010

Hope is a hot bath that has just had its stopper pulled. It is comforting but fleeting, draining away until the inevitable emptiness.

There is no more hope that Manny Pacquiao and Floyd Mayweather Jr. will fight, not in 2010, at least. That plug was pulled weeks ago, hope edging closer each day to the abyss, struggling against the current but ultimately succumbing. The fight has gone down those proverbial tubes.

"I'm not really thinking about boxing right now," Mayweather, coaching a charity basketball game Sunday, told the Associated Press. "I'm just relaxing. I fought about 60 days ago, so I'm just enjoying myself, enjoying life, enjoying my family and enjoying my vacation."

That would have to suffice for the reason why Mayweather will not fight Pacquiao. It was an explanation that failed to explain, just as Mayweather turned down a Pacquiao fight without ever officially turning it down.

There had been subtle signs that this would be so.

Three weeks ago we were told negotiations for a fight between Pacquiao and Mayweather were over, that the hard part was done.

On the surface, this was progress.

Half a year ago the negotiations had sputtered out spectacularly. They had agreed on the money (a 50-50 split), a weight limit (welterweight), and the size of the gloves (8 ounces). They could not agree on drug testing.

They would not agree on drug testing. It was a matter of ego that masqueraded as a matter of principle. Pacquiao went on to defeat Joshua Clottey. Mayweather went on to beat Shane Mosley.

Talk again turned to Pacquiao-Mayweather. This time, discussions would have to be different if the fight were to be made — THE fight, a bout pitting not only the two best welterweights in the world, but the two best fighters, pound-for-pound, of the past decade. Something would have to change. Strong stances would have to weaken. Egos would have to be put aside.

There was hope. How can you miss out on a chance to be in the biggest fight of your career? Of your generation? Of your sport? How can you miss out on a chance to make tens of millions?

They chose against it once. How could anyone make the same mistake twice?

Some reports came out a few weeks ago that this most recent round of negotiations had concluded successfully. All that remained now was Mayweather's signature on the contract. The easiest element. The most essential element.

Those reports didn't come from Mayweather's camp, but from Pacquiao's promoter, Bob Arum. Another report, however, warned that not everything had been agreed to. That kind of news wouldn't have come from Arum, but from other sources close to the negotiations. That report portended trouble, and even if you weren't inclined to believe it over those originating from Arum, there was still a simple but important issue:

Mayweather had not yet signed a contract.

Why announce that the fate of the fight was now in Mayweather's hands unless Arum was waiting —

keyword: waiting — for Mayweather to sign? It was but a public relations ploy, one designed not only to spotlight that Mayweather hadn't yet put his signature on the contract, but to convince observers that Mayweather was the only obstacle remaining.

And so Arum waited. So did we. Hope took the form of cautious optimism: Mayweather will sign. He has to. Doesn't he?

Arum's company, Top Rank, soon placed a countdown clock on its website, ticking away the days, hours, minutes and seconds under the heading of " 'Money' Time: Mayweather's Decision." The deadline: Saturday, July 17, 3 a.m. Eastern Time, midnight Pacific Time for those, like Top Rank and Mayweather, based out of Las Vegas.

Hope still floated, but there was a sinking feeling. Mayweather hadn't signed in the past couple weeks. Why would he sign now?

Top Rank scheduled a stunt of a conference call for the moment the deadline passed.

The deadline, Arum explained, was merely when the exclusive negotiating period would end. The promoter would pursue matches pitting Pacquiao with other members of the Top Rank roster, perhaps a rematch with Miguel Cotto, perhaps a fight with Antonio Margarito. Those fighters would have 10 days to accept a bout with Pacquiao, which would be scheduled for Nov. 13.

If Mayweather were suddenly to accept the Pacquiao fight, that would take precedence. But only if a deal had not already been made for Pacquiao to face Cotto or Margarito.

Sliver of hope.

Mayweather was silent through all of this. He had

essentially turned down the fight without saying yes or no. He had essentially turned down the fight without explaining why. And then the AP asked.

"I'm not interested in rushing to do anything," Mayweather told the AP.

Hopeless.

This second negotiating process had been set up to avoid making the same mistakes as the first time, when too many combustible elements involved caused the fight to implode. According to Arum, Top Rank spoke this second time to Pacquiao and then communicated with Mayweather through what amounted to a 21st century game of telephone. Top Rank spoke with a mediator — HBO Sports executive Ross Greenburg — who in turn talked to Mayweather's adviser, Al Haymon, who then would speak with Mayweather.

Arum has not been shy in the past about communicating his separate displeasures with Greenburg, Haymon and Mayweather. This time he had no ill will toward the first two and no ire for Mayweather.

"Obviously the problem was that Floyd, for whatever reason, and I'm sure he has a valid reason, didn't want to commit," Arum said. Perhaps, Arum speculated, Mayweather was uncertain about fighting without his trainer and uncle, Roger Mayweather, whose criminal trial on assault charges was to begin in August. Such concerns would be understandable, Arum said.

It was not a surprise that Arum played nice. He had already proven with Pacquiao-Clottey in March that Pacquiao could star in a large event and a successful pay-per-view without Mayweather. There was no need to underscore that point a second time. Such provocation could prevent Mayweather from ever stepping in the ring with Pacquiao. Arum could move on to Plan B without shutting the door completely on Plan A.

PR takes finesse. Arum was attempting to thread a needle. Mayweather also knows how to play the game. Keep your words spare. Don't over-explain. People will ask questions, but you still choose what to answer — and when, and how.

Within the subtext of what little he told the Associated Press, Mayweather essentially said he would not fight Pacquiao in 2010 but did not take away the possibility of fighting him again later. Increasing the suspense. Increasing the desire. And also increasing the discontent.

If Mayweather didn't want to fight Pacquiao in November, why not say so earlier? Why let your adviser continue to negotiate if your end of the negotiations isn't being conducted in good faith?

For all the improvements in the negotiating process, this remained a PR war. Top Rank wanted to put the pressure on Mayweather, and Mayweather didn't want to be pressured into giving Top Rank what it wanted.

Never mind what the fans wanted. Never mind what it would add to the fighters' already historic legacies. Never mind what it would add to the fighters' already sizable bank accounts.

Top Rank will go on to put Pacquiao in against Cotto or Margarito, its proceeds smaller but its profits kept in-house. Mayweather will go on to face whomever he decides to face, whenever he decides to face them. As with Pacquiao-Clottey and Mayweather-Mosley, neither fight will be the fight fans had hoped for.

Hope, after all, is a hot bath that cannot overcome a cold business.

'Iron' Deficiency: Tyson Lawsuit A Gold Mine of Laughs

August 9, 2010

This is the story of a former boxer hoping to score the biggest upset in the history of the sport.

Michael Wayne Landrum Sr. is attempting to surpass Buster Douglas and that legendary 1990 knockout of Mike Tyson in Tokyo. He is suing Mike Tyson for $115 million, claiming the former heavyweight champion stole his nickname, took away his opportunity, pilfered any possibility of fame and fortune for a welterweight who said he was "Iron Mike" first.

Landrum is 52 years old now. Nearly three decades have passed since he became a pro boxer. Some 25 years have gone by since the Californian had his last pro fight. That year was the same year Tyson turned pro as a New York knockout sensation.

Tyson retired five years ago. No matter. Landrum wants justice now, in the form of nine figures.

Landrum once only wanted $5,000 from Tyson and Tyson's promoter at the time, Don King. That was 1996 and 1997, when Tyson was still active but Landrum was not. Landrum was merely pondering a comeback in 1997, filling out paperwork for the California State Athletic Commission seeking a boxing license.

Landrum tried the small claims court in Los Angeles back then. He included three copies of that legal paperwork in this most recent lawsuit, but did not provide any indication of what happened in that case. He has gone bigger this time — a payout 23,000 times larger, litigation filed in a bigger venue.

He went to the U.S. District Court in Riverside, Calif., setting legal wheels in motion June 28. Later, he filed 29 pages attempting to detail his case.

It didn't get national attention until last week, when the TMZ tabloid website published a short story. TMZ got his age wrong, and it also had where he filed the lawsuit incorrect. No matter. Numerous news outlets picked up on TMZ's piece and followed suit with articles of their own.

Landrum said he had trademarked "Iron Mike" before his first pro fight, which came a few years before Tyson got paid to punch. Once Tyson took the nickname, Landrum's career had about as much chance of succeeding as Peter McNeeley did.

Landrum told TMZ he was "hindered from getting any major title fights or sponsorships because of the name confusion."

Those opportunities should have been limitless for a man of Landrum's ability. As he had noted when applying for a boxing license from California in 1997, he had fought seven times in the amateur ranks, winning four times, including twice by knockout, and only losing in three of those bouts. Upon turning pro, he had steamrolled through the opposition and built up a wealth of experience, getting in the ring 11 times, winning six, including three by knockout, losing but four bouts and fighting to one draw.

Landrum even listed all of his professional boxing matches when asked to on the application. In that section he was even more impressive than on the previous page, winning eight fights in California between December 1983 and February 1985 and losing none. Down went Roberto Hernandez, Miguel Miranda and Eddie Johnson, all by knockout. Up went Landrum's gloves following decision wins over Rodolfo Gonzalez, Otis Rogers, Rubin Guero, Rod Stevins and Steven Bell.

None of those fights are listed on the BoxRec.com online database. BoxRec also has no record of any boxing matches taking place in California on the days of Landrum's victories.

The website is not always completely correct with its listings. That has to be why the only Mike Landrum in its system is a man who was 0-2, who fought once in San Jose, Calif., in April 1982, losing by first-round knockout to Steve Acosta, and once in Carson, Calif., in April 1985, losing by second-round knockout to Kevin Payne.

Landrum is a humble man. Rather than include proof of any of his victories in his filing with the court, he instead attached a photocopied page from the September 1985 issue of THE RING magazine, noting Kevin Payne's win over Landrum in a welterweight bout. He also included three fighter contracts in which he committed to facing a trio of opponents: Acosta, Payne, and Hector Martinez, the last bout apparently one that never happened.

This noted veteran had a strong claim to the name. Two letters dated from 1996 and 1997 were signed by Rob Lynch of the California State Athletic Commission, noting that Landrum was last licensed to box by the state in 1985, and that "[h]is professional ring name was 'Iron Mike Landrum.' "

He has proof of the trademark, too. A certificate from California's secretary of state showed Michael Wayne Landrum Sr. as the registrant of "Iron Mike." He is not the kind of man to procrastinate; he had trademarked the nickname with the state on April 22, 2010.

Landrum told the state the trademark hadn't been used anywhere until Nov. 23, 1983. Transcending time and space, the trademark was first used in California on Nov. 10, 1983, he said.

With that trademark registration filed just this year, the Spike TV television show "Knockout Sportsworld" should have known better than to use the "Iron Mike" nickname in a national poll without Landrum's permission. That is why he has sued the company that produces the show, which features knockouts from the various combat sports, for $1 million. If Tyson using his nickname deprived Landrum of making money two decades ago, then the television show's galling behavior is costing him money now.

Now is the proper time for justice for Michael Wayne Landrum Sr. Now, when the complaints are fresh and the damage is raw, is when he deserves payback. Now, when Tyson is broke and retired, is when Landrum can resuscitate his career, never mind his bank account.

Now is the time to root for "Iron Mike" Landrum. After all, he is a man of truth, a man who knows it is best to wait to take action, and to take action only when he has all the right reasons for doing so.

Pascal-Dawson:
A Clash in Styles, A Dynamic Duel
August 16, 2010

MONTREAL — There are enemies and there are rivals. Jean Pascal and Chad Dawson were both.

Theirs was a rivalry born out of competition. Dawson was regarded as the number-one light heavyweight in boxing. Pascal was a spot or two behind him. Their signatures swirled upon dotted lines, setting a night to determine who was truly better.

Theirs was not a friendly rivalry. Their personalities were too different.

Dawson speaks impassively, a soldier who believes in his training and ability and quietly accomplishes his missions. He is self-assured but not assertive, camouflage trunks, defiant rap anthems, a boxer who hits and moves on fight night and is then rarely heard from in-between bouts.

Pascal boasts effusively, a performer who not only believes in his training and ability but wants everyone else to as well. He is swagger personified, hot pink splashed on his trunks, operatic bursts leading off his ring walks, an aggressor outside of the ring and between the ropes.

They went nose-to-nose after weighing in, Dawson clasping his hands together behind his back, Pascal's hands at his sides, two rams communicating nonverbally and unblinkingly but not yet butting heads.

After separating, each flexed a bicep at the crowd, Pascal tapping the muscle on his left arm with his right index finger before looking toward Dawson and smirking. Later, Pascal turned, faced fully outward, posed with both arms and stepped in front of Dawson. Dawson just shook his head and turned away.

"Anything you do, I can do better," Pascal's actions were saying.

"Anything you do won't mean a thing," Dawson's responses promised.

Theirs was a clash in styles, personal and professional, that spawned a dynamic duel.

Rivalry. Speed against speed, skills against skills. Dawson came forward, flicking out jabs, seeking to close the distance and create an opening. Pascal moved away before exploding at Dawson, a cobra rearing his head and suddenly striking. Both would try to duck or dodge each other's shots. When Dawson missed, he would cautiously reset and begin anew. When Pascal missed, he would often throw caution to the wind and continue his attack, targeting wherever Dawson's head or body had reappeared.

Neither had much success in the first three rounds. Pascal threw 46 punches in each of those three-minute periods, or 138 total, landing 9, 7 and 14, or 30 total. Dawson went 7 for 26 in the first, 8 of 40 in the second, and 10 of 30 in the third, totaling 25 landed punches out of the 96 thrown in the opening nine minutes of action.

Pascal took those three rounds on all three judges' scorecards, throwing more and hitting harder. He would duck his head down and charge forward with a lead right hook or cross, some aimed at the body, others at the head, and then would follow with left hooks. If Dawson ducked or blocked but remained in range, Pascal would punch more, sending shots out from unorthodox angles, not giving Dawson any respite.

Rivalry. Smarts against smarts. Dawson attempted to break his habit of ducking incoming right hands. Doing so would not keep him from harm. When he didn't duck, the hooks hit his body. When he did duck, the hooks hit his head. And Pascal would then keep throwing. So Dawson began to take a step back before moving in again to return fire, just as he had done in past victories over Antonio Tarver and Glen Johnson.

Pascal adjusted, too, though. When Dawson moved away, Pascal still followed up, punching where he thought Dawson was going.

Through six rounds, Pascal had landed 53 of 267 punches, about one landed for every five thrown, a connect rate of just 20 percent. Dawson had landed 62 of 224, about one landed for every four thrown, a connect rate of 28 percent.

Though Dawson had landed more, the judges favored the heavy shots Pascal delivered, even when most missed or were blocked. Pascal was ahead five rounds to one on a pair of scorecards, and ahead four rounds to two on the other.

Pascal was already an aggressor, and he remained so, even when it was Dawson who was coming forward. Dawson was already a boxer, and he remained so, but he could not mount a sustained, effective attack because of Pascal's aggression. Unorthodox punches from odd angles force a fighter to look for where the next shot is coming from, to think about what could be coming at him next, and when. Such a style can take a proactive fighter and make him reactive.

Pascal has speed, the ability to pounce at a good boxer such as Dawson and hit him. Pascal also has power.

Pascal followed a blocked jab with a right hand that

143

landed hard about a minute into the seventh round, catching Dawson as he ducked his head down. Dawson tried to get away and regain his senses, but Pascal pursued. Another Pascal right hand about halfway through the round made Dawson's knees buckle.

Rivalry. Pride versus pride. Dawson took that shot, dropped his gloves at his sides and walked straight at Pascal, his legs steady, his passions inflamed. He sent out combinations to Pascal's head and body, including a couple of low blows, taking control as Pascal took a breather.

Dawson, who had remained on the outside for most of the fight, returned inside two minutes into the eighth. A hard right hook to the body landed, as did a left hook to the body and two more rights downstairs. He then sent out a southpaw jab at Pascal's head followed by a straight left, but Pascal dodged and rolled into a hard right hand counter that hurt Dawson even worse than he had been hurt the previous round. Dawson held for much of the remaining minute.

That put Pascal ahead six rounds to two on a pair of scorecards and seven rounds to one on the other. Dawson didn't know the exact scores, but he knew he was losing, that he needed to mount a comeback, and soon. Pascal didn't know the exact scores either, but he knew not only that he was winning, but that he could hurt Dawson again.

That's what Pascal tried to do in the opening seconds of the ninth, throwing heavy shots that backed Dawson to the ropes. Dawson bounced off with a right hook that hit Pascal's left temple. Pascal put his gloves at his side and backed away. Now it was Dawson who had Pascal holding. But Dawson wouldn't make the same mistake of leaving himself open for a counter, as he had done in the eighth. Instead, he stalked patiently.

When they were in the center of the ring, Dawson looked for an opening for another big, single shot. When Pascal was maneuvered into the ropes, Dawson smothered him with hard, fast combinations. Pascal could not punch back so long as he had to cover up. Once the action moved back away from the ropes, Pascal, hurt and tired, loaded up on sporadic shots that the rejuvenated Dawson easily dodged.

Rivalry. Heart versus heart. Pascal took the momentum back in the 10th, returning again to his strategy of moving away from Dawson to minimize Dawson's offense and then charging forward to put Dawson on the defensive. Pascal landed 18 of 36 in that round, the most he'd landed in a round all night and his best connect rate as well. Dawson threw just 26 in that round, tied for the fewest he'd thrown in a round all night. He landed 11.

Yet momentum shifted back to Dawson in the 11th. He pummeled Pascal with 18 of 59 punches, while Pascal could only muster 4 landed out of 15 thrown. The defining moment came when Pascal charged in with a jab and was about to throw a right when Dawson countered with a perfectly timed left uppercut that hit Pascal on the chin and stood him up straight, stunned.

There were 82 seconds left in the round. Dawson paused for one of them, saw that Pascal was hurt, and shuffled forward at his foe. Pascal shuffled back to the ropes and grabbed a hold of Dawson. They broke free of each other, Dawson following, Pascal jabbing to keep him away. Then both moved toward each other at the same time, ducking their heads and starting a shot.

The accidental head butt opened up a bad cut over

Dawson's right eye, one that was about two inches long, horizontal along the eyebrow, and bleeding badly. The fight was over. It went to the scorecards, with Pascal taking the technical decision. Two judges saw it 106-103, or seven rounds to four, while the third saw it 108-101, or nine rounds to two.

Their rivalry had made them opponents and enemies. Their differing demeanors made for a dynamic duel, one in which their speed, skills, smarts, pride and hearts created 11 rounds of attacks and answers.

Both took shots in this duel. But this duel ended with bullets still in their chambers, an ending that was clear in that Pascal was the deserving winner but inconclusive in that Dawson had not yet been decisively beaten.

The remaining four minutes could have run out and brought about a Pascal decision win. They also could have been enough time for Dawson to keep the fight from going to the scorecards.

That Pascal had done more and won more rounds earned him the number-one spot in the light heavyweight division. That Dawson had previously been number-one had earned him enough sway in the fight negotiations that he can redeem a contractual rematch.

It was Dawson who landed more punches on the night, going 134 of 436 to Pascal's 114 of 430. But it was Pascal who landed the first shot in the rivalry, and it is Dawson who will be gunning for revenge.

Randy Couture and James Toney: 'The Natural' and A Disaster
August 30, 2010

BOSTON — It was only natural that this would happen. All of the pieces fit together as expected. All of the actors played their roles to a tee. All of the events transpired precisely as imagined.

There was James Toney, defenseless and flat on his back, his left arm trapped, the pressure preventing blood from flowing forth to his brain. Consciousness — like his prospects of winning once both he and the fight hit the ground — was vanishing rapidly.

There was Randy Couture, dominant and mounted atop Toney, his left arm curled under the back of Toney's neck, his left bicep cinching Toney's blood vessels and airway, his right hand grabbing the left and closing the choke. Victory — like Toney's head and neck — was firmly within his grasp.

It was only natural that this would happen.

James "Lights Out" Toney had spent more than 25 years in the sweet science, more than two decades as a professional boxer. He had been paid to fight 83 times within a boxing ring, compiling a Hall of Fame career as a middleweight champion and a titleholder at super middleweight and cruiserweight. He continued to fight until he had slipped into the fringe, a rotund 42-year-old no longer considered a viable heavyweight contender.

He had spent less than a year attempting to be a mixed martial artist. The marketing said he had been training in MMA for nine months. He had signed to fight in the UFC just six months ago. Couture was selected as a stiff test for

Toney's foray into the cage, a noteworthy foe who, despite his age, would provide credibility on the off chance that Toney actually won.

Toney might have been attempting to be a mixed martial artist, claiming to be taking a crash course in a combat sport that incorporates wrestling and Brazilian Jiu-Jitsu and Muay Thai and judo, but his talk centered around using the one element of mixed martial arts that he was already most familiar with — boxing.

Randy "The Natural" Couture had spent more than 13 years in mixed martial arts. He had been paid to fight 28 times within an Octagon or a ring, compiling a Hall of Fame career as a light heavyweight and heavyweight champion and then continuing to fight upper-level opposition, a robust 47-year-old who less than two years ago had regained the heavyweight throne.

He had taken up amateur wrestling as a teenager and continued into adulthood, not making his mixed martial arts debut until he was 33 years old. He succeeded in incorporating new skills into his wrestling background, and he often implemented the perfect strategy for getting the win.

Couture would be the overwhelming favorite no matter how hard Toney trained over these months. Toney would still be judged, first by what kind of shape he arrived in, then by what kind of form he showed in the fight.

The final media workouts tend to be more about the media than about the workout. Toney arrived first on Thursday afternoon, two days before UFC 118. He promptly sat down on the platform ringing the exterior of an Octagon set up at the Hynes Convention Center in Boston.

He did not train that day, saying he never did so at such events — "I don't want nobody to see what I'm doing," he said. Instead, he kept on his black shirt, black pants, a hat turned slightly sideways that still had its sticker attached, and what he said was hundreds of thousands of dollars worth of jewelry. Instead, he held court for 25 minutes with the assembled mass of video cameras, digital audio recorders and notebooks.

"What's your prediction?" a writer asked.

"What's your prediction?" Toney retorted.

"I'm asking you," said the writer.

"No, I'm asking you," Toney volleyed back.

"Nobody wants to know what I think."

"I want to know what you think. Because you the reporter."

"I'm the reporter. You're putting me on the spot?"

"I'm putting you on the spot."

"Alright, I'm going to say Randy Couture. Submission."

Toney didn't say anything.

"Don't hit me," the writer said to break the tension. He was mostly joking.

Toney glared, then laughed, lightening the mood once more. Then he gave the writer grief.

"Why would you say that shit to my face?" Toney said. "Don't you know what the fuck I can do to you?"

Toney shook the writer's hand and then finally offered his prediction.

"I'm going to knock his ass out. First round."

Randy Couture came into the expansive convention center room at about 2:30 that afternoon, quickly stripping down to short black and red boxer briefs, showing off a tanned, toned, 6-foot-2, 220-pound physique that should not belong to a man just a few years away from 50. He gloved up and stepped into the Octagon. His fists pounded pads. One-two. One-two-three. A right leg kick.

The workout was brief. He walked over to the same spot Toney had been sitting, talking for half the time Toney talked. He offered volumes of insight within those 13 minutes.

"I don't want to come right out and get into that range of exchanges and try to get into a firefight with James, especially early on. That would be stupid," Couture said. "I have to stay away and be more patient, be a little bit less aggressive than I'm used to being. And then it kind of depends on how James wants to play it.

"Is he going to come out and stand in the center like he does in boxing and kind of wait and see what his opponent does? Or is he going and try and walk me down and pressure me to land that shot? I've got both things ready to go. One's going to be easier than another, I think."

He broke down the story of the fight:

"I take James very seriously," Couture said. "He's obviously a very dangerous striker. How much of the other stuff he's learned is the question. Is he going to learn enough to survive? Can he make it three rounds? If we hit the ground, how's he going to do? Those are all questions everybody's asking. I'm not worried about it. I'm prepared to go as long and as hard as I need to go."

How long would he need to go?

"I'm not big on predictions," Couture said as the session wrapped. "It's a fight. I'm training to go out and do my job, and I think it's going to go well. I feel the peak here, and I'm ready to have a good performance. But anything could happen."

It was only natural that it happened the way it happened.

Their walks to the Octagon in the TD Garden arena lasted longer than the actual fight.

Toney came to the center of the Octagon with his left arm dropped, his right hand cocked, hunched down in anticipation of Couture attempting to shoot forward for a takedown. Couture feinted such a move several times before sending out a half-hearted jab from a distance, a punch that was merely meant to distract from the single-leg takedown that followed.

Toney flailed his arms in a downward reach but grabbed nothing. His rear end hit canvas. His back was on the mat. Couture was mounted on top of him. Less than 20 seconds had passed. Nearly all of the five-minute round remained.

"Exactly how I saw it in my head," Couture would say following the fight. "I had no illusion to stand around and trade any blows with James. I had to pull out the low single. It's hard to counter-punch that. You've got to be within arm's length to counter a double-leg. And guess what, he's got arms."

As for kicking at Toney's legs?

"Counter to those things is a good, hard right hand" Couture said afterward, noting that Toney has a good, hard right hand. "I didn't spend time thinking about it."

Toney, who is 5-foot-9, had weighed in at 237 pounds, matching the highest weight he'd ever been in a boxing ring, back nearly four-and-a-half years ago when he fought to a draw with Hasim Rahman in their first bout against each other. He had reportedly lost considerable weight since signing with the UFC, but not enough to keep flab from flowing over his shorts.

"He's got two handles ready for Randy to grab," one writer had joked after the weigh-in.

Couture was eyeing something else: Toney's footwear, which partially covered his feet and came up to his ankles.

"I got something I can grip," Couture recalled thinking. "If it gets dicey and he tries to step [out of the takedown], I've got something to grab onto other than his sweaty leg."

Toney, once taken down, was trying to grab onto Couture, too. He tried to pull guard, bringing Couture down to him to try to keep him from raining in punches from above. He didn't have much success with that.

Toney's training camp partners had been training to teach him technique. Their level of resistance couldn't compare to that of Couture.

Couture had been training to teach Toney a lesson.

Couture dug punches to Toney's ample body, sent shots from up top, pushed Toney toward the cage and sank in an arm triangle choke, wrapping his own arms around Toney's neck and left arm.

Toney had been resting on his right arm during Couture's initial submission attempt. Soon he would be on his back. Soon it would be over. Less than 200 seconds into the fight, with 1 minute and 41 seconds remaining in the first round, Toney waved his free right hand, signaling that he was tapping out.

Toney never even threw a single punch.

"I didn't expect him to be so aggressive at first," Toney said immediately afterward. "He just caught me."

Couture didn't just catch him. Toney had given Couture the equivalent of a fastball grooved down the middle. Toney was a boxer in a mixed martial arts bout. Couture was a mixed martial artist facing someone who only knew how to box.

"I didn't feel like he demonstrated any real solid skills once he hit his butt and his back," Couture said. "He didn't close his guard. He didn't protect himself that well. I was able to maneuver and get to mount easily. I could hear what they were trying to get him to do, but I think he was more interested in trying to punch me in the head from his back."

Toney didn't say much to Couture afterward — "He said 'Good job,' and that was it," Couture recalled. "At least I think that's what he said." — and aside from his very brief interview in the Octagon immediately afterward, Toney would say nothing else, skipping the post-fight press conference.

Toney had both the hubris and the courage to step into the cage, and he took his lumps for his trouble. He now must take the embarrassment that comes along with overconfidence, the consequences of picking the kind of fight he never could truly be prepared for.

Toney already respected mixed martial arts but did not realize the competitive advantage a mixed martial artist has when fighting involves more than punching. Couture respected boxing but recognized the difference between the two combat sports. He would not be foolish enough to fight Toney in a boxing ring. Couture is an all-around fighter, but that does not make him a boxer.

"I will respectfully decline such an offer," Couture said. "That would be as silly as I think it is for James to step into mixed martial arts here. It would go probably the same way. James would knock me out in the first round."

Toney was a great boxer. Couture was a great mixed martial artist. In nearly 30 MMA fights, Couture has long shown that he is a natural. In one night in MMA, Toney proved that he was a disaster.

It Is No Longer 'If' For Manny Pacquiao, But 'How'
November 15, 2010

He can do it with 400 punches, and he can do it with one. He can do it with power, and he can do it with speed.

It is no longer "if" for Manny Pacquiao, but "how."

He has been a champion in four weight divisions, a beltholder in four more. He has gone undefeated for the past five years, lost just once in the past decade, and won 14 times against 13 world titlists. Nine of those victories came by knockout or technical knockout.

No obstacle is insurmountable, no opponent unbeatable.

He has stood in with more powerful punchers and taken their hardest shots. He has broken down men who said he could not hurt them.

Pacquiao did both on Saturday against Antonio Margarito, demolishing a man who, a decade ago, was fighting five weight divisions above him. Pacquiao was a junior featherweight then, soon to capture a 122-pound title, Margarito was a welterweight then, still a couple of years from holding a belt in the 147-pound division.

Pacquiao weighed in at about 144.5 pounds on Friday, 148 pounds on Saturday. Margarito made the contractual limit of 150 pounds on Friday and had rehydrated to 165 pounds by Saturday.

This was a size advantage — for Pacquiao.

So many boxers starve and sweat to make weight, using the period between the weigh-in and the opening bell to pack the pounds back on. They strive to have advantages in size and strength in a division that they do not belong in for but for those few moments they step on the scale.

Pacquiao counts calories, too, but he adds them up rather than subtracting them. Those 7,000 calories per day help him pack on muscle — but not too much mass — so that he can carry his power into higher weight classes without losing too much of the speed that makes his punches all the more effective.

Pacquiao used to be a one-handed fighter, powerful but predictable, throwing out two southpaw jabs with his right hand and then following with a fierce left cross. He was often off-balance, but he often got away with it. As HBO's Larry Merchant once described him, "He's one dimensional, but it's a hell of a dimension."

He added a right hook. He absorbed the technique and training imparted to him by Freddie Roach. His improved footwork turned what was a fearsome puncher in the lower weight classes into a formidable boxer-puncher, one with the offensive and defensive skills necessary to compete with — and defeat — opponents who were now much larger, but also much slower.

He ducked and weaved and bounced and dodged against lightweight David Diaz, hitting him with jabs and crosses and hooks and uppercuts and the final overhand left that sent Diaz crashing face-first to the canvas.

He darted in and out and pot-shotted and delivered combinations against a welterweight Oscar De La Hoya, limiting De La Hoya to only one landed punch for every five thrown. Pacquiao, meanwhile, couldn't miss. His lowest power-punch connect rate on the night was 50 percent.

He countered junior-welterweight Ricky Hatton with

right hooks and then set him up for a perfectly placed left, knocking Hatton unconscious within two rounds.

He traded punches with a welterweight Miguel Cotto for four rounds, then cranked into a higher gear, and then an even higher one. Cotto had thought he could overwhelm Pacquiao with power, but Pacquiao overwhelmed him with speed. Pacquiao's punches came from odd angles and in blistering, bruising flurries.

That hand-speed paralyzed a welterweight Joshua Clottey, who stayed in a defensive shell for nearly the entire 12-round bout. Clottey never went down, but he didn't go down fighting either. Pacquiao threw more than 1,200 punches on the night, more than 100 per round.

Pacquiao was the overwhelming favorite against Margarito. His foot speed had proven to be too much for fighters who box better than Margarito does. His hand speed had proven to be too intimidating for fighters with better defense than Margarito has.

And yet the closer we got to the fight, the closer we were made to think the fight could be.

Clottey had thrown only 399 punches, hitting Pacquiao with just 108. But he had hurt Pacquiao with single shots and marked up his face with what little did land. Margarito, a pressure fighter, was bound to throw and land more punches than Clottey did.

Pacquiao's training camp had been beset by distractions, particularly his role as a congressman in the Philippines. Word had leaked out that trainer Freddie Roach had been unhappy with how Pacquiao looked in some sparring sessions.

If Pacquiao couldn't keep Margarito off of him, Margarito could break him down as he had done to other smaller, faster foes.

It is no longer "If" for Pacquiao.

The farther we got into the fight, the farther Pacquiao pulled away.

Margarito worked behind a jab in the opening round, trying to establish distance between himself and a shorter man who would need to get closer to land. Except Pacquiao would back away, stretching Margarito forward and bringing his head in range for counter shots.

Margarito ratcheted up the pressure in the second round. But it was Pacquiao's volume of punches that would give him fits. Margarito would throw a three-punch combination. Pacquiao would respond with three punches of his own, then four, then more. Margarito would come forward or cut off the ring. Pacquiao would send out single shots, then move, then send out another barrage, then move again.

"He has no power," Margarito told his trainer after the third round. "He can't hurt me."

Pacquiao had landed 70 punches through three rounds. One punch in the fourth would imprint a sizable welt under Margarito's right eye. Another single punch in the fourth would hurt Margarito to the body, forcing Margarito to drop his right elbow and retreat in hopes of recovering.

Pacquiao would land 49 punches in that fourth round, including 43 power punches out of 62 thrown, a 69 percent connect rate. His punches always seemed to have the perfect placement, the perfect timing, the perfect amount of torque and speed behind them.

Margarito would have the rare moments, trapping Pacquiao on the ropes, digging heavy hooks and uppercuts to Pacquiao's body and head. Those moments seemed to coincide with portions of rounds that Pacquiao was taking off. And then Pacquiao would explode off the ropes and regain control with firepower and flash.

Margarito's past rise to welterweight prominence had come as a result of heavy pressure and a sturdy chin. No obstacle is insurmountable, no opponent unbeatable. Both Margarito's willingness to throw punches and his willingness to take punches would be favorable to Pacquiao's chances.

Margarito, never a defensive dynamo, would be in front of Pacquiao throughout the fight and open to the hundreds of shots that pierced his porous guard. And while Margarito would take punches in order to deliver his own, these punches from Pacquiao had speed that amplified their power. These punches added up.

Forty power shots in the fifth round; 32 in the sixth; 39 in the seventh; 36 in the eighth. Pacquiao seemed to take the ninth round off but still landed 25 power punches out of 48 thrown. He was 57 of 89 in that category in the 10th and 51 of 75 in the 11th.

It was one-sided. But what a hell of a one side it was. Pacquiao turned to referee Laurence Cole three times in that 11th round, silently imploring the third man in the ring to stop him from hurting Margarito any more. During a clinch in that stanza, Pacquiao stood inactive, seemingly not out of a need for rest, but rather out of a need for mercy.

Margarito's right eye was almost completely closed, and even he could see that this fight had been decided. But he didn't want it to be over. He went back out for more punishment in the 12th.

Pacquiao wasn't willing to give it to him. He boxed for much of that final round, letting Margarito last the remaining three minutes behind an offense of 50 jabs and only eight power punches. Pacquiao would still flurry, but he would not seek a finish.

There was no need to prove something that had already been proven.

Pacquiao would land 474 punches out of 1,069 thrown, sending out 713 power punches and landing 411, a 58 percent connect rate. A brutal 401 went to Margarito's head, including the one that left the welt and the subsequent shots that opened a cut, raised swelling and fractured his orbital bone.

Pacquiao had also taken 229 of Margarito's punches, including 135 power punches. He stood in with a more powerful puncher and took his hardest shots. He broke down a man who said he could not hurt him.

Some withhold credit from a fighter for beating an opponent he should have beat. But judgment should not rely merely on whether a fighter wins, but the manner in which he does so.

Pacquiao demolished Margarito. What impressed was not if Pacquiao could do it. It is no longer "If" for Manny Pacquiao, but "How."

Martinez Leaves Williams and World With Eyes Wide Open
November 22, 2010

ATLANTIC CITY, N.J. — This is how a man falls — suddenly surrendering himself to gravity, quickly crashing to canvas, his bearings briefly settling him somewhere between pained and paralyzed.

This is how a man rises — by making other men fall.

This is how it ended, with Paul Williams falling, rag dolled face-first in the center of the ring, his arms lying limply at his sides, his head turned to the left.

His eyes wide open.

This is how it begins, with Sergio Martinez rising to the top of a crowd within the ring, perched atop someone's shoulders, a crown placed atop his head, blowing kisses to the fans with his still-gloved hands to his lips.

This was as much a crowning achievement as it was an ascension. Martinez is the middleweight champion. He is one of the best boxers in the sport.

He was once an unknown to the boxing world. That was as recently as two-and-a-half years ago.

On an evening in a Connecticut casino, before the arena filled and the cameras rolled, Martinez had battled with Archak TerMeliksetian, seven rounds of men exchanging bravado, machismo and punches.

Coincidentally, the broadcast that night featured Paul Williams' first-round stoppage of Carlos Quintana.

By that point, Williams had been featured on televised cards or pay-per-view shows for two years. He had received a title shot, won a belt, lost it and, with the victory over Quintana, regained it.

By that point, Martinez had toiled in obscurity for more than a decade.

Prior to 2007, Martinez had fought just once in the United States, losing in 2000 to what was then a welterweight prospect named Antonio Margarito. Martinez had, at the time, been a pro fighter for less than three years, and he'd taken up the sweet science later in life.

He'd have to learn on the job. And off the radar.

For the next seven years he'd fight in his native Argentina, in Spain, and in the United Kingdom. He'd return to the United States in '07, the winner of 22 straight, a junior-middleweight who was rising in the WBC's rankings of fighters but not in the Q-ratings measuring fame.

That'd change after the TerMeliksetian fight.

HBO spotlighted Martinez on an October 2008 broadcast, one in which Martinez landed 212 punches while his opponent, Alex Bunema, landed 31. Martinez was a flashy, skilled boxer. Beyond the trinket he'd earned with the win — the WBC's interim 154-pound belt — he was worth seeing again.

Martinez was back on HBO in February 2009 for a bout with Kermit Cintron, one that Martinez essentially won twice, even though he left with a majority draw. What should have been ruled a knockout was not, and then two judges somehow saw Cintron winning rounds that, well, he didn't.

Williams, meanwhile, was being positioned for a bout with then-middleweight champion Kelly Pavlik. When Pavlik's health issues forced him to withdraw from that fight, Martinez stepped in to face Williams. The momentum swung throughout 12 rounds in a fight that was one of the best of that year. The scorecards could've gone either way. Williams got the decision.

But Williams balked at facing Pavlik in early 2010, unwilling to sign a contract without financial considerations in case Pavlik were to postpone or pull out of the fight again. Once again, Martinez stepped in, this time to face Pavlik.

Martinez won. He was the middleweight champion. Yet he still had to prove himself to be the best at 160, recognition that could come by beating Williams.

Two things can happen in a rematch of a great fight. Either both boxers, familiar with the danger his opponent poses, will fight more cautiously — or both boxers, familiar with the danger he poses to his opponent, will pick up where he left off in the previous bout.

Martinez and Williams chose the latter option.

There would be no feeling out process. Williams threw the first shot, a southpaw right hook, coming forward aggressively behind jabs and hooks. Martinez backed up, evading shots, countering misses, and then stepping forward between Williams' lengthy arms to land punches to his body.

The inside was one place Martinez could choose to work against a man with Williams' wingspan. The other was far outside, out of reach. Williams moved forward, jabbing and following with left crosses, and Martinez retreated, setting up traps. When Williams punches, he punches low and long, leaning his head down and leaving himself open for hard counters over the top.

Martinez countered with left hands and right hooks. Williams kept coming, landing punches of his own as Martinez opened up, then digging in uppercuts from underneath when they clinched.

Each believed he had truly won their first fight. Each believed himself to be better and came out with confidence.

For Williams, that confidence took the form of activity and aggression against a strong counter-puncher. For Martinez, that confidence took the form of dropping his arms to his sides with 36 seconds still to go in the first round, doing so against a fighter who was capable of throwing 100 shots in a round and capable of using his lanky frame as a conduit for power punching.

Martinez countered Williams with left hand after left hand in the opening minute of the second round. Moments later, Martinez closed the show with that same punch.

He backed across the ring, drawing Williams forward. Nearing the ropes, he moved to his right, changing angles, then shuffled his feet quickly — moving farther to the right and opening up the angle even wider. He was right in front of Williams, who was now basically squared up.

Williams threw a left. Martinez threw a left. Martinez's left landed first. And hardest.

There is nothing more electric in boxing than a man's lights being turned out.

The punch was heard before it was seen. The sound of the shot filled the arena. Then Williams began to fall, his body contorting as he surrendered to gravity.

The crowd reacted with a combination of shock and suspense. Williams couldn't get up from a punch like that. They waited, though, as the referee counted to 10. Once he did, they roared.

Martinez ran back and forth as if he had just won the lottery. There was no luck in this, though. He had created his own opportunity, just as he had against TerMeliksetian, against Bunema, against Cintron, against Williams the first time, and then against Pavlik.

This is how a man rises. This was as much a crowning achievement as it was an ascension. His knockout punch left Williams with his eyes open from a shot Williams had never seen.

That punch left the world with its eyes open from a fighter they will want to see again.

Khan-firmation? After Marcos Maidana, Can Amir Survive, Thrive at 140?

December 23, 2010

He was derided, disparaged and doubted, even though he was favored to win.

"Weak chin," they said of Amir Khan. And they were right.

He had not only been knocked down twice and knocked out in less than a minute against Breidis Prescott, but he'd also been put down on the canvas by lesser fighters in Willie Limond and Michael Gomez.

"If Marcos Maidana catches him clean, Khan's going to get hurt," they said. And they were right.

A little more than a minute into the 10th round of their fight, Maidana countered over Khan's left jab with a looping right hand, catching him directly on the chin. Khan's right leg splayed away from him. And as Maidana continued to attack, Khan attempted to retreat with all the grace of a wounded gazelle trying to outrun a lion.

"If Maidana hurts him, the fight will be over, and it will prove that Khan has been protected, that he doesn't belong among the best in his division," they said.

And they were wrong.

There were three possible storylines that Khan-Maidana could follow. Khan could beat Maidana without ever having his chin tested. Khan could have his chin tested but still beat Maidana. Or Khan could have his chin tested and lose.

Khan undoubtedly would have preferred the first option, preferred that his skills and speed made for an easy night. But rare is the athlete who is so good that he never has to overcome bad moments.

The moments Khan had Saturday were about as bad as could be without being completely catastrophic. But those bad moments on one night were all the better for what is yet to come in his career.

Those moments gave Khan confirmation that he can survive when in with the best in the junior-welterweight division. And those moments will give Khan the confidence he needs if he is to thrive among the rest of the best.

Khan proved more to himself and to his detractors by going all 12 rounds than he would have had he won the fight in the first round — which he nearly did.

Khan has advantages in size and speed and a style that demands he use those advantages.

At a lanky 5-foot-10, he sends out fast, long jabs and right crosses, working from a distance that is close enough for him to land when he's throwing but far enough away that defense often merely requires a quick step backward. And this positioning is made even more necessary because the way Khan uses his length makes him less effective when he is in close, where his chin also makes him more vulnerable.

Maidana, meanwhile, is 5-foot-7, shorter and slower, with power put into a plodding package. Against Maidana, Khan would look even faster than he normally does. Against Khan, Maidana would look even slower.

Khan exploited his advantages in hand and foot speed in the first round, using blinding jabs to set up right hands, then moving away from an opponent who would then have to follow and set his feet to throw. Maidana tried to compensate with timing, sending wide right-hand counters around Khan's jabs.

But as Maidana was trying to see if he could crack the glass supposedly in Khan's chin, Khan would attempt to snuff out the fire in Maidana's belly.

Khan followed a jab to Maidana's head with a left hook that didn't have much force behind it. That hook served to distract Maidana upstairs from what was to come below — a right hook to the body and then a left hook to the liver. Maidana closed his eyes and opened his mouth and fell to the canvas.

A year before, another fighter had to overcome his demons and others' doubts about whether he could handle the pressure and power of an opponent who couldn't match his ability or athleticism.

Lucian Bute had been moments away from a knockout loss in the final round of his first fight with Librado Andrade, surviving for the victory. In their November 2009 rematch, however, Bute would encounter no such strife, digging a left to Andrade's liver and putting him down for the count.

Maidana would get up from Khan's body shot, though.

Khan's speed was the telling factor in the first half of the fight. Rather than Khan being cautious of a single powerful punch from Maidana, it was Maidana who had to be cautious of the fusillade that would come from Khan.

Khan landed 162 punches in those first six rounds to Maidana's 62. Of those, Khan landed 114 power shots, compared to 41 from Maidana. The difference was most telling in those first two rounds, when Khan landed 63 punches, including 45 power punches, while Maidana landed only 10 punches, including just four power punches.

But as Khan saw that Maidana wouldn't go away, he began to pace himself. And that gave Maidana more opportunities go give Khan problems.

What Maidana lacked in technique, he made up for in tenacity.

While Khan has fast feet, he does not always show the best footwork, the ability to maneuver out of bad situations and into better locations. Sometimes when he finishes working, he ducks shots and shuffles away. But on other occasions he rests and covers up, passively defending himself instead of proactively doing so.

Maidana seized the opportunity when Khan stopped punching, getting in close, squaring up and sending uppercuts between Khan's gloves and hooks around them. In the seventh round, Maidana landed nearly as many punches as Khan, with 17 to Khan's 18, but he landed more power shots, with 14 to Khan's 11.

Khan took the momentum back in the eighth, while Maidana seemed to be losing steam. Khan used uppercuts to stifle Maidana's advances, and he landing 24 punches in that round while Maidana could only land four. Maidana appeared to limp back to his corner after that round ended, and his trainer could be heard telling him, "If you want, I'll stop the fight."

The ninth round followed the pattern of the one preceding it. Khan landed 34 punches this time, including 21 power shots, while Maidana had eight and four.

Khan had control. But Maidana still only needed to land a single shot to change that.

He did.

That the looping Maidana right in the 10th hurt Khan was bad enough for Khan. What made it worse for him was that he would not hold Maidana and could not keep him away. Maidana teed off with 23 power punches in the 10th to Khan's seven.

And as with Lucian Bute's first win over Librado Andrade, Amir Khan was able to survive Marcos Maidana's onslaught because of some controversial refereeing. In the case of Bute-Andrade 1, it had been a long count from Marlon Wright that gave Bute extra time to recover. With Khan-Maidana, Joe Cortez seemed to step between the fighters at moments that were unnecessary and, for Maidana, inopportune.

None of those 23 punches sent Khan down, however. As Khan made it through two tough minutes, he appeared dazed but not discombobulated.

Maidana would be revitalized, however, out-landing Khan 39 to 23 in those final two rounds, including 36 power shots to Khan's 17. Still, while Khan endured being hurt again in those final six minutes, he was not hurt as badly he was before.

Khan took the first half of the fight, Maidana the second — not the best method for sending a message of superiority. Khan won enough rounds early to give him the decision, taking the fight by scores of 114-111 from two judges and 113-112 from the third.

Normally that kind of outcome means that there are more questions about a fighter than answers.

Not in this case.

The first question entering the fight had been if Maidana could hit him, not whether Maidana could hurt him. One would dictate the other. The second question entering the fight had been whether, if Khan were hurt, he could withstand it.

Maidana hit him and hurt him. He withstood it.

Against lesser punches and lesser fighters, the

170

knockdowns Khan had suffered had raised valid questions about his chin. And against Breidis Prescott, the one-minute drubbing Khan had suffered had raised valid questions about his composure.

Marcos Maidana had entered his fight with Khan having scored 27 knockouts in his 29 victories. Khan stood in the ring for 12 rounds with a vaunted puncher. His chin cracked, but he never crumpled.

He was doubted, disparaged and derided. He would not be defeated.

As with other flawed fighters, Khan will need to continue to compensate for his weaknesses by playing to his strengths. He now knows he can handle being hurt by a big puncher.

He also knows he should not put himself in a position to prove that again.

A Reminder Of What Boxing Also Is
February 14, 2011

GLEN BURNIE, Md. — For one moment, go beyond the gloved combatants in the ring hell-bent on hitting each other as hard as they can and as many times as they can.

Go beyond the simplest of premises and examine boxing, starting from its philosophy and reaching to its periphery, and you will find that it is an institution in conflict with itself.

It is a savage pursuit, this casting aside of humanity for a predetermined amount of time so as to bash and bruise and cut and concuss, and to do this to another man who is not seen as a mortal enemy but merely as a momentary opponent.

It is a scientific practice based on fundamentals of technique and talent and skill and discipline. One must train and work and sacrifice to improve, and one must continue to do so just for a chance to succeed. He must release himself into battling with ruthlessness yet restrain himself by behaving within the rules.

The best must work for years to reach that level. Yet being the best doesn't always mean others — the promoters who will pay them, the people who will pay to see them — will immediately recognize their talent and reward them for it.

But before there can be the few who find fame and fortune in the professional spotlight, there are those thousands toiling in the ranks of amateur anonymity for free.

There are the trainers at the gyms and clubs and

storied holes-in-walls who take kids — many of whom come from troubled homes and neighborhoods — and deliver them into this constructive conundrum:

The boxers are bettering themselves through actions that, when undertaken in any other setting outside of those four ropes, would be deemed viciously criminal.

Outside of the ropes, so many of them are anything but. Trained to use their hands to hurt, they understand the power of that privilege, the reality of responsibility.

It is easy to become distracted from that fact, to let the caricatures and the cases of chaos and corruption speak for the rest:

Those who speak softly and without the salesmanship and showmanship of a Muhammad Ali or a Don King.

Those who live in a manner that will not bring headlines from a mainstream press that thinks boxing stopped when Mike Tyson retired.

Those who give soft, limp handshakes with the same hands that form clenched fists.

It is easy to become distracted by the soap operas of professional boxing: the fighters who will not fight each other, the glut of sanctioning bodies issuing a confusing abundance of title belts, the controversial endings to bouts that in turn take precedence over the actual action that came before.

Sometimes we must bring ourselves back into focus.

*   *   *

For one moment, go beyond those complications and return to where boxing is at its simplest: at the local level.

There, a writer who has been ringside in stadiums and arenas and clubs and casinos can see boxing where it is still more of a sport than it is a spectacle.

There, a person will find little of the disconnect between fighter and fan seen at the bigger of boxing cards, those events where the cost of a ticket alone will set them off at a distance from the ring — and they will be pushed farther still from the ring by rows of VIPs protected by metal barricades. Also, the best boxers might have known names, but celebrity does not truly equal familiarity.

This writer had traveled far to see the best boxers and the biggest of boxing cards. But until this past Friday he had never been half an hour from his hometown to see the quality of simplicity at a suburban Maryland ballroom.

There have long been regular professional boxing cards at Michael's Eighth Avenue in Glen Burnie. Until recently, those cards had come about half a dozen times each year. But there were but two in 2009 and two in 2010.

This was an amateur card put on by two local promoters: Scott Wagner, who has run the Ballroom Boxing shows in Glen Burnie, and Jake Smith, who has promoted in the area under his Baltimore Pro Boxing banner.

Doors opened 90 minutes before the first fight. Those arriving early could walk in to see boxers spilling out of the cramped, curtained-off area at one end of the ballroom that was serving as a makeshift dressing room for about two-dozen fighters, plus their trainers and an assortment of suitcases and duffel bags. Several wore jackets with the names of their boxing clubs emblazoned on them.

On a table at ringside, three boxes held more than two-dozen trophies of varying sizes, each with a picture of dangling pair of red gloves and the words "The Future" — not coincidentally the name the promoters had given the event.

Nearby, one boxer sat at a table underneath one of four chandeliers, wrapping his own hands — two of those institutional conflicts appearing in a single place. This savage pursuit would take place in a room also used for weddings and proms and banquets. And fighters trained to hurt others with their hands must first follow the delicate art of cushioning those hands with gauze and tape and gloves, protection for their fists, yes, but also for their foes.

Two boxers changed and tied their shoes outside of a stall in the men's bathroom, speaking to each other in Spanish as others occasionally entered to use the facilities for their designated purpose.

They represented athletic participation when it is still fun and not work. They presented boxing where it is still organic — there are flaws, granted, but it is easier to overlook imperfections when there is such an abundance of passion.

* * *

Smith was a visible presence, the show's co-promoter working to organize the event and announce the fights and energize the fans. He wore a black T-shirt with an image imitating the lapels and undershirt of a tuxedo, casual gear necessary when you are being summoned around the building.

Earlier in the evening, the man taking the tickets up front kept yelling Smith's name — "Jake!" "Jake!" — every time he had a question. Later, Smith was in the back with the boxers, ensuring that everything was set before the card was to get under way.

Finally, he was in the ring, microphone in hand, not at all trying for the ceremonial smoothness of a Michael Buffer, but sounding rather like the front man of a rock and roll band whose concert set was about to start and who wanted to get the fans ready to have heads banging.

"The louder you cheer, the harder they fight," he told what had become a filled ballroom.

He announced the first bout, which would be for the amateur Maryland state championship, open-class, 165-pound division.

"That's how we start a night," Smith said. "Start it right."

Reggie Lucas was from Baltimore. Most of the fans cheered. Monreco Goldston was from Salisbury. Most of the fans booed.

"Reggie, get out to the ring," Smith said.

Lucas and Goldston did. Soon came the sound of a ring bell, which apparently was patched through the speaker system.

They were not going to be the best boxers. There are enough layers at the professional ranks — champion, titleholder, contender, prospect, gatekeeper, measuring stick, designated opponent, tomato can — never mind the amateur tiers.

But these fighters not being refined can make their fights all the more entertaining. Many tended to cast aside foot movement in favor of throwing punches and exchanging combinations. They are still developing, coached heavily during the bouts by vocal trainers.

Hal Chernoff, who works with touted professional prospect Fernando Guerrero, had made the two-hour drive from Salisbury, Md., just for his one fighter on the card, Goldston, who appropriate wore gold trunks. Of course, unlike the pro ranks, these amateur fighters also donned tank tops and protective headgear.

"Five! Five! Five! Five!" Chernoff yelled during the third and final round, the number corresponding to whatever punch the trainer wanted his fighter to throw. Goldston and Lewis exchanged haymakers in the round, attempting either to knock the other out or at least to leave an indelible impression on those scoring the fight.

The bell rang over the speaker system. Smith stepped back into the ring.

"Who thinks the blue corner?" Smith asked. "Who thinks the red corner?"

A few in the audience insisted that he get to the result. Goldston won the split decision. Both he and Lucas were handed trophies.

The Salisbury contingent cheered. At many major boxing cards, most ticket buyers don't file in until the later fights despite spending so much money, because they are conditioned not to care about anyone beyond the upper tiers of boxers. But early on at those shows there will be the pockets of fans who traveled in support of their local heroes, support that is not conditioned upon accomplishment.

These at Michael's Eighth Avenue were friends and family and also area residents who just appreciated a night at the fights. Though they seemed out of place with the music that played between bouts — hip-hop in a room of old and/or white faces — their enthusiasm didn't wane, and it contributed tremendously to the atmosphere.

Simpler. More organic.

Even the ring card girls — likely two local strippers —

went without the typical heels, instead wearing tube socks over their feet.

One explained that they were warned that heels would poke holes in the ring canvas.

*   *   *

For one moment, look beyond the tube socks, the simulated ring bell, the tuxedo T-shirt and the amateur action.

Ours is a culture caught up in the blockbuster: the big summer movie, the big concert, the big game, the big fight.

We designate a level of importance to those, but we must not denigrate that which cannot — and need not — live up to that billing.

There are art-house flicks and local club bands and minor league baseball teams and regional boxing cards. They are neighbors and everymen and homegrown talents whose efforts are all the more honest and nonetheless entertaining.

It is easy to become distracted by celebrity and its requisite controversy and chaos. Sometimes we must bring ourselves back into focus.

Yes, boxing is the expensive event at the stadium or arena or club or casino. It is the thrill of extraordinary boxers and exhilarating action, and it is the frustration of fights not being made, bad decisions and rampant confusion brought about by the sheer number of sanctioning bodies and title belts.

It is more than the champions and titleholders and contenders and prospects. It is the gatekeepers, measuring sticks, designated opponents and tomato cans who won't find fame and fortune but who still take plenty of punches for a few bucks.

It is the amateur fighter who comes away with little beyond the thrill of competition, and a little recognition, and maybe a trophy, but also the improvement — and the proving — of self.

Go beyond the gloved combatants in the ring hell-bent on hitting each other as hard as they can and as many times as they can.

This might seem a savage pursuit, but those rewards bring more sweetness to this sweet science.

Sergio Martinez: A Cut Above
March 14, 2011

MASHANTUCKET, Conn. — Boxing, like baseball, is a five-tool sport. And in the sweet science you cannot get away with merely being a designated hitter.

In this fight game, a boxer who is great at one thing is not necessarily great overall. Conversely, a boxer can be great even if some of his tools are merely good.

The fight between Sergio Martinez and Sergiy Dzinziruk pitted a boxer who is more great than he is good against a boxer who is more good than he is great.

Dzinziruk's greatness is in his jab, the kind of jab befitting of his "Razor" nickname, the kind of jab that left bruising around Sergio Martinez's left eye and opened up a cut above that same eye.

It is the kind of jab that forced the dashing Martinez to cover his face with sunglasses after the fight and sent him seeking medical attention to see if he needed stitches.

Similarly, Martinez's goodness is in his jab, the kind of jab that earned the respect of Dzinziruk, a master of that punch himself, early in their fight.

It is the kind of jab that isn't just pushed out merely to establish timing or measure distance, but is popped out with force, setting up follow-up shots and stopping his foe's forward progress.

Dzinziruk appeared to have a good left hand — except what appears to be a good left hand is one that all too easily disappears in favor of the southpaw jab. When Dzinziruk did throw his left hand, and when it landed flush, it got Martinez's attention.

Martinez has a great left hand, however — and it not

only appears often, but it also often appears out of nowhere. It is the punch that hit Kermit Cintron so hard that Cintron thought he'd just suffered a head butt. It is the punch that sent Paul Williams into unconsciousness before he'd even crashed to the canvas.

And it is the punch that — with the assistance of a good jab — led Martinez to five knockdowns and a technical knockout in an impressive victory over Sergiy Dzinziruk.

Martinez does not have that razor jab, but he is nevertheless a cut above the rest.

In the past 11 months, he has outpointed Kelly Pavlik for the middleweight championship, then successfully defended the throne twice by knocking out Williams and stopping Dzinziruk.

In order to stop Dzinziruk, he had to stop what Dzinziruk was great at.

"Nullify his boxing. Nullify his jab. Nullify his punches," Martinez said after the fight. "Little by little we did that."

He did that with his defense — head movement and distance — and with his offense, with the irritation of his own jab and by intimidating Dzinziruk with the possibility of what could be coming back at him.

Martinez felt cocky enough in his ability that it was merely a minute or two into the fight when he first did his characteristic dropping of his arms to his waist. Against a fast, capable jabber, that decision should fall somewhere between stupid and suicidal. But Martinez didn't need his gloves to block the jabs so long as he could use his reflexes to avoid them.

He ducked his head low, inviting Dzinziruk to jab at the open target. But when the jab came, Martinez would either duck downward and forward to send the punch harmlessly past him above, or pull straight back just enough that the shot fell short.

Martinez also circled to his right — usually a no-no when one is moving toward a southpaw's left hand. Dzinziruk's left wasn't what Martinez was worried about, though. And as a southpaw himself, the move gave Martinez better angles for landing his own left hand — a similar movement to the one that preceded the Williams knockout — and his right hook.

In the fourth round, Martinez landed a left hand through Dzinziruk's guard, buckling his knees. A follow-up left hand landed high on Dzinziruk's head, and his knee touched the mat. That would be Dzinziruk's first time down — and not just in the career of a boxer who claimed that he'd never been floored as an amateur or as a pro.

Martinez would knock Dzinziruk down a total of five times in eight rounds.

The next knockdown came in the next round. Dzinziruk, for all of his skills, sometimes brings his right hand back low. Martinez already had shown an advantage in speed and timing. This was merely an additional opening.

With Dzinziruk's jab hand starting low, Martinez felt less threatened to move in as the punch began its course. He beat Dzinziruk to the punch with a left hand, perfectly — and painfully — placed.

For those first five rounds, Martinez had been using his jab to knock Dzinziruk off his rhythm. Martinez used the jab to keep Dzinziruk at a comfortable distance. And he used the jab to reset the timing, allowing him to set up counter shots and the occasional hard lead.

182

Martinez had landed 150 punches in the first five rounds, the jabs accounting for 103 of those. The power shots didn't need to land often — they just needed to land right.

Though both Martinez and Dzinziruk have spent the majority of their careers in the junior-middleweight division, Martinez has thrived since going up to middleweight. Though he is not as large as some of the other fighters who compete at 160, he carries the weight well and has six fewer pounds to lose before stepping on the scale.

He has power that is amplified by the speed at which the shots come and the location on which they land.

And with his hands down, those punches came from unorthodox, unexpected angles.

But Martinez opening up on offense meant he also left himself more open on defense. Dzinziruk was able to seize the opportunity. Previously he had landed just 10 jabs in the first round, nine in the second round, 12 in the third, eight in the fourth, and four in the fifth.

The sixth round saw him land 16 jabs, however, and the seventh round had him landing 18.

Martinez's left eye had already been bruised. Then a jab opened a cut over that eye with less than 30 seconds remaining in the seventh. Martinez dabbed at his eye with his glove, and between the seventh and eighth rounds he was heard talking of trouble seeing out of the eye.

Martinez's corner went to work before the eighth got under way. And once the round began, so did Martinez.

He went back to lowering his head and bobbing it up and down, looking up, waiting, setting a trap.

Dzinziruk sent out jabs. Martinez moved to his right —

Dzinziruk's left — then distracted him with jabs and followed up with a straight left hand.

Down went Dzinziruk. He got up, but as the referee was finishing his mandatory eight count, Martinez was rushing in. A left landed directly on Dzinziruk's chin. Down he went again. He rose once more but had little ability to stop what was still coming. Dzinziruk's high guard meant nothing when the shots were pummeling him through and around the gloves.

He fell back, and the referee stepped in.

"The knockdowns were not from hard punches," Dzinziruk said after the fight, sounding at first like he was trying to take away from Martinez's accomplishment. And then he finished his sentence with due credit. "Just perfect shots. And I got caught."

Dzinziruk's great jab was less effective on this night than his power punches were — he landed 80 of 242 jabs, compared to 81 of 171 power shots.

Martinez, meanwhile, landed more jabs than he did power punches in six of the eight rounds, with the fourth and eighth rounds being the only exceptions.

On the night, he landed 147 of 384 jabs, compared to 79 of 209 power punches.

With his one tool limited, Dzinziruk was merely a good fighter who could not contend with a great one.

Martinez, meanwhile, is a five-tool player who decided to keep hitting singles until he had the chance for those big swings that would send everyone home.

Erik Morales: He Asked For It
April 12, 2011

He asked for it — and he asked for it at a time when we were asking questions of him.

What little did Erik Morales have left? Why would he choose Marcos Maidana as his latest comeback opponent? How long would he last against Maidana? And how badly would he get hurt?

Morales asked for it — and he asked for it because he already knew the answers to those questions.

He had enough left after a great but grueling career that he could still pose an honest challenge to one of the top fighters at junior welterweight, that he could still pose a hard challenge against one of the toughest fighters in the division.

He had enough left, at least, to face Maidana, a fighter whose power made up for his predictability, whose unrelenting advances made up for his unrefined skills.

Except Morales saw it the other way around. Rather than those traits being flaws that Maidana had succeeding in overcoming, they were weaknesses for undermining Maidana, weaknesses that others had failed to fully exploit.

Morales would last, then, for as long as his strategy allowed, and for as long as his body did, too. What remained physically would be key for applying the mental aspects of the fight game. And the mental aspects of the fight game would help him make up for what was no longer physically there.

This, after all, was a fighter older than his 34 years, a fighter who'd turned pro 18 years ago and had fought 57 times, going to war in trilogies with Marco Antonio Barrera and Manny Pacquiao and waging battles with so many others over so many years at junior featherweight, featherweight and junior lightweight.

This, after all, was a fighter who'd retired in 2007 after moving up to lightweight to challenge David Diaz, a limited but rugged beltholder who'd overcome his flaws and overachieved. Morales said after the close, unanimous decision loss to Diaz that his head rang every time Diaz hit him.

This, after all, was a fighter who'd only returned to the ring a year ago and had only faced second- and third-tier opponents since coming back. Maidana, for all of his flaws, was still far more accomplished and able than Jose Alfaro, Willie Limond and Francisco Lorenzo.

This was why we were asking questions of Erik Morales. And this was why we were uncertain of what the answers would be to what Marcos Maidana would ask of Morales in the ring.

Morales' legs looked stiffened with age and rust, slowed by the burden of additional weight on his frame. Maidana laid into him in the first round with heavy left hooks to the body and head and hard uppercuts upstairs.

Morales didn't appear to have the ability to keep Maidana off of him. In clinches, he would hold Maidana's right arm but allow Maidana to punch away at him with the left. Morales didn't throw much either — just 46 punches in the first three minutes, about half of the 91 that Maidana threw. Morales only landed seven, of which only four were power punches. Maidana landed 24, of which 21 were power shots.

One of those power punches brought out significant swelling over Morales' right eye. Maidana alone is a difficult opponent. Morales would spend the duration of the bout half-blind and less able to see shots from Maidana's punishing left hand.

Maidana saw a wounded warrior waiting to be put down. He trapped Morales against the ropes in the final minute of the second round and hit him with the left, then chased him to another side of the ring and hit him with that left hand again.

And then Morales gave the first glimpse of what he had left — and what he had planned.

He fought off the ropes with a few right hooks, then a left hook, then a right cross, and then another right hand, and then another. And then it was Maidana who was backing away and Maidana who was trying to battle back.

Maidana is powerful and unrelenting. But his style means that he would be there in front of Morales the entire time. Morales could see him coming, and Maidana is slow enough that Morales could see what was coming, too.

For an aging fighter who can no longer use his legs as much and no longer throws his hands as much, an opponent who hits harder is much easier to deal with than an opponent who moves quicker and throws faster.

Morales was less active and used less footwork, but he was able to compensate for Maidana's pressure and power with head movement, ducking and weaving and rolling with punches, limiting the damage if the punches landed. He put forth jabs and one-twos to throw Maidana off his rhythm and sent out counters and flurries in response and retaliation.

Maidana kept coming.

Through four, Maidana had thrown 301 punches and

landed 64, including 53 power shots. Morales had thrown 185 total shots, landing 37, including 25 power punches.

Everyone thinks they see something in Maidana. They see the wide arm punches that don't look like they should hurt as much as they do. They see the lack of fundamental skills, the slow offense and the porous defense.

But only two men had been able to beat him. Andriy Kotelnik managed a close split decision. Amir Khan had to survive a frightening late rally en route to a close unanimous decision.

Khan had remained mobile and relied on speedy feet and hands to keep hitting Maidana and keep moving afterward. He was the one expending energy while Maidana stalked. It was only when Khan rested that Maidana was able to hurt him with damaging uppercuts.

Victor Ortiz had stood in front of Maidana after scoring three knockdowns in the first two rounds, leaving himself susceptible to Maidana. If Maidana can hit you, he can hurt you. Ortiz called it a night after six rounds, unwilling to take more punishment and unable to prevent himself from taking it.

Maidana is aggressive, and so Morales threw between Maidana's wide punches with straight, clean shots. This forced Maidana to recuperate. And Maidana was more active against what he perceived to be a lesser threat in Morales. This forced Maidana to rest.

Morales sent Maidana moving backward in the fifth with right hands, left hooks and combinations, slightly outlanding Maidana in the round, 20 to 19, with each landing 17 power punches.

Morales had handpicked Maidana as his opponent. Yet it was Morales who had to earn Maidana's respect.

He did that in the fifth, and he did it again at the end of the sixth, letting Maidana finish his own combinations and then sending out several flurries of his own, just as Morales had during his three back-and-forth battles with Marco Antonio Barrera. And he earned his respect again in the beginning of the eighth, hurting Maidana with a lead left hook.

Now it was Morales asking questions of Maidana.

How much energy did Maidana have left to deal with the vintage Morales moments? How badly had Morales hurt him? How long would it take for Maidana to get his second wind?

Maidana answered in the ninth, bursting forth with a tremendous attack that went unanswered for the first minute of the round. Then Morales dug in, reminding Maidana that there would be return fire — even if the volleys came less often, even if the ordnance was less explosive.

Morales outlanded Maidana in the eighth. Maidana outlanded Morales in the ninth, going 22 of 99, though Morales was still an exceptionally effective 18 of 26.

Maidana needed a round to rest after that. The 10th would be the only round in the fight in which Morales threw more punches than Maidana, sending out 57 punches and landing 22. Maidana, meanwhile, sent out 49 punches and hit Morales with just eight of them.

It was a closer fight than most expected. The ending was in question.

Maidana had the solution.

Maidana summoned the stamina for the championship rounds and targeted Morales' closed right eye with more left hands.

For 10 rounds, Morales had shown what he had left in

189

him — one more great fight. But he didn't have enough left in the final two rounds for one more great victory.

Morales threw just 25 punches in the 11th round, landing four. He threw 45 punches in the 12th, landing 11. Maidana threw 197 punches in those final six minutes, landing 39 and taking the two rounds that would earn him the majority decision victory.

The scorecards: 114-114 once, or six rounds apiece; and 116-112 twice, or eight rounds to four.

Like Sylvester Stallone's Rocky, Erik Morales had fought through a closed eye.

Like Rocky, Morales came up short.

Erik Morales had asked for this, for a chance to prove that his year-old comeback was not about vanity, not about money and not about trying to hold onto the sport when you can no longer handle the competition.

We asked questions of Morales, thinking that we already knew the answers. We were wrong, and Morales made us glad to be wrong.

His fight with Marcos Maidana went from ugly to beautiful. And we went from dreading what could happen to delighting in what did.

Pacquiao-Mosley:
Intimidation Preceding Domination
May 9, 2011

Thirty-six minutes segmented over 12 rounds is not a guarantee, not when a fight can end in the blink of an eye and the flash of a fist.

The bout between Manny Pacquiao and Shane Mosley was scheduled for 12 rounds, and that is exactly how long it lasted. The fight, however, was essentially over by the third round. The outcome was decided even earlier.

"Everyone has a plan until they've been hit." A variation of that quote has been attributed to Mike Tyson, though it predates him by generations of heavyweight champions, dating back, at the very least, to Joe Louis.

The quote has been axiomatic of Manny Pacquiao's fights since the days when all Pacquiao had was one hand and one gear, relying on blazing speed and blasting power in a left hand that left few standing. Whether his foes planned for that left hand didn't matter; he would still pummel them with it. Knowing what had hit them did not lessen the consequences.

Preparing for Pacquiao has required much more strategizing in these past few years, a run that has completed his growth beyond a one-dimensional but overpowering force and into a multifaceted and overwhelming fury.

No amount of planning, though, could prevent David Diaz, Oscar De La Hoya, Ricky Hatton and Miguel Cotto from losing before those scheduled 12 rounds could be completed. No strategy could save Joshua Clottey and Antonio Margarito from being dominated and defeated throughout the duration of that 36-minute distance.

Manny Pacquiao would not stop Shane Mosley as he had done to Diaz, De La Hoya, Hatton and Cotto. Nor would he badly batter Mosley as he had Margarito.

As with his decision victory over Clottey, Pacquiao's ability to deliver punches with speed and power and volume intimidated Mosley. The effect on Mosley wasn't submission, but rather inaction.

It was Pacquiao pitching a near-shutout — the scorecards read 120-107, 120-108 and 119-108 — in which Mosley struck out looking instead of going down swinging.

"When you take more risks, then you're susceptible to get knocked out," Mosley said following the fight. The reputedly sturdy fighter pointed to the obvious turning point, the third round, when Pacquiao sent him to the canvas with a left hand.

"He kind of surprised me with his punching power," Mosley said. "That's the most legitimate knockdown I got hit with in a long time. I said, 'Well this guy must really have some power.' "

Mosley's post-fight conclusion served as confirmation to what had been a surprising pre-fight evaluation.

"I don't know if I have any advantages," he'd said earlier that night, hours before he'd step into the ring.

He fought as if he believed that to be true.

Pacquiao and Mosley both came out cautiously, keenly aware of the inherent danger. Each was facing an opponent who was looking to use fast, powerful counters and quick combinations, key shots that could turn control of the action in their favor. Each, then, felt it necessary to feel the early rounds out, intent on preventing the inherent danger from transitioning into impending and inevitable.

Both probed with the jab in the first round, Pacquiao sending out 28, Mosley throwing 26, each landing two apiece, according to CompuBox. Neither wanted to over-commit and open himself up, and so the power punches came rarely — Pacquiao threw nine, landing six, while Mosley threw eight, landing two.

Mosley had said he wasn't sure whether he had any advantages, but he did believe in his skills. "I know that I'm very fast," he said in that pre-fight interview. "I have good hand speed. I'm very powerful in my punches. And I'm ready to go."

He was ready to go until he saw someone who was faster, who had better hand speed, who also had power in his punches and who wasn't just ready to go, but was also ready to turn up the pace to a level for which Mosley wasn't ready.

Mosley saw what he had in front of him and knew that caution was necessary. Pacquiao saw what he had in front of him and knew that Mosley's caution meant he'd close up and go defensive, allowing Pacquiao to open up on offense.

Mosley remained jab-heavy in the second and third rounds, landing 5 of 23 in the second round and 1 of 17 in the third. Before the fight, his team had spoken of how Pacquiao had the perfect style for Mosley, how Pacquiao would come forward and be there to be hit. But Pacquiao's style is one of motion, darting and ducking in and out and to the side.

Pacquiao had little lateral movement in this Mosley fight, but he was still easily able to move away or under Mosley's punches or pick the shots off with his gloves. Mosley landed none of the 12 power punches he threw in the second round and four of the dismal six he threw in the third.

Through the first three rounds, Mosley had thrown just 26 power punches, landing six, and he had thrown just 92 total punches (about 30 per round), landing only 14 (less than 5 per round). Pacquiao, meanwhile, felt comfortable committing more, throwing 21 power shots in the second (landing 14) and 31 power shots in the third (also landing 14).

Pacquiao took advantage of Mosley's defensiveness in that third round. He feinted before throwing a southpaw jab, followed by a straight left hand. Mosley's timing was thrown off; the left hand caught him as he tried to duck beneath it. The punch caught Mosley on the side of the head and sent him down.

Mosley rose at the count of five, clearly disappointed. He'd seen the punch coming. That fact hadn't made a difference.

Hockey players can't score if they don't put shots on goal. And a boxer's hand speed and power don't mean much if he doesn't throw punches. Mosley rarely opened up from his shell, leading with the occasional hook to the body or right hand upstairs. He rarely threw counters either, not against a Pacquiao who would lead with different punches and from different stances and on different rhythms.

Mosley had gotten in the habit of throwing fewer and fewer combinations over the past several years, instead loading up on power. He couldn't throw with as much power against Pacquiao, however, not when he saw a need to move or dodge, wary of what could be coming back at him.

From round four through round nine, Mosley threw

just 178 punches, an average of about 30 per round, landing just 42, an average of 6 per round. Mosley was throwing just one punch every six seconds, and he was landing only one of every five punches thrown.

Most of those were jabs: Mosley was 28 of 141 with that punch during rounds four through nine, and 14 of 37 with his power shots.

Pacquiao had a hesitant, moving target in front of him, but one that was potentially dangerous still because he had not yet been physically broken down. Instead of five-, six- and seven-punch combinations, Pacquiao's flurries were shorter bursts divided up by single shots. He was consistent with his strategy and his activity, throwing enough that Mosley expended more energy reacting instead of acting.

From rounds four through nine, Pacquiao was 110 of 359, or about 18 of 60 a round. The jab rarely landed (30 of 190 during those rounds), but it blinded Mosley between Pacquiao's power punches (80 of 169 in that time).

Even Mosley's luckiest moment would work against him.

Pacquiao fell to the canvas with about a minute left in the 10th round, going down due to Mosley's left foot being on top of his right. Referee Kenny Bayless incorrectly called it a knockdown, and Pacquiao worked to make up for the ruling. He attacked Mosley for the remaining 60 seconds, forcing him to retreat and convincing at least two of the judges to award Pacquiao a round in which he'd been "knocked down."

Not that the result would ever be in question.

Mosley landed 10 total punches in the final three rounds, throwing 60. Pacquiao landed more than Mosley threw, hitting him with 70 of 226. Two of Mosley's landed punches were power shots. Sixty-three of Pacquiao's were power punches.

Mosley never landed in double digits on the entire night, averaging just five-and-a-half landed punches a round, including less than four landed jabs per round and less than two landed power shots. He was cautious to a fault, not fighting to survive, but rather surviving instead of fighting.

He was intimidated to the point of being dominated.

Bernard Hopkins Won
With Table Talk
May 23, 2011

He head butts, seemingly unintentionally, definitely otherwise. He crashes the point of his hip into his opponent's body before initiating a clinch. He punches his opponent's legs while the referee stands on the opposite side.

Bernard Hopkins knows the tricks. He also knows the trade.

He is a technically proficient fighter whose timing is still there on offense, whose reflexes are still there on defense, who does all the little things that add science to the simple premise of hit and don't get hit. He is tough. He is strong.

He is smart.

For all of his physical abilities, it is Hopkins' mental game that has made him victorious, a lock for the Hall of Fame with more than 50 wins, with a run that saw him win a title belt at 160 pounds in 1995 and not relinquish it for a decade until 20 fights later, with a career that has included championships won at middleweight and light heavyweight.

It is his mental game that has made him durable, a 46-year-old man who can compete and defeat men two decades his junior in large part due to his conditioning and his strategy. He knows he must approach each training camp with discipline and dedication, and he knows that he must approach these fights differently than he would have when he was younger.

It is his mental game that has made him the oldest man

ever to win a legitimate world championship, a distinction that came with his rematch win over top 175-pound fighter Jean Pascal.

He did it in the ring with his tricks and his trade, his skills and his smarts. But before then, he'd won this bout with the mental game outside of the ropes.

Bernard Hopkins won with table talk. He won with what he said, with confidence in concentrated bursts from the dais at press conferences promoting the fight, and with verbal jabs unleashed in a spoken salvo at a small table that HBO had set up for a filmed face-off with Pascal the network had shot in advance of the bout.

On the surface, Hopkins was breaking down what had happened in the first fight between himself and Jean Pascal. Between his lines, he was breaking Pascal's façade down weeks before the first punch in their rematch had even landed.

Pascal had landed the first big shots in their first bout, knocking Hopkins down in the first and third rounds. Hopkins had come back and taken control down the stretch. The fight, however, would be scored a majority draw, with two of the three judges seeing the action even.

Pascal didn't argue the result and accepted a rematch, willing to work for a different outcome the second-time around. Hopkins reminded him that the first fight still mattered. Sure, Pascal had shown that he could hurt Hopkins. But those two knockdowns didn't deliver him to victory. Hopkins called Pascal a four-round fighter, a derogatory description in an era of title bouts scheduled for a maximum of 12.

"It's not what happened, it's what happens next," Hopkins said at the face-off with Pascal, looking intensely across the table. "And what happened next is you bitched. You ran. You didn't fight.

"I forced the fight, and from the fifth round to the 12th round I was in your ass and you was ready to quit and you was blowing and puffing and went to your corner like a rag doll, done, defeated and knew that you lost the fight. I guarantee that you won't be able to do it because you don't have it in you."

Pascal had reached the top due to his power and speed. In the first bout with Hopkins, though, the cards didn't turn out in his favor. He had already gotten a good idea in that first fight of what Hopkins would be bringing to the ring in the rematch. And while Pascal still had confidence in his hands, Hopkins had instilled some doubt in him.

The best boxers hold themselves in supreme esteem. No one can be better, and that is why post-fight interviews are often laden with excuses.

Before the first Hopkins fight, Pascal had beaten all but one person in his pro career, and at light heavyweight he had gone undefeated and ascended to the top. For a man nearly two decades his senior to fight him to a draw wasn't only unexplainable — it was unnatural.

"It's not me. It's the fans asking: Are you willing to take the test?" Pascal asked Hopkins at one press conference several weeks before the fight.

Pascal was insinuating, less than subtly, that Hopkins could only have given him trouble in their first fight due to the use of performance enhancing drugs — not the tricks, trade, skills and smarts that others have credited for Hopkins' success deep into his 40s.

Pascal had signed a contract for this rematch without insisting on extra drug testing. It was an attempt at a mind game, to bolster his own confidence and to get under Hopkins' skin.

The premise ate at Pascal more than it ate at Hopkins.

"You're a fucking cheater," Pascal said at the press conference. "You're a cheater."

Pascal had given a crucial tell. Hopkins' pre-fight talk, meanwhile, wasn't bluffing.

Hopkins knew what he had in hand for Pascal. He said what he did to Pascal in the first fight, and then he did what he said he'd do in the second fight.

Pascal didn't fight much in the first two rounds, landing 10 punches out of 69 thrown. He was hesitant as a continuation from how his first run-in with Hopkins had ended, and there was also Hopkins' usual ability to shut down his opponent's offensive effectiveness.

Hopkins did even less in those two rounds, landing six of 38. He out-landed Pascal in the third round, a reminder that he hadn't gotten old in the interim, that a difficult and potentially long challenge was still ahead.

Pascal appeared to hurt Hopkins in the fourth with a looping right hand to the neck. From there, from that fourth round beyond, Hopkins asserted control.

In his losses to Jermain Taylor and Joe Calzaghe, Hopkins had minimized their landed punches but had been too frugal himself, falling behind on the scorecards. Against Pascal, Hopkins landed more punches than his opponent from the third round through the 12th and threw more punches than him in all but two of those rounds.

Hopkins made Pascal question himself outside of and within the ring. His feints had Pascal reacting rather than attacking, and his leads — straight rights, looping rights, jabs, quick flurries — left Pascal uncertain of what would come and when.

Pascal had a few moments, but they were short-lived, and the chips — and points — were quickly stacking against him.

Hopkins landed 131 punches, or about 11 per round, to Pascal's 70, or about six per round. He landed more power shots, 80, to Pascal's 51. And, most important, he won more rounds, getting tallies of 116-112, 115-114 and 115-113 from the judges at ringside.

It didn't even seem as close as that.

Bernard Hopkins' physical feats in the first fight had allowed for his mental game to be played out against Jean Pascal prior to their second bout. That mental game, in turn, allowed for Hopkins' to beat Pascal in the rematch.

I Will Not Fight:
Complaints, Demands
May 30, 2011

I want to be world champion. I want to be seen as the best in boxing. And I want fortune to go with my fame.

I am the fighter. I leave the rest to my team, to my manager and promoter and trainer. You hear me say this after every victory. They line 'em up and I knock 'em out.

Except it's never truly that simple.

I want everything to be perfect. I want everything to go my way, for every promotion to cater to me. I have a list of demands longer than a rock band's list of contract riders.

I want everything but a six-pack of water, chilled, and a bowl of nothing but green M&M's.

I want the ring to be small when I face someone with much less power than me.

I want the ring to be large when I face someone with far more power than me.

I want 12 rounds for a non-title fight, not 10 rounds, and I want 10-ounce gloves, not eight ounces, and I want the gloves for both me and my opponent to be Winning Gloves, not Reyes.

I won't take a fight with George Foreman III unless I can get a free George Foreman Grill. Oh, and also an autographed picture of the man himself.

I will not fight without a rematch clause. Or maybe I will not fight unless there is a rematch clause.

I will not fight if there are contractual options. Or maybe I will not fight unless my opponent gives up contractual options.

I want to walk to the ring second.

I want the weigh-in to be even earlier than usual so I have more time to rehydrate. And I want a limit on the number of pounds my opponent can gain after making weight.

I will not fight unless it is in my hometown. Or, barring that, I will not fight unless it's in my home country. Or at least a part of my opponent's country that is easier to travel to should my fans want to come see the fight.

I won't fight because I refuse to be tested for HIV. In fact, I believe that the burden of proof is not on me to take the blood test every other fighter takes. No, it's the commission that needs to prove that I have the virus.

I want to be able to drink Gatorade in my corner between rounds.

I will not fight unless I have neutral judges. Or maybe I'd be okay with having one judge from my country, one judge from my opponent's country and one judge from somewhere else.

Oh, and I will not fight if a certain referee is assigned to be the third man in the ring.

I will not fight Chad Dawson because I don't want to ruin yet another prospect.

I will not fight certain fighters because they don't deserve to fight me. I'm undefeated, and they have losses on their record. So instead I'll fight other fighters who also have losses on their records.

I will not fight certain fighters because they haven't beaten anyone as good as me. I will not fight them until they beat the guys I've beaten. And then, after that, I will not fight them because all they will have beaten are my leftovers.

I will not fight unless my fans have more tickets made

available to them.

I will not fight Jermain Taylor because I've abruptly decided to retire. I actually won't fight him because my promoter didn't offer me enough money. I'll come out of my so-called retirement less than a week later.

But even then, I might not fight because I'm being set up to be the opponent to Amir Khan.

Or maybe I won't fight because I'm waiting for a shot at the title or a big payday. I won't fight because I recognize that this sport often rewards those who don't stay active and don't have another fight on the horizon.

I won't fight because I have a back injury, except in reality I'm in the middle of a dispute with my manager. When that's over, I won't fight because my promoter owes me money.

I want a catch-weight, a contractual limit that will disadvantage my opponent, a demand he will acquiesce to because I have the drawing power and he can't earn anywhere near as much money without me.

I won't fight unless my opponent takes part in random drug testing to answer suspicions that started with my baseless accusations. I won't fight him without this drug testing because I want to clean up the sport, even though I haven't called for similar drug testing to be done on the undercard fighters participating in my pay-per-views, and even though I've been on sabbatical for more than a year and haven't exactly been spending that time getting my blood drawn at random times.

I won't fight because demands that I take a drug test have offended me and are intended to be a mind game and a negotiating ploy. No amount of money, no matter how many millions are on the line, will be worth compromising my principles, even if doing so could mean shutting my accusers up.

Most importantly, I will not fight unless I get more money.

I will not fight without more percentage points in relation to what my opponent is getting. I will not fight if I feel I've been low-balled. I will not fight without a bigger cut. I will not fight unless I get what someone else who turned down the fight was offered. I will not fight unless we also have an even split of the television license fees.

It doesn't matter if I actually bring less money to the table. It doesn't matter if I'm coming off a loss. It doesn't matter if I've been inactive. It doesn't matter if I've not been on television in a while. It doesn't matter that my saying no to this fight means I'll be sitting on the sidelines even longer.

These complaints and demands don't matter to the fans. All that matters to them is the fights.

That doesn't matter to me. I will not fight.

Klitschko-Haye: Power Outage
July 4, 2011

The everlasting allure of heavyweight boxing lies in the exercise of power. They are the biggest men and the hardest punchers. There is supposed to be danger in their delivery and excitement in their execution.

Wladimir Klitschko and David Haye were two of the three best heavyweights. Klitschko had become the true heavyweight champion, resurrecting his career after dramatic failures in grit and stamina, finding confidence through his superior skills, strategies and strength. Haye was seen as a legitimate challenger. He had a world title around his waist, speed and power in his punches, cockiness in his countenance and swagger in his step.

Klitschko's fists had handed him 49 knockouts in 55 victories. Haye's had brought him 23 early nights in his 25 wins. Their records promised pain. Their words did the same.

Haye had sought a clash with the Klitschkos — Wladimir and his brother, fellow heavyweight titleholder Vitali — from the moment he'd cast aside his cruiserweight championship and entered boxing's marquee division. He'd even worn a shirt depicting him holding the decapitated heads of the brothers.

After years of talk, he was finally fighting Wladimir, whose style, Haye said, was ready made for him. It was he, Haye said, who would crack Klitschko's questionable chin and leave him flattened and shattered. It would be over quickly, he said.

Klitschko felt disrespected — by the shirt, by the words, by Haye's repeated refusal to shake hands — and he vowed to make Haye respect him. He promised to make Haye his 50th knockout. He questioned whether Haye would show up for the fight to back up his words. He asserted that it would be a night of extended punishment, ending only once he was ready to put Haye down and away.

Their fight should have been a power struggle between two big punchers with questionable chins. The winner, many thought, would be the first fighter to land a clean, hard shot.

The power struggle never developed. Instead, it devolved into a power outage.

The everlasting allure of heavyweight boxing lies in the exercise of power. Neither seemed willing to exercise his.

After all the threats, and despite the knockouts on their records, the fight lasted the entirety of its 12 scheduled rounds, a majority of the minutes lacking the inherent danger in delivery and excitement in execution.

In total, they landed but 65 power punches on the night. Broken down, that number becomes even more depressing. The biggest men, the heaviest hitters in the sport, averaged about five and a half power punches landed per round — combined. On average, each of those 36 minutes included less than two total landed power shots.

Haye threw 119 of them in those 12 rounds, about 10 per round. He landed just 36, three per round, one per minute. Klitschko threw 133 total power punches, about 11 per round, landing just 29, about two and a half per, or one every 74 seconds.

The most either ever landed in a single round was five.

Klitschko, as has been his norm, relied on his jab, a thudding left that helps maintain distance, softening his opponents up for the occasional left hook or right cross. He threw 376 on the night, more than 30 per round, more than 10 per minute. Haye's movement minimized its damage — he shifted from side to side, dodging Klitschko's probes and forcing him to reset, and even when the jab was on the mark, he'd often deftly pull his head back and make it miss by mere inches.

Klitschko landed just 105 jabs, but as his trainer, Emanuel Steward, had told interviewers before the fight, the punch did not need to land for it to have an impact.

Indeed, Haye concentrated more on minimizing Klitschko's chances of a knockout than he did on maximizing his own. Each round, on average, saw him throw just two dozen punches. Sometimes they were overhand rights with exaggerated loops. Sometimes they were left hooks. Sometimes those two punches were put together in combination.

Haye did not blitz Klitschko, preferring to remain at a distance, seeking to counter Klitschko with faster return fire or to extend him and bring the chin lower. On occasion he burst forth with a single overhand right for which the follow-through included him ducking his head down and allowing himself to be off-balance on the inside.

Neither man had any interest in fighting in close. Klitschko was willing to direct a ducking man lower; Haye was willing to be pushed downward to the canvas.

"He fought the perfect game plan against someone who had my particular style," Haye said afterward.

Klitschko is no lumbering giant. His height advantage is enhanced by good footwork that quickly pulls him out of range of attacks, and his hand speed and power keep foes at a distance — and on defense.

The total punches Haye landed — 72, split evenly between jabs and power shots — is actually less than what other Klitschko opponents were able to do.

Calvin Brock went 77 of 280 in seven rounds. Lamon Brewster, in his rematch with Klitschko, landed 70 of 248 in six rounds. Sultan Ibragimov went 97 of 316. Tony Thompson went 150 of 408 in 11 rounds. Samuel Peter, in his rematch with Klitschko, landed 100 of 440 in 12 rounds.

Not that Klitschko was an offensive dynamo himself.

"It was very hard to hit this man," Klitschko said afterward. "He was definitely fast. He didn't give me a lot of opportunities. He was very backed up and super cautious, so I couldn't really land a good shot."

Neither fighter was trying to dominate with his own offense. Each was more intent on trying to defend against that of his opponent.

It was incumbent on Haye to make the fight. For him, cautiousness meant falling behind on the scorecards. His strategy — and Klitschko's defensive abilities — wasn't giving him many opportunities. After the fight, Haye blamed a broken right toe, injured three weeks prior to the fight, for his not being able to be more aggressive.

Klitschko didn't put Haye away, but the onus wasn't on him to do so, not so long as he was winning, and not so long as Haye was still capable of harming him. With Klitschko's jabbing not softening up Haye as it had done to other opponents, he settled for winning rounds clearly. Haye only landed in double digits in a round once. Klitschko did so eight times.

They are the biggest men and the hardest punchers. Because of that, even a bad heavyweight fight has the potential for danger, for a thrilling knockout to erase memories of the dullness that preceded it.

Not this time. In a fight between a champion nicknamed "Dr. Steelhammer" and a challenger who calls himself "the Hayemaker," the continued potential for devastation meant that the only knockout scored was on those watching.

Kelly Pavlik: 'The Ghost' Makes Himself Disappear

August 8, 2011

His popularity grew out of a wealth of power and a dearth of pretense. There was nothing artificial about Kelly Pavlik. He need not box and weave and move, not when he could just get hit and then hit back even harder. He was blue collar, punching in and punching out, true to his roots in the steel city of Youngstown, Ohio. He still lived there, even after the championship, the spotlight and the seven-figure paydays.

Celebrity can uproot even the most grounded. Sometimes the symptoms don't present themselves until the fame has begun to fade.

"Kelly Pavlik is still one of the biggest names in boxing," Pavlik said last week, resorting to the third-person in an online radio interview with Alec Kohut of MaxBoxing.com. "It is," he added, in case he hadn't yet convinced his audience.

Pavlik was in the news last week because he'd decided not to fight in two fights. He would not face Lucian Bute, one of the three best 168-pound fighters in the world, in November in Montreal. Nor would he face Daryl Cunningham in what was to be a tune-up bout to help Pavlik prepare for Bute.

The Cunningham fight was supposed to take place in Youngstown. It was supposed to take place on Aug. 6. Pavlik pulled out on Aug. 2.

"It's not about fighting for Youngstown," Pavlik said. "It's about me."

It's about money, no matter how many times Pavlik

said he can afford to go without paydays he'd have received for Bute and, to a lesser extent, Cunningham.

It's about principle. Just because Pavlik said he doesn't need money doesn't mean he doesn't want more of it if he's going to get in the ring.

The tipping point, he said, came when he found out what he was getting for the Cunningham and Bute fights — a minimum of $50,000 and a minimum of $1.35 million (the latter amount supposedly negotiated up from a $1.1 million minimum).

The Cunningham payday would be much less than what he'd gotten for past lesser fights. The Bute payday would be much less than what he'd gotten for past big fights.

And, to make it worse, Pavlik insisted that another super middleweight, Mikkel Kessler, had been offered much more money to face Bute, $3 million, an offer Kessler reportedly turned down.

Pavlik turned his ire toward his promoter, Top Rank.

He would fight Bute in Atlantic City for $1.1 million, he said, but not in Montreal, where he'd have to "put the guy on a stretcher to win the fight."

"It's kind of like Top Rank is cashing in on me, like 'We're going to make our money off of him. We're done with him.' And that's it," he said.

"I'm not going to fight Bute in his hometown to get beat so Top Rank can cash out on me," he said. "I'm not doing that. It's kind of stupid. I'm selling myself short by doing that."

He got paid $2.5 million to face a lesser opponent, Gary Lockett, in front of a smaller crowd in Atlantic City than would be there in Montreal, he said.

He got paid $3 million to face Bernard Hopkins, an

opponent of Bute's caliber but not Bute's drawing power, in front of a smaller crowd in Atlantic City than would be there in Montreal, he said.

He even got paid $350,000 to face a lesser opponent in Miguel Espino, $275,000 to face a lesser opponent in Alfonso Lopez, and $1.5 million to face Marco Antonio Rubio, a good opponent but one without any true market value.

"How can you pay me 2.5 or 3 million to fight Hopkins or Gary Lockett, but you can't pay me $2.5 to go fight Lucian Bute in Montreal with a sold out arena?" he said. "$3 million is there, but that's what they're cashing out on. 'We're going to pocket $2 million. He's going to lose the fight, and we're done with him.' "

It's about money.

It's about principle.

And it's about incorrect information and misguided decisions.

Kessler was never offered $3 million to fight Bute, according to several reports following Pavlik's withdrawal. Pavlik had that number on his mind in June, though, when his local newspaper, the Youngstown Vindicator, noted that Kessler had said no to that amount.

Ben Thompson of FightHype.com asked Pavlik where he heard about such an offer.

"It was posted on the Internet. It's not a lie," Pavlik answered. "If you put in Google 'Mikkel Kessler $3 million offer from Bute's camp,' you'll pull it up."

Thompson's interview with Pavlik links back to the Vindicator article. An in-depth search of the Internet cannot find any reliable sources to bolster Pavlik's claim.

The Vindicator article received the information about Kessler's $3 million offer from three sources in Pavlik's camp, one of whom was Pavlik himself, according to the Vindicator reporter, Joe Scalzo, speaking to BoxingScene.com via email.

"Obviously, that was inaccurate," Scalzo said.

Pavlik said last week that he'd yet to receive his contract for the Cunningham fight, a questionable claim coming just days before a bout that was to be broadcast on Showtime, a questionable claim coming from a world-class fighter who would know not to get so close to fight time without having the business end taking care of.

The Cunningham fight was a tune-up requested by Pavlik himself, Top Rank officials noted. We learned more last week from various reports: that the Youngstown show was doing poorly, selling around 1,000 tickets; that Pavlik's $50,000 fee was more than what fighters appearing on Showtime's "ShoBox" broadcasts typically get, and that the payday would've increased if the live event profited; and that the Bute-Pavlik fight would've seen the proceeds split 60-40 between InterBox (Bute's promoter) and Top Rank, with Pavlik entitled to 82 percent of Top Rank's revenue.

He very well could've gotten more money. And while most were predicting Pavlik would have little shot of beating Bute, Pavlik himself was self-defeating, complaining about the insurmountable disadvantages of fighting in Bute's adopted hometown.

Pavlik was paid very well during his time as middleweight champion. HBO dished out the cash for the Lockett fight. The bout with Hopkins was on pay-per-view. The fights with Rubio and Espino were on smaller pay-per-views. And the Lopez tune-up was on a pay-per-view undercard.

If he wanted a tune-up with Cunningham on short

notice, he'd have to settle for a slight jump above Showtime's usual "ShoBox" budget. And he'd have to settle for Showtime's money for the Bute fight.

Instead, he's fighting nobody and getting paid nothing.

"I'm not trying to be one of them cocky people," Pavlik told Kohut. "Kelly Pavlik is Kelly Pavlik. My name still draws. … Until I get what I deserve, until I'm happy, then I'm not going to fight."

There was nothing artificial about Kelly Pavlik. Though his nickname was "The Ghost," he was hard to miss in the later part of his career, both in the ring and on the screen. He need not box and weave and move. He could just get hit and then hit back even harder. He was the champion, receiving the spotlight and the seven-figure paydays.

His championship was lost more than a year ago. His fame has faded. His paychecks are diminishing.

Celebrity is temporary, especially so for athletes, incredibly so for boxers who are only one punch, one injury away from obsolescence.

For his next act, Kelly "The Ghost" Pavlik is making himself disappear.

215

After The Last Round
August 22, 2011

Arturo Gatti and Micky Ward swing in the glorious ninth round of their first fight. Gatti's face contorts with each clean, hard punch that lands from Ward. And all of Ward's punches are landing, every single one clean, hard and damaging.

These are men, the epitome of strength and bravery.

We montage through vicious knockouts, the victims collapsing and crashing, the victors exultant, the losers lifeless.

We transition from a gladiator arena built in Europe more than 2000 years ago, now empty, to a bullring in present-day Mexico, a crowd roaring. On this night within, a boxer floors his opponent.

We hear the insight of those long involved in what is called a sweet science but remains a brutal trade.

"You put your life on the line when you get in the ring, and that's the bottom line because somebody is trying to kill you, and the object of boxing is to render the other guy unconscious," says Johnny Ortiz, trainer, manager, radio host and writer.

"A caveman can understand boxing," says George Chuvalo, former heavyweight contender.

"It's barbaric, but people love that," says trainer Manny Steward. "It's still the epitome of excitement."

We turn to an often unspoken reality.

Alex Ramos of the Retired Boxers Foundation: "There's another side of boxing that people should know about."

We see what he means.

An elderly man wearing a black helmet sits in a chair,

unresponsive. "Phil," a woman says. "Look at me," she says. "Come on champ."

She is a caretaker in a Portland, Ore., nursing home. He is Phil Moyer, a middleweight who fought five decades ago, once defeating Sugar Ray Robinson. So, too, did his brother, Denny Moyer, also helmeted, shown living in the same facility and in similar condition.

These are men, mortal and vulnerable. Denny died last year. Phil is now confined to a wheelchair.

These are the opening minutes of "After the Last Round," a documentary examining how fighters suffer damage, life-altering and life-taking; why they continue to step into the ring despite this; and what happens to them once they stop taking punches and try to continue with life after boxing — what remains of it.

The film's executive producer is Tom Moyer, who is Phil and Denny Moyer's cousin. The narrative is pieced together by Ryan Pettey (who also is the director) and Patrick Moyer, Tom's son.

Their subjects are gladiators only for a few nights a year, and only for an hour or so on those nights. Though they spar and train and live for those nights in the ring, they also have families, sides of them we do not see during their careers. We only think of them as performers. We rarely remember them once they retire. Our attention turns to those younger, better, relevant.

DaVarryl Williamson watches his kids swim in a Denver pool, a heavyweight of recent vintage who has delivered others into unconsciousness and been sent there himself.

"For me, the safety of my husband is my first priority," says his wife, Shalifa, in the documentary. "There are places you go in your mind that you don't wanna go. My biggest fear is taking that plane ride home by myself. I can't do that."

"Boxing is like having a bad girlfriend," DaVarryl says. "The girl's not good for you. You know you shouldn't be dating her or hanging out with her, but you keep calling her back."

There are the pro fighters who keep returning to the ring when they shouldn't have, seduced by the prospect of another title shot, another payday, drawn back by the allure of conquering another man, another challenge, and being adored for it. There are many who should've quit earlier, who should've known better, if only it were that easy.

We watch Muhammad Ali being interviewed before his final fight, in 1981, against Trevor Berbick.

"Do I sound like I have brain damage?" he asks, defiant.

He is slurring his words. The symptoms of the Parkinson's that has long since crippled him were clearly evident before his last rounds.

Boxing is not the only sport in which the participants suffer serious injuries or die. Football is in the middle of a paradigm shift, with coaches and players and doctors increasingly aware of the consequences, of the cumulative damage from years of hits and numerous concussions. Rules are being changed, even if the changes are a detriment to the nature of the game. Athletes are being protected, even if they don't want to be.

But as the documentary reminds us, boxing is one of the few sports in which the intent is to incapacitate.

"The intent is to knock the other person out," says Freddie Roach, a trainer and former fighter who is also battling Parkinson's. "We don't want to intently hurt somebody, but we know it's possible."

This is our guilty pleasure. This is regulated combat, less savage than gladiators and street fights and war, allowing men to make money through violence and through our predisposition to watching it unfold. We would never do away with it, just as we would never do away with football, even as more players are diagnosed with brain injuries, deteriorating early and dying young.

We have watched through moments such as Emile Griffith punching Benny "Kid" Paret until Paret would no longer wake. We have watched through fighters taking unnecessary punishment that, as we see it, shortens their careers. We barely think about what follows.

We institute rules to protect them. The rules are inconsistent, depending on where the fight is and who is fighting. A once-great boxer whose legs and chin have since departed will still be allowed to lace up the gloves. Sometimes he will hear and heed the call to retire.

The notable fighters are the only ones we notice as being in danger. The journeymen and lower-tier foes are done in by their anonymity. There is no memory of what they once were, no measurement of how much they have slipped. They are expected to lose, interchangeable opponents few know enough about to tell them it's time to stop.

Sugar Ray Seales told the filmmakers he boxed blind for 18 months. "I didn't know it," he said. "Why? I was winning."

A majority of those afflicted with pugilistic dementia are found, after their deaths, to have evidence of past brain bleeds, neurosurgeon Dr. Robert Cantu says on screen.

Sometimes the symptoms don't show until 10 or 15 years after a fighter has retired, Dr. Margaret Goodman, respected ringside physician, says in the documentary.

This is why — while the rest of us stand and cheer and exhort the fighters to be like Micky Ward and the late Arturo Gatti, strong and brave — family members at ringside cover their mouths or their eyes and sit stone-faced, afraid of their loved ones ending in similar states as Phil and Denny Moyer, mortal and vulnerable.

"When DaVarryl got knocked out that first round," says Shalifa Williamson, recalling her husband's loss to Joe Mesi, "I immediately jumped up and ran towards the ring."

Says Alex Ramos: "Some of them are scary. You never know if you're going to wake up."

Life continues after the last round. But only a fraction of fighters make and save enough to retire. Some have given nearly their entire lives to boxing and know little different. Some have given so much of their bodies to fighting and cannot do anything else.

The latest collective bargaining negotiations in professional football included talk of supporting retired players, who earned far less money than players today but nevertheless suffered significant damage.

There is no organization representing active boxers. It is a competitive pursuit, not just in the ring, but for finite resources — television dates, spots on cards, money and attention. Their sport is one-on-one by definition, and it's not often enough that a trainer or manager or promoter forgoes money and advises a fighter to retire.

We, as fans, seek the warriors and the winners, supporting them with a percentage of the proceeds from pay-per-view purchases and ticket sales.

It is a lot easier for us to give and get in return than it is for us to give and expect nothing back. Life does continue after the last round, however. There is that other side of boxing that people should know about, the side Alex Ramos mentioned, the side he and others are working to support through donations to the Retired Boxers Foundation.

There are boxers who turn to alcohol and drugs, who lose their homes, whose bodies and minds, once weapons in the ring, begin to turn against them.

These are men whose next fight begins after the last round ends.

Ortiz-Mayweather: As Always, Money May Makes 'Em Pay

September 19, 2011

The subplots were manifold, each presented, digested and dissected: the acrimonious relationship between Floyd Mayweather Jr. and his father; the abandonment of Victor Ortiz as a child by his parents; the falling out between Ortiz's trainer, Danny Garcia, and Garcia's brother, Robert Garcia, who once had trained Ortiz himself. There were mentions of Mayweather's idol, money, and Ortiz's idol, Oscar De La Hoya. There were references to Floyd Mayweather's legal problems and Roger Mayweather's health issues.

Those secondary storylines supplemented the primary conflict. But for those shelling out hundreds or thousands of dollars to see Ortiz vs. Mayweather in person or spending $60 to $70 to watch the fight on television, it was "Money May" who made them pay.

For six years he has made them pay with his mouth. He is abrasive and aggressive, a boisterous braggart. He captured those characteristics, augmenting his marketability by making himself into "Money Mayweather." Then he amplified himself further, turning from character to caricature and ensuring he was a man boxing fans either wanted to see or wanted to see humbled.

For 15 years he has made his fighting foes pay in the ring, making them look offensively impotent, making himself seem defensively impenetrable, making defeating him appear to be patently impossible.

For all of the subplots — the ugly argument with his

father caught on camera, the numerous criminal and civil cases against him, the constant conversation about why he and rival phenom Manny Pacquiao are yet to fight — Floyd Mayweather Jr. remains unparalleled in dedication to his craft and discipline in the gym. He tunes out the distractions, then disrupts and sometimes destroys his opponents.

Victor Ortiz gave in to distraction, to a costly lapse in discipline. He would be made to pay for it.

With Mayweather pinned against the ropes toward the end of the fourth round, Ortiz decided to stop launching punches and instead launched himself, blatantly propelling the top of his head into Mayweather's face. The referee, Joe Cortez, pulled Ortiz away, then turned away to pause the clock with nine seconds remaining. Ortiz walked back over to Mayweather, placing his right arm over him in an embrace and planting a kiss to his right cheek.

Cortez again brought Ortiz away, taking him around the ring and taking a point away from him, a penalty for the foul. Mayweather walked out toward a neutral corner, glaring at Ortiz incredulously. The two tapped left gloves, and Cortez positioned Ortiz in the neutral corner opposite Mayweather.

"Let's go," Cortez said, and he turned away from the fighters and toward the timekeeper. As Mayweather and Ortiz approached, Cortez, standing to their side, asked an official ringside if the bell had rung to end the round. Ortiz placed his gloves out toward Mayweather's hips, apparently attempting to apologize once more, and stepped forward for another embrace. Mayweather placed his gloves on Ortiz's shoulders, then planted his feet as Ortiz backed away, hands at his sides.

Mayweather threw a left hook that dazed Ortiz and finished with a right cross that downed him. Cortez caught the sight of Ortiz falling to the floor, then counted to 10 as he failed to rise.

Ortiz had fouled in the heat of battle, forgot he was in the heat of battle and was felled in the heat of battle.

It was both an opportunity and an opening for Mayweather, who did as he had done for the previous four rounds, taking Ortiz's aggression and using it against him.

Never should the game plan against Mayweather call for out-boxing him; he is too smart too swift, too gifted, too great. Rather, the strategy is to overwhelm him. If Mayweather's mastery is in making you miss more often than not, then you must keep on throwing. Mayweather's defense discourages his opponents, opening them up for his own offense.

Mayweather had been criticized by some in the past for his mobility, for moving away from slower or stronger fighters, preferring a momentary retreat that makes him almost untouchable over staying in the line of fire and rendering himself more vulnerable. He vowed to stand in with Ortiz, taking aim not at the naysayers — Mayweather tunes out all distractions — but at Ortiz's flaws.

Conventional planning when an orthodox fighter faces a southpaw calls for right crosses, the punch less likely to be parried by his foe's front hand. Ortiz has been particularly susceptible to right hands in the past. That would be no different against Mayweather.

Mayweather would lead with the right hand, or he would jab with his left — "blindingly fast" an apt description when considering its intent — before following with the right cross.

Neither man landed often in the first round. Mayweather's reflexes remained quick enough to dodge or duck Ortiz's power punches. Ortiz, younger at 24 and gifted himself, albeit to a lesser degree than Mayweather, also had success at evading these earliest attacks. Mayweather landed but 9 of 41 punches in the opening stanza, a 22 percent connect rate, a far cry from the 46 percent connect rate he'd averaged in his previous five fights. Ortiz landed less, though, 5 of 42, the 12 percent connect rate even lower than Mayweather's past opponents' paltry average of 16 percent.

If Ortiz were to overwhelm Mayweather, he'd have to do much more — and much better — than that.

The first round is traditionally the time for fighters to feel each other out, to see what the other man has and what he hasn't. Mayweather and Ortiz both picked up the tempo to start the second. Ortiz moved forward, slightly closing the distance between himself and Mayweather, seeking either to catch him at the end of his punches or to get inside and send hooks to his body and head.

Mayweather, too, picked moments to move forward. A power-puncher in the mold of Ortiz is less comfortable when he is not leading the action. And that, in turn, led Ortiz to come back at Mayweather, leaning forward with lefts that left Ortiz's chin exposed to Mayweather's rights.

Ortiz walked through those punches and forced Mayweather against the ropes, Ortiz putting his head down and pushing it into Mayweather's. Mayweather landed three right hands in succession in the final minute of the second round. Ortiz again walked into them and through them, and twice more he dug the top of his head against Mayweather's face.

Prior to the fight Ortiz's camp had complained about Mayweather's tactics in the clinch, about the forearms and elbows Mayweather had wedged against Ricky Hatton's neck to create space between himself and Hatton. It was Ortiz that went dirty against Mayweather, limiting the room between them and attempting to send a message of Ortiz as bully.

Ortiz was actually the bull, and Mayweather's sword thrusts would become increasingly pointed and punishing.

In the second round Mayweather landed 15 of 47 punches, a 32 percent connect rate, but on power punches he was 13 of 27, hitting Ortiz with nearly one out of every two. Ortiz remained in single digits: 8 of 41, or 20 percent, in power shots, 8 of 46, or 17 percent, overall.

Ortiz tentatively sent out three jabs in the opening seconds of the third, none landing. Mayweather showed him up by retorting with three of his own, all three landing. Ortiz, knowing he'd shaken off Mayweather's counter right hands in the previous rounds, attempted to charge Mayweather into a corner once more. Now Mayweather responded with a check left hook, and then a second as Ortiz tried again.

A gunfight isn't won by the deadliest weapon, but the most accurate. Ortiz couldn't hit Mayweather, and he was taking fire whenever he tried sending out shots. Defense discourages and opens up for offense. A minute into the third round and Mayweather had Ortiz backing up again. That lasted for about 40 seconds before Ortiz tried coming forward with a left hand — and moved into Mayweather's cleanest, flushest right hand yet.

It happened again. And again. And then another check hook. With 20 seconds to go in the round, Mayweather had landed 17 punches. Ortiz had landed two. Mayweather would go 22 of 53 on the round, 42 percent of his shots landing, including 16 of 29 power punches, more than half of what he threw. Ortiz was 4 of 33 overall, just 12 percent. After throwing 36 power punches in the first round and 41 in the second, he could only get off 14 in the third.

Mayweather, as promised, stayed in front of Ortiz in the fourth. Prior to the fight Ortiz might have thought that would be precisely where he wanted Mayweather. Now he knew better. Mayweather hit him with a jab and a right hand, then a right hand and a jab, then a jab and a right uppercut, followed by a left hook, a right hook, a left hook and a right uppercut. Ortiz tried to grab Mayweather, and Mayweather stepped back and hit Ortiz flush with another left hook and right hook combination.

Ortiz weathered the barrage, and with Mayweather momentarily stopping, Ortiz bulled him back to the corner, ducking his head down against Mayweather's face, looping a couple of right hands toward the rear of Mayweather's head, and then butted his head into Mayweather. It was not as blatant as the foul that would come a couple of minutes later, but it was enough to draw a warning from Cortez.

Mayweather kept landing. Ortiz kept coming. You must keep on throwing. And he did, landing a right hook here, a left hand there, all when Mayweather was against the ropes. Mayweather shook his head and brought the fight back into the center of the ring.

Mayweather walked Ortiz down, pot-shotting him until Ortiz, unwilling to keep moving backward, sought to retaliate. He came forward with a flurry of punches, driving Mayweather back to the ropes. Mayweather was on defense but not in danger. Ortiz ducked his head down, just as he had done throughout the round, just as he had done throughout the fight. This time he jumped up with a head butt and followed with a left hand.

The post-apology knockout soon followed.

Victor Ortiz lost his cool in the heat of battle and lost the fight because of it. As with after every Floyd Mayweather fight, the critics would make themselves heard. His left hook and right hand had been cheap shots, they said. He didn't need to end the fight this way, they said.

They were right. Mayweather was winning the fight, and he very well could have stopped Ortiz later without throwing punches when Ortiz was least expecting them.

This was the heat of battle, though. Ortiz had just fouled Mayweather, drawing blood from his mouth. Mayweather might not have done what some consider to be the right thing, but in no way was what he did wrong.

We ask soldiers to shoot to kill the enemy on the battlefield but to show mercy if the other side is captured alive. We ask fighters to step into the ring with the intent of sending his opponent into unconsciousness, and we ask them to be sportsmanlike.

Mayweather knocked down Arturo Gatti on a break. He punched Shane Mosley when Mosley tried to touch gloves. This is a sport, but it is a sport at odds with itself. Fouled and furious in the heat of battle, Floyd Mayweather Jr. had every right to pull the trigger.

Still Missing Arturo Gatti
September 26, 2011

I was a fan of Arturo Gatti back when I could still be a fan of a fighter, back before I was a writer, back when it was just my father and I bonding over boxing on Saturday nights.

I'd often return home from work to find the television tuned to HBO, the undercard already under way. Many of those evenings I'd acquiesce to exhaustion in the middle of the action, "just resting my eyes," I'd say, submitting to unconsciousness on the couch some time before a boxer would do the same on the canvas.

Not when Arturo Gatti fought.

I had to stay awake — not that you could do anything but keep your eyes open, and your mouth, too. His skin swelled. His flesh bruised. His eyebrows cut. His knees shook. And his punches somehow kept coming.

He was an action hero.

He wasn't an invincible Arnold Schwarzenegger, nor was he an ass kicking, wise cracking Steven Seagal or Jean Claude Van Damme. Rather, he resembled Bruce Willis as John McClane or Sylvester Stallone as Rocky. There was no doubt that he would take a beating. And there was no doubt that he'd find a way to still be standing.

But it was hard to watch when the action became more one-sided, when the beatings got worse, and when it wasn't just skin swelling, flesh bruising, eyebrows cutting and knees shaking. It was hard to watch when it was also his body succumbing, when his punches were no longer coming and he no longer could find a way to remain upright.

And so it was better when the final credits rolled on our action move, when the Human Highlight Reel looked at the camera, waved, and said "Hasta la vista, baby." There he was, minutes after another devastating defeat, quoting the Terminator.

"I can't be taking this abuse no more," he had said. It was a bittersweet moment. He had taken that abuse for our entertainment, because he knew no better, because it was who he was in the ring and in life, because it was what had made him our hero, both to his benefit and at his expense.

An athlete ceases to exist, remembered only for his profession, thought of only on occasion. New action heroes take to the screen.

We had hoped Arturo Gatti would retire to comfort, to a life he had fought for, as literal a life of blood, sweat and tears as one could have. But it is difficult for former athletes to adjust, particularly so for boxers. Gatti had lived a turbulent life even during his career. Without routine, without the daily discipline of training, he was left to his vices.

"He partied like he fought — hard and heavy," said fight photographer Tom Casino. "I knew if he continued drinking something bad was going to happen. It was inevitable."

Casino spoke those words on an episode of "48 Hours Mystery" that aired this past weekend on CBS, a broadcast that looked into Gatti's death more than two years ago in Brazil. Initially ruled a homicide, police concluded it to be suicide, a difficult conclusion for all to stomach, an impossible conclusion for many to accept.

"My gut says he didn't take his life," said Micky Ward,

whose last three pro fights were the legendary trilogy with Gatti. "I just can't see him taking his own life," Ward told the television crew. "That's just not him. Everything in life was going good for him."

Other notable boxers have died tragically in recent years. Diego Corrales left us too early after crashing his motorcycle in 2007. Vernon Forrest chased after a man who had just robbed him and wound up being shot and killed. Alexis Arguello is believed to have killed himself. Forrest and Arguello, like Gatti, died in 2009.

Gatti's death has remained an open wound. His widow, once a suspect in his death, was set free. Many of those close to him set out to prove that police had made a mistake. They funded a private investigation that recently concluded. They said the investigation found, with certainty, what they had felt all along — Arturo Gatti didn't take his own life.

"48 Hours" presented both cases: that made by Gatti's widow and that made by those who blame her for his death.

That the last fights of Gatti's career had been so hard to watch was because they showed him more vulnerable than ever. We prefer to think of our heroes in memorable montages, recalling them in their greatest moments.

"48 Hours" proved difficult to watch because it humanized Gatti even further. We saw his body lying prone, heard about his many personal problems, and realized that the man boxing fans idolized for his pugilistic pursuits was now having all of his flaws and follies publicly aired.

This was not how we wanted to remember him. This was not how we wanted others to know him.

He had alcohol and drug problems, and a temper, and

drunk-driving charges, and fights with police officers. He had a troubled marriage, battled depression and had been accused of domestic violence.

"He got depressed. He didn't know what to do. He started drinking a lot," Amanda Rodrigues Gatti said of Arturo after his retirement. "There was the man I fell in love, the funny, the romantic, the lovely husband and father, and then there was this person that would change when he was drunk. He would become aggressive, nasty. He was a completely different man when he was drinking."

She remains the suspect in the minds of Gatti's fans, members of his team and nearly all of his family and friends. They look to the changes in his will just weeks before his death, changes which left his money to her and their son. They recall how she treated him, the threats they heard her make, the mean text messages she sent him when the couple had separated. They point to the blood on the floor, to the wound on the back of his head, to the flimsiness of the purse strap which he supposedly used to hang himself.

They point to the brief Brazilian police investigation that absolved her of blame, and to the extensive private investigation that found that Arturo Gatti's death wasn't a suicide. "If not him," they think, "then it must be her."

One longtime friend and one of Gatti's brothers think Arturo committed suicide, however.

With authorities in Brazil yet to reopen the case, Gatti's family sought to make his death part of the civil court battle over the late boxer's estate.

It is a battle in which there are no real winners. He is still gone.

I am still missing Arturo Gatti. I will never stop

recalling that ninth round in his first fight with Micky Ward, recalling how he fought through a broken hand in the trilogy's finale, recalling the hooks out of nowhere and the bravery and the warrior mentality.

He was what we wanted to be: strong and courageous and victorious. But he was also what we all are: imperfect in his better moments, troubled in his worst.

His was a turbulent life, one that was taken too early, whether it was by someone else's hand or his own. I will miss him for how we went to war, and I will always miss him as he rests in peace.

Kirkland-Angulo:
The Flick of a Switch
November 7, 2011

The expectations that fueled more than three years of anticipation were fulfilled within the first three minutes of action.

The first knockdown — Alfredo Angulo's right hand sending James Kirkland firmly onto his rear end — came less than half a minute into the opening round. The second knockdown — Kirkland retaliating, Angulo reeling, then collapsing — came with less than half a minute remaining.

That one round brought two knockdowns, two shifts in momentum, 200 punches in three minutes. That is how long it took for Angulo and Kirkland to bring a fantasy fight into the realm of reality.

That one round made it easy to forgive how long it had taken to get them there.

There was symmetry in that first round, and there was symmetry in what had come before it, in what had kept them apart and what had brought them together.

Years ago they both had been prospects promoted by Gary Shaw, bruising brawlers knocking nearly everyone out. They shared broadcasts, first on Showtime's "ShoBox" series designed to spotlight up-and-coming fighters, then on HBO's "Boxing After Dark" series designed to feature exciting fights.

Promotion is the art of long-term investment at the expense of short-term satisfaction. It is better to have two potential sources of income rather than one. Angulo and Kirkland would not fight so long as both were in Shaw's stable, not at least until it was worth it. Then Kirkland departed Shaw for Golden Boy Promotions, and the possibility of their pairing became even less likely, not when one promoter's risk could lead to the other's reward.

Kirkland went to prison in 2009; a convicted felon, he'd been caught with a gun. By the time he was out from behind bars, it was Angulo in trouble, immigration issues sending him back to Mexico and rendering him unable to fight in the United States.

Angulo signed with Golden Boy a few months ago. Kirkland had lost in a shocking upset earlier in the year, getting knocked down three times by an opponent who'd been thought to be a light-punching sacrificial lamb. Kirkland had won twice since then but needed a big win to take him from junior-middleweight prospect to 154-pound contender. Angulo, too, had been rebuilding since his own surprising defeat, a decision loss in 2009, and now needed to establish himself in the division.

Golden Boy Promotions has another young star in the weight class, Saul Alvarez, who is exceedingly popular in Mexico. The promoter had one stream of income guaranteed. Angulo-Kirkland, then, was the right bout for both the promoter and the fighters — the winner would be better positioned for the future, the loser would potentially remain where he was before, a fan-friendly prospect not yet at the next level.

For more than three years, the expectation had been of an electric battle, two power-punchers vying to turn his opponent's lights out.

They knew no other way. Each had only three decision victories on his record.

It was not surprising that Kirkland was the first to fall.

He can be as reckless as he is ruthless, his viciousness leaving him vulnerable. Kirkland's pressure and punching pushed Angulo into a neutral corner. Kirkland, a southpaw, threw a right hook to the body, a right uppercut upstairs and then a left cross, but he brought his head straight back up, his chin in range and exposed. Angulo hit it with a right hand. Kirkland hit the floor.

With one moment, the fight was in Alfredo Angulo's hands. Within one minute, Angulo's hands had made that no longer the case.

Kirkland, in his upset loss earlier in the year to Nobuhiro Ishida, had been overconfident and underprepared. He had tried to respond to the first knockdown rather than recover from it, leaving himself open to the punches that would floor him twice more.

Angulo knew his own power and thought he knew Kirkland's weakness. Kirkland, however, was also aware of both.

Kirkland rose from Angulo's right hand, clear-eyed but clearly on the defensive. He tried to hold on to Angulo, but failing that he covered up, taking some shots, blocking and rolling with the others. Angulo expended too much energy loading up on power punches, tiring out with time to spare in the first round, with Kirkland's legs returning and senses remaining.

Kirkland had a second wind. Angulo had none.

For all the symmetry of the action, it was better to be on the right side of the round, to end it better than you began. Kirkland had been knocked down from one punch. Angulo had crumpled from sustained punishment.

After the Ishida loss, Kirkland had returned to Ann Wolfe, the trainer who had worked with him until his prison term and whose training methods were designed to put her fighters through hell.

Kirkland knew how to survive a grueling war, incorporating boxing into his brawling. Rather than overwhelm an opponent with indiscriminate volume, he set up his punches, putting together hard combinations and dodging Angulo's shots. Angulo had tried to blow Kirkland away with one gust. Kirkland set out to break Angulo down with a sustained beating.

Angulo landed more punches in the first round than he would for the next five rounds combined. Kirkland's connect rate kept getting better — 27 percent in the first round, 34 percent in the second, 35 percent in the third, 39 percent in the fourth, 47 percent in the fifth and 56 percent in the sixth.

Angulo was still throwing, but the battle was being beaten out of him. Kirkland pinned him against the ropes in the opening minute of the sixth round, peppering him with combinations, chipping away at a granite chin atop an unsteady foundation. The referee jumped in and Angulo wobbled backward.

The symmetry of the first round had been followed by a one-sided beating for the next five.

For more than three years, the expectation had been of an electric battle, two power-punchers vying to turn his opponent's lights out. Angulo was running out of power before the first round ended. Kirkland, with the flick of a switch, turned himself from a reckless bruiser to a relentless boxing brawler.

It had taken more than three years to get them together. Within three minutes, Kirkland set himself apart.

Pacquiao-Marquez 3:
A Rivalry Without a Resolution
November 14, 2011

It's impossible to settle a score when the scores don't settle anything.

Juan Manuel Marquez had a draw with Manny Pacquiao in 2004 and a narrow split decision loss to Pacquiao in 2008. The final scorecards showed Pacquiao to be just a little bit better. Yet the parts that made those sums tilted the conclusion in the other direction — with 12 rounds a fight, and three judges for each, Marquez had been marked down as winning 41 out of 72 rounds.

Pacquiao, meanwhile, had been a one-point scoring error away from victory in 2004. Though one point gave him the edge in 2008, he'd considered himself the winner without controversy. He'd knocked Marquez down four times in two fights. Two of three judges tabbed him in the second fight, and that should've been the same result for the first.

These were the justifications Marquez and Pacquiao carried with them for years, evidence underlying assertions that one was better than the other.

Theirs was, and still is, a rivalry without a resolution.

Marquez turned down an immediate rematch with Pacquiao in 2004 and instead had to wait four years for a second shot. He was forced to wait again after the 2008 battle as Pacquiao moved on to bigger opponents, bigger paydays, bigger exposure and bigger stardom.

They were featherweights in 2004 and 130-pound fighters in 2008. Marquez followed Pacquiao to lightweight, hinted he'd do the same with 140, and waited while Pacquiao went in against welterweights and a junior middleweight.

Their rivalry had been heated and historic, but its future seemed to be in the past, destined to be lost to history. In 2011, they could look back at their time together like alumni at a class reunion.

"That was who we were then" — younger, the same size, Pacquiao a hard-to-tame whirling dervish, Marquez a hard-to-conquer technician.

"This is who we are now" — Marquez at 38, a smallish lightweight who'd recently been getting hit more and hurt more; Pacquiao at 32, still fast and ferocious despite the additional pounds on his frame, but also more skilled and savvy.

It seemed a mismatch to many, to the writers, boxing trainers and other observers who believed Pacquiao to be too good and too much to handle, particularly at a catch-weight of 144 pounds. Marquez, in his lone fight weighing in at 142, had looked too slow and too off-balance.

This reunion would show otherwise. Though Pacquiao is a more well-rounded student than he was in 2004 and 2008, he is still not in a higher class than Marquez.

This would neither be a blowout nor a knockout, not with a professor still capable of taking Pacquiao to school.

Marquez looked measurably better at 142 against Pacquiao than he did against Floyd Mayweather Jr.. Much of that could be credited to Marquez's new conditioning coach, Angel Heredia, who has an infamous past as a supplier of performance enhancing drugs but who also introduced Marquez to different training methods to prepare him for the bout.

Pacquiao also wasn't going to force Marquez to lead

the way that Mayweather had. Nor was Pacquiao going to be able to lead the action as he had against every single opponent he'd faced since the last Marquez bout.

Those fighters had all been bigger and slower. They had all deluded themselves into thinking that Pacquiao wouldn't be that fast and wouldn't be that strong. They had all been subdued by his speed and chastened by the number of shots they'd take for every punch they threw and missed.

Marquez had adjusted to the whirling dervish version of Pacquiao in their first fight. He had stood in with the improved version of Pacquiao in their second fight. He knew the right distance and timing for facing Pacquiao, how far he would need to move back to evade Pacquiao's double-jab and left-cross combination, where he'd need to move his head to avoid Pacquiao's left hands.

Pacquiao was also well aware of what Marquez was capable of. There would be far fewer multi-punch combinations against Marquez, who remains capable of landing perfectly placed counters from any angle at any time. Marquez would respond immediately after every Pacquiao flurry, and if Pacquiao opted to remain inside instead of moving back out, Marquez would dig hooks to his body.

Pacquiao would not load up on power shots either. At times, he was moving out of range before finishing with following through on a punch, instead dodging Marquez's counters.

By CompuBox estimates, the 578 punches Pacquiao that threw this past Saturday were 149 fewer punches than he threw against Shane Mosley, 202 fewer punches than he threw against Miguel Cotto, 491 fewer punches than he threw against Antonio Margarito and 653 fewer punches than he threw against Joshua Clottey.

It was only about 50 fewer than Pacquiao threw, on average, in the two previous Marquez fights. But the action was more measured, more manageable for Marquez.

Marquez had disrupted Pacquiao's recent rhythm. He still got hit, though this time he never was knocked down. That was because he, too, was cautious against Pacquiao. He'd exchange, but he wouldn't leave himself out of position and open to a shot he couldn't see. He'd land pinpoint shots and connect them together into combinations — a left uppercut lead followed by a left hook, for one, or a jab followed by a looping right hand, for another — but would pick his spots.

Each was trying to set a trap, trying to make an opening, trying to catch the other with a shot that would change the tone of the fight. Each was keeping the fight close but unable to pull away.

It was high in drama but not high in action. Many of the rounds could reasonably have been scored for either man. Pacquiao's trainer, Freddie Roach, sensed this and told his fighter before the 10th round to go for the knockout. Meanwhile, Marquez's trainer, Nacho Beristain, told his fighter that he was winning.

Pacquiao threw fewer punches in the final round than he had in the previous 11, according to CompuBox. Marquez threw one punch fewer in that round than Pacquiao did.

Their first two fights had ended in debatable decisions. They sent it to the scorecards once again.

The three judges agreed on six of the first seven rounds — one, three and six for Pacquiao, four, five and seven for Marquez. The judges agreed on none of the final five rounds.

Two judges, Robert Hoyle and Dave Moretti, agreed on the 12th round, giving it to Pacquiao. The judge who gave the last round to Marquez, Glenn Trowbridge, scored the fight eight rounds to four for Pacquiao, 116-112.

Hoyle had it six rounds apiece, 114-114. Moretti had it seven rounds to five for Pacquiao, 115-113.

Had Marquez won the last round on their cards, the final scores would've been 116-112 for Pacquiao, 115-113 for Marquez, and an even 114-114 — a three-way draw, just like the first fight.

Marquez, as with the first two fights, felt he'd won. A sampling of press scoring the fight at ringside and on television had many scoring the fight for Marquez, some tallying up a draw, and a stray scorecard or two for Pacquiao.

The marketing before the fight had been that this bout would decide who was better. That marketing seemed misguided — those fights had taken place years ago, when the fighters were different than they were thought to be now.

Marquez proved people wrong, though. He was the same fighter who could trouble Pacquiao like no other fighter has consistently been able to. He was the same fighter who'd leave with the same result — no victory, only a debatable decision.

Marquez has two losses and a draw in three fights he believes he won — three fights that Pacquiao believes Marquez lost.

It's impossible to settle a score when the scores don't settle anything.

Pacquiao was guaranteed $22 million, but he left the ring to a chorus of boos and left the post-fight press conference after his promoter cut off reporters after three questions.

Marquez was guaranteed $5 million, but, for a man with his pride, all those zeroes on his paycheck won't make up for the zeroes in his win column after three fights.

Theirs is a rivalry without a resolution.

Miguel Cotto Secures His Most Satisfying Career Victory

December 4, 2011

NEW YORK CITY — For three-and-a-half years, Miguel Cotto sought revenge — for the first loss he had ever taken, for the brutal beating he had received at the hands of Antonio Margarito, for the belief that Margarito's hand wraps had been tampered with, amplifying the extent of that beating.

For nine rounds, Cotto exacted that revenge, working to guard the weaknesses that Margarito had taken advantage of in 2008 — and taking advantage of Margarito's own weakness, one that dated back to a year ago and had been a topic of both conversation and concern in the weeks leading up this rematch.

Margarito's right eye — where an orbital bone had been broken by Manny Pacquiao in November 2010, where vision had been blurred, a cataract removed, a lens replaced — swelled up due to the targeted punching of Cotto. Though expert physicians had ruled that Margarito's surgically repaired eye left him fit to step in the ring, the ringside physicians have a stricter criteria when it comes to being fit to stay in the ring.

His eye was shut, the doctors saw. His vision was impaired, the doctors ruled. The fight was over, the doctors decided.

Cotto had his revenge, and an announced 21,239 in attendance — nearly all of Puerto Rican heritage, but some with Mexican blood — were there to see it.

Cotto had come out boxing in their first fight, only to be broken down under Margarito's pressure. Margarito had dug hard uppercuts down into Cotto's body and brought them up into Cotto's face. Bloodied, his face misshapen, Cotto eventually wilted after 11 rounds, taking a knee and taking the loss.

That was July 2008. Six months later, Margarito was discovered with tampered hand wraps prior to his welterweight title fight with Shane Mosley. Speculation ran rampant after Mosley knocked Margarito out. Had Margarito used tampered hand wraps in previous fights? Had tampered hand wraps made his punches hurt more? Had Cotto lost to someone who had cheated?

Cotto believed so and said so. Margarito denied it and said he would beat Cotto the same. Their dispute over what had happened in 2008 would never be settled. But their continued rivalry could be decided.

Cotto decided not just to think about what might or might not have been in Margarito's gloves, but to put his fate in his own hands.

Cotto's first true punch of consequence on Saturday was a blocked left hook, but otherwise he came out as expected, boxing for the duration the first round. He jabbed and moved to his left, occasionally switching his movement and going forward with left hooks and right crosses. Every clean shot received an approving roar from the Puerto Rican faithful — and a smile and a shake of the head from the man they'd decided was a Mexican villain.

Once again against a mobile opponent, Margarito went to the body, throwing hooks underneath Cotto's hooks and to his ribs. Cotto moved early to avoid a repeat of the first fight — he pulled away from clinches, bounced away from the ropes, wrestled Margarito away when he tried to keep Cotto in place.

Margarito had always had a reputation of taking many

in order to land his own. He would take what Cotto threw and exact a tariff on him, body shots placed within Cotto's flurries. After three rounds, he was hitting Cotto's body with increasing success — but his right eye was already beginning to swell.

Try as he might, Cotto could not put in a flawless performance. He would be forced to the ropes by Margarito's pressure. He would stand in close with Margarito in the middle of the ring. He would be hit with hard body shots and uppercuts.

He would not be hit with as many. He would not stay on the ropes or in tight quarters. And he would not let Margarito get him without Margarito then getting it back even worse.

After Margarito had more success in the fourth, Cotto fought with more control and at more distance in the fifth, not getting suckered into a firefight and not making the same mistakes.

Margarito tried to trap Cotto back in the sixth, landing several hard body shots and uppercuts. Cotto again seized firm control in the seventh, making Margarito miss, ducking his punches and moving away. When caught on the ropes, he would grab Margarito and spin him, their positions switching.

This rematch was not following the pattern of Cotto's first fight with Margarito. Rather, it was closer to Margarito's bout with Pacquiao. By the end of the seventh, Margarito's right eye looked shut.

Now when Cotto was moving to his left — Margarito's right — he wasn't so much moving toward Margarito's power hand as he was moving toward Margarito's bad eye.

His jabs and left hooks were heading in the same

direction, just as he had promised.

Ringside physicians checked Margarito's eye before the start of the ninth round. The crowd stood, thinking the fight was over, that revenge was there — and theirs — and now.

They would have to wait.

Cotto went back to the jabs, more than one at a time, and followed them with hooks and crosses. With Cotto staying in one place longer, Margarito was able to land more body shots.

He could not stop Cotto's momentum. He could not stop his eye from swelling. He could not stop the fight from ending.

Two physicians stood in front of Margarito before the 10th round could begin. Margarito and his corner pleaded for one more round, argued that the fight should not be stopped.

Margarito's fate did not rest in his hands, but in those of the doctors and the referee, who waved off the bout.

The judges all had Cotto firmly in control. Julie Lederman had given Cotto the first eight rounds and Margarito the ninth, scoring it 89-82. John Poturaj had only given Margarito the seventh and had the same score. That tally also was on the scorecard of Steve Weisfeld, who only gave Margarito the fourth.

This fight — and this night — belonged to Cotto. All Margarito would see was Miguel Cotto raising his gloves in the air and turning to the cheering crowd.

Their hero was triumphant. The villain had been vanquished.

Cotto-Margarito 2: An Eye For An Eye
December 5, 2011

NEW YORK CITY — No wound pierces deeper or heals slower than a wound about which nothing can be done.

Miguel Cotto no longer showed the physical toll his face and body had taken from Antonio Margarito in July 2008. Three and a half years later, however, the mental scars had yet to fade — rather, they were more noticeable than ever.

Cotto could never truly prove that Margarito had cheated, that the tampered hand wraps found prior to Margarito's bout with Shane Mosley had been previously used.

Cotto never needed to convince anyone but himself.

That belief first placed him in the role of victim, of a man wronged and not willing to allow Margarito to further benefit from it. The action in the first fight promised profit in a rematch. The drama of the subsequent scandal meant even more money could be made.

That belief cut to his core, though. The wound could pierce no deeper.

His resolve against a rematch softened. The millions he'd be paid helped.

His rage against Margarito remained. No number would be worth as much to him as revenge.

Miguel Cotto had allowed the perceived injustice to infect him with vitriol, hatred that festered until, like a scar, it was always at the surface and also ingrained within him. He no longer needed to wait for the wound to heal — not when he could tear off the bandage and allow his anger to flow forth.

And yet the best way for him to channel that rage was to remain in control.

The build-up to the rematch between Cotto and Margarito was one of legitimate rivalry, of one fighter who'd blamed a beating on cheating, and of another fighter who said it did not matter what accusations flew, that all which would decide defeat would be the punches that landed.

Theirs was a blood feud so hostile that there was no ceremony, just acrimony. There would be no final face off at the pre-fight weigh-in. There would be no sportsmanlike touching of gloves before the bell rang.

Try as Margarito did to goad Cotto into battle, Cotto boxed, not empowered by emotion but driven to victory through discipline, strategy and smarts.

No wound pierces deeper or heals slower than a wound about which nothing can be done. Cotto had the right plan in his first fight with Margarito, boxing, throwing punches, then moving and doing it all again. He merely needed to do it better.

That would not necessarily be simple. Margarito's pressure — and punching — had broken him before.

Cotto had similar success in the first six rounds of the rematch as he did in the opening half of the first bout. In July 2008, Cotto had landed 174 of 409 punches, or about 43 percent. On Saturday, Cotto landed 134 of 333, or about 40 percent. He was throwing less and landing less, which in this case was a good thing.

Cotto was not tiring himself with activity, with attempts to keep Margarito off him. Instead, he was capitalizing on moments — jabs and combinations of hooks and right hands, planting his feet for flurries, then moving away. Throwing any more punches would leave him in more danger of being caught. Focusing on footwork left fewer chances for Margarito to trap him on the ropes, where body shots and uppercuts had weakened him in the first fight.

Cotto still got hit but had methods to minimize the impact. He circled smartly to his left, then abruptly changed direction when caught on the ropes. When the fighters fought inside, he would grab Margarito and wrestle him in another direction, changing their positions. He also would leverage Margarito backwards; while on the move, punches from Margarito that once had torque were now closer to taps.

Margarito, too, had success in the first fight and would seek the same in the second. That meant Cotto knew what to expect — and how to react.

Technically and physically, Margarito's style fit perfectly into Cotto's counter-punching.

Margarito keeps his hands low when working in close, the better for sending out his body shots and uppercuts. Cotto, then, could throw left hooks and right hands over Margarito's punches. And at a distance, the downward jabs from the taller Margarito brought openings for right hands from Cotto in return.

In those opening six rounds of the rematch, Margarito landed 102 of 450 punches, or less than 23 percent. He landed 79 of 229 power punches; the other half of what he was throwing tended to be range-finding jabs.

Cotto was incredibly accurate with his power punches, landing 96 of 197 in rounds one through six. Margarito has a reputation of taking punches in order to deliver punishment. But his right eye had been cut in the third round and was swelling shut — the same eye where he'd suffered an orbital bone injury a year ago against Manny Pacquiao and had needed surgery to repair a cataract.

With many of Cotto's clean punches, Margarito, relishing his role of villain, would taunt Cotto with words or noises or a shake of the head or a grin or a tap to his own face.

Margarito was trying to break Cotto down mentally — except that Cotto had only retreated and then surrendered in the first fight as a result of not being able to sustain any more punishment.

In that first fight, Margarito had his best round in the seventh, landing 46 of 104 power punches in those three minutes alone, and a total of 134 out of 344 power punches from rounds seven through 11.

In the rematch, Margarito went 16 of 47 on power shots in the seventh and 11 of 40 in the eighth, and — facing the possibility of the fight being stopped due to injury — went 25 of 78 in the ninth. Many of those in the ninth had little behind them, lesser punches thrown while tied up or forced backward in clinches.

Cotto landed the same number of power shots as Margarito in the final nine minutes — 52 — but he was landing more than half of what he threw. Many of those were hooks targeting Margarito's right eye, which the ringside physicians were watching closely.

After the ninth, the doctors spoke of stopping the fight. Margarito's team protested.

"That was the best round!" someone said. "One more!"

They didn't listen. Margarito's face showed a combination of disgust and disbelief.

Margarito felt that he was not given a fair chance, that he still had the ability and opportunity to win. He felt that he was never hurt — that is, he was never rocked, never in danger of being knocked out. It was his skin that betrayed him, he felt, not his chin, not his muscles and not his heart.

There was nothing he could do about it.

Any win would have been satisfying for Cotto. The most emphatic revenge would have come via knockout. But that would have taken only a temporary physical toll on Margarito rather than leave mental scars.

Cotto gave Margarito an eye for an eye. Margarito suffered a loss he felt he did not deserve.

No wound pierces deeper — or heals slower.

On Freddie Roach:
Once Again, A Winner
January 16, 2012

The fighting stopped for Freddie Roach, but the battling continued.

He retired at 26, none the richer from a sport that had given him enough punishment to literally last his lifetime. He stayed in the sweet science, moving from the center of the ring to the corner, a young trainer who had never challenged for a title now trying to guide his peers to the prize. He became a man behind champions, a teacher sought out by fighters from around the globe.

He has done all of this despite the very visible effects of Parkinson's disease. This has been said often. There is much more to the story.

Freddie Roach's struggles have been covered many times before, mentioned in Cliff's Notes form during the various "24/7" documentary/commercial series featuring his star fighter, Manny Pacquiao, and covered in more depth on "Real Sports with Bryant Gumbel." HBO is well familiar with Roach, but his story has never been told like this.

No narration. No script. Just a camera that cannot help but capture a man and his battles.

"On Freddie Roach," a six-episode HBO documentary series premiering at 9:30 p.m. this Friday, follows the trainer from a morning in Las Vegas looking on as one of his star students, Amir Khan, runs on a track just days away from a bout — to another evening, when he's left the boxing gym he owns in Los Angeles and has returned home to watch footage on his computer, studying in

253

advance of yet another fight for yet another fighter.

Boxing, like life, is a battle between chaos and control. It is fitting, then, that Roach's gym is called the Wild Card. He has no choice but to take what life has dealt him. He has taken that, though, and turned it into a winning hand, thanks in large part to what he can do with others' gloved fists.

He retired early after too many beatings, which gave him the same disease that felled the great Muhammad Ali. He will enter the Hall of Fame as a trainer, not as a fighter.

"If you knew then what you know now about the game," Roach is asked early on in the first of two episodes sent out for review, "could you have made it all the way?"

Roach waits several moments before answering: "I think so."

A fighter never truly leaves the ring. This is why Roach became a trainer at 27, working with his first world champion, Virgil Hill. This is why Roach tells his fighters to sprint in the last leg around a track and then joins them in the final stretch.

He is no longer a fighter, however, gasping for breath by the end. He is still battling, though.

He has riches and respect because of what training has brought him. He still faces questions about his health.

In one scene, we see Roach teaching Khan angles, working on adding technique to take Khan's superlative speed and give him even greater advantages in the ring. The footage, by now six months old, is the kind rarely shown on television, not with fighters and their camps so careful about giving away any inside knowledge to the opposition. The footage also shows why Roach is so often praised for the work he does preparing his fighters.

In another scene, we see a press conference before Khan's fight with Zab Judah. We hear Richard Schaefer of Golden Boy Promotions talking about the Cleveland Clinic and its study into the effect of punches on a boxer's head. We note that Roach is the only person looking up and listening to what is being said.

With no narration, and with a spare soundtrack, the quiet moments speak volumes.

In an arena, Roach tells a woman to bet on Khan to defeat Judah by knockout. "Come on, Freddie. Really?" she says. "Of course," Freddie responds. He is not only confident, but correct.

In a locker room, Roach prepares the tape that he will use to wrap Khan's hands. His breathing is audible. His shaking becomes even more visible. Khan soon sends out punches. Everything is fluid and fast for him. Nothing is easy anymore for Roach.

At ringside, he is trembling while watching Khan fight Judah. His voice isn't very strong, so he gives instructions via Khan's strength and conditioning coach, Alex Ariza, who yells them out to their fighter in the ring. Khan wins by knockout. Ariza, not Roach, is the first to run into the ring and pick Khan up.

"When I can't do mitts anymore, I'll quit," he says later. "Because I really won't be able to get the fighter, inside his head, make him believe in himself — and in me also."

Nothing is easy anymore for Roach, but he finds a way. The trainer has figures of the Popeye cartoon character in his home, a character with no grievances about the hand life dealt him: "I am what I am, and that's all that I am."

Says Roach: "Outside of the gym, I'm just an average

person. I'm not going to change the world. I don't think about Parkinson's. I just go one day, day by day, and live through it."

Trainers are seen only in the minute segments between rounds. For those like Roach who work with the most famous fighters, there are the moments and vignettes featured before fights and on shows such as "24/7." Roach has become famous in the Philippines thanks to the stardom of his prized pupil, Manny Pacquiao. That success has brought him even more work, more fighters coming to the Wild Card for his wisdom and perhaps a better shot at the top.

All of the work wears on him. With commitments to the American amateur boxing team and to Pacquiao's coming training camp looming, he turns to an assistant, an ex-girlfriend of his, to help schedule his life. In-between doctor's appointments, he takes a nap. She admits to needing one, too. Their relationship is still somewhere between business and personal. At a group dinner, he chides her for being on the phone. She soon cries.

He rises early on another morning to go to the Wild Card. Other loved ones are also working with him, spreading his success to his mother and Pepper, both employed at the gym. Pepper points to old family photos on the walls, relics from the time when the Roach men were all fighters. His pugilistic past, too, has been harsh for his health. While Freddie looks fit at 51, life has been rougher for Pepper, who is a year older. He'd suffered strokes in the past, and has another one during filming.

Roach, trainer to stars and prospects, owner of a gym that has become a Hollywood attraction, tends to his brother, contacts his sister-in-law, then moves off camera, where his voice cracks and some tears presumably flow.

He comes back out. The quiet is telling, and then the rhythm of the gym begins again, the hands striking pads and bags, Roach returning to work.

The work is never over. He drives home, puts a DVD into the computer and watches a fight. His left hand shakes until he brings it to his chin, intently studying. His life — for good and bad — is consumed by boxing.

Freddie Roach has triumphed through 24 years as a trainer and battled through two decades with his disease. This documentary series details how he does it. "On Freddie Roach," like its namesake, is a winner.

Salido-Lopez 2: Juanma's Last Stand
March 12, 2012

The boogeyman was an idea, a seed of doubt planted 11 months before, growing until it towered over him, casting darkness that he would either have to outrun or break through.

The nemesis was real, a man who had sown that seed and who now stood before him again, ready to return to digging to his body and drilling his chin.

Juan Manuel Lopez tried to dodge the darkness, tried to box Orlando Salido, tried to keep what Salido had done to him 11 months before from being done once more. But the boogeyman kept stalking. The nemesis, however, was not a mere idea but rather was real, a man who could be broken. And so Lopez confronted his demon and took his fate into his own hands.

And, in a flash, it was taken away from him. The darkness returned. The boogeyman was back.

Every fighter has his limits, a realization he never wants to reach. Every loss lingers, then, from the first moments of regret through months of self-reflection: What went wrong during the fight? What could I have done beforehand to make myself more ready, mentally and physically? What can I do better?

Lopez had 11 months to think about it and up to 12 rounds to put it into action.

He had patched together a friendship with his ex-wife, the mother of his children and his cook in camp. Gone was the personal turmoil that might have distracted before he first fought Salido. He would be mentally ready. Back was the personal chef who would help him be in the best possible shape. He would be physically ready.

He came in with a strategy. He would use movement to offset Salido's pressure, just as another Puerto Rican hero, Miguel Cotto, had done in a rematch against another Mexican conqueror, Antonio Margarito. Cotto was able to stick to his strategy for nine rounds, as long as that bout lasted. Lopez had never been a stick-and-move fighter, however.

Lopez started off the bout moving to his right, away from the looping right hand that Salido had caught him with again and again in their first fight. That would keep his right foot on the outside of Salido's left, of utmost importance when a southpaw faces an orthodox fighter. And it would allow Lopez more opportunities to land lead right hooks.

Cotto had remained in high gear in his rematch with Margarito, jumping in and out with combinations before retreating from a fighter noticeably slower than him. Lopez did not have a distinct advantage in speed against Salido, who began to time his hardest shots for when Lopez stopped moving, moments that came when he was within range. Lopez was not dictating the action, but rather was delaying it. He was not so much defending against Salido's attacks as he was merely fending them off.

Lopez had thought he knew what it'd take to beat Salido, but it wouldn't be this. Salido knew what it'd take to beat Lopez, and thought it wouldn't be long before he could turn the rematch into a replay. A right hook from Salido in the first minute of the second round lifted Lopez's left foot off the canvas. He kept closing the distance and caught him with an uppercut in the third.

Salido was landing more and more each round: 8 of 28 in the first, 19 of 49 in the second, 30 of 66 in the third. All but two of those landed shots were power punches. Lopez, meanwhile, was landing at a steady, lesser rate: 9 of 41 in the first, 11 of 67 in the second, 9 of 46 in the third. A majority of those, too, were power shots, but not at all enough of them.

Lopez wasn't going to out-box this boogeyman, but he could try to take out his opponent. You cannot out-run an idea, but you can break a man. Salido was neither impervious nor impossible; he'd been knocked down and hurt badly in December against Weng Haya. He'd won that fight, but he was far from undefeated in his career.

Lopez opted to return to that which was comfortable, even if it meant walking a pugilistic tightrope. Rather than retreat, he opted to come forward with combinations, standing longer in front of Salido and leaving himself vulnerable to the shots he knew would come and knew would hurt.

That meant hitting Salido a total of 19 times, all but 2 of those power punches, in the fourth round — and getting hit by 27 hard shots in return. That meant getting hit with 21 hard shots in the fifth, too, but Lopez landed 14 of his own, including the one punch that would make all of this seem worth it.

Salido had just pegged Lopez with two hard left hooks, clean and flush, visibly and audibly effective. He followed Lopez around the ring and went forward again, walking directly into the path of a short counter right hook to the chin, a well-placed, well-timed shot that sent him to the canvas.

He rose and made it to the end of the round. But what seemed to be a turning point in favor of Lopez was also one in favor of Salido.

The knockdown emboldened Lopez, who went back to war with Salido as he had in their first fight, even though his headlong aggression meant going forward chin-first. Salido obliged, returning fire and catching Lopez pulling straight back. Salido's looping right hands, not the most technically sound, lent themselves to effective placement, more likely to alight on Lopez's shaky chin.

This was where Juan Manuel Lopez would have to make his stand. Boxing hadn't worked. Brawling was all that was left. Their battle had heated up in rounds six and seven, fueling the firefight in the eighth and ninth, six minutes of torrid toe-to-toe trading. Lopez had a history of fading late in fights, but he could only lay everything he had out there, particularly with the pace Salido was setting.

Salido went 35 of 100 in the eighth, more than he'd thrown and landed in any of the previous seven rounds, then out-did himself in the ninth, going 37 of 114. He was outworking Lopez, who landed about half of what Salido did in those two rounds.

Despite this, it was Lopez whose chin was holding up, and Salido whose eyes were beginning to swell shut as the ninth round ended. Lopez was confronting his demon, taking his fate into his own hands.

And, in a flash, he was taking fire again, and the fight was taken away from him. The end began just seconds into the 10th round with a right hook, followed by a left uppercut, then a right uppercut, and finally a jab that pushed back a teetering fighter. Lopez rose quickly, yet his legs and eyes showed his true condition. It was one last act of defiance, but at last he'd been rendered defenseless.

Every fighter has his limits, a realization he never wants to reach. Every loss lingers, from the first moments of regret through months of self-reflection: What went wrong during the fight? What could I have done beforehand to make myself more ready, mentally and physically? What can I do better? Juan Manuel Lopez had done everything he could. He made his stand until he could stand no more.

Mike Tyson is Happy, and I'm Glad
April 2, 2012

Maybe I identified too much with Mike Tyson. After all, I'd grown up with two loving, providing parents in middle-class suburban utopia, not as the poor son of a single mother who packed her family into a tenement in the Brooklyn slums. Never mind that I'd never been the heavyweight champion, never been in prison, never had millions of dollars and never spent myself into insurmountable debt.

But when Tyson had yet another incident, yet another tirade or loss of self-control, I knew better than those who said he was stupid. He was smart but troubled, and I had been, too, once again to a lesser extent. My youth had been one of antidepressants and psychologist visits, of failing grades and wasted potential.

Maybe I still identify too much with Mike Tyson, but it makes me relieved to see that he is the two most basic things I'd eventually aimed for: happy and healthy.

It also makes me relieved because I was there when it all ended for Tyson, when the former youngest-ever heavyweight champion now showed his age, when the one- or maybe two-time "baddest man on the planet" now was getting beat up by an unexceptional formerly anonymous opponent named Kevin McBride.

I watched as a fighter who had once instilled so much fear in his foes now sat on the canvas at the end of the sixth round, seeking the internal strength just to return to his corner. The referee motioned for Tyson to get up. Within a minute, the fight was over.

His career was over, too.

"I just don't have this in my gut anymore. It's just not in my heart anymore," Tyson said at the post-fight press conference. "I'm not trying to take anything away from Kevin McBride. We know his record. We know his credentials. And if I can't beat him, I can't beat Junior Jones."

He no longer had boxing. That left us worried about him no longer having anything remaining at all.

His financial and marital woes had been well documented, as had his brushes with the law. Tyson was broke, with massive debt to pay and with no more chance of the seven- or eight-figure checks that could help chip away at what he owed. He was resigned to this fate, to yet another obstacle that wouldn't fold in front of him.

"My career has been over since 1990," he said.

"I look good, I feel good but then when I went out there, I can't do it. I felt like I was 120 years old," he said.

"I'm not too interested in these swan songs," he said.

Instead, he pondered the prospect of doing missionary work abroad.

"I just want to do something that has a more tangible effect for people," he said.

Some of the fans that had found their way into the press conference tried to console him with applause. Some of the writers tried to have him look back at what he had accomplished in his career, not at how it had ended. He told those who stood up with an ovation to sit back down. They were embarrassing him, he said.

"You have to deal with the real, man. Don't live in fairytales," he said. "I'm comfortable with my stigma. I know who I am. I know what you think about me. I may be bizarre sometimes, but I'm very rational. I'm extremely rational. I understand my situation ... I'm not going to lie to myself, and you shouldn't allow me to do this as well." But he was back in the ring 16 months later for the October 2006 launch of what was supposed to be Mike Tyson's World Tour, a proposed series of pay-per-view exhibition bouts. He went four rounds with Corey Sanders in Youngstown, Ohio, in what would be the lone stop on his world tour.

This could have been the beginning of a sad ending, the kind seen too often when professional athletes are forced to retire, when the spotlight fades, the bank account dwindles and the hangers-on disappear.

And it seemed for a bit that it would be that way for Tyson, too.

There was the drug addiction, particularly even more worrisome with a man who had never been known to exercise much control over his urges.

There were brushes with the court system: an arrest in Arizona on charges of driving under the influence and cocaine possession, then the paparazzi photographer in California who accused Tyson of attacking him at an airport.

And then Tyson found his own version of normal.

His career had brought him from fame to infamy, from accomplishment to embarrassment. His name was no longer just synonymous with sport, but with his in-ring and out-of-the-ring meltdowns.

That meant there was interest in Tyson, intrigue in his appearances, particularly after his time in the sweet science ended and he began to speak with more perspective, more introspection.

A documentary was made about him. He appeared on "The Oprah Winfrey Show" to speak about his life. And his appearances weren't all serious. Previously he had been a punch line — "What now?" was the set up. Now he was able to laugh at himself, singing on "Jimmy Kimmel Live," showing up on an episode of a foreign version of "Dancing With the Stars," stealing scenes in movies "The Hangover" and "The Hangover 2," telling jokes on a televised roast of Charlie Sheen, even spoofing presidential candidate Herman Cain in comedy sketches.

There was nothing to be embarrassed about. He had become a different person, a man who found healthier ways to enjoy life. Once mythical, he'd now mellowed. He became more at ease with who he is, with his situation, with his struggle.

"I was Iron Mike Tyson then," he told CNN's Piers Morgan in an interview last week. "Now I'm not."

His induction into the International Hall of Fame in 2011 was but the final chapter that allowed for him to officially close the book on boxing. He'd already been dedicating his life to more important things, particularly after the tragic, accidental death in 2009 of his four-year-old daughter.

In the years after boxing, his wife had brought him the strength and stability to start a new life he'd never envisioned himself surviving to see. He returned that, dedicating himself to responsibility, to living for more than the present and building a future.

It will never be easy. Not for a man who has seen and done regrettable things, who never truly rose above adversity because he kept on creating it for himself. It will never be easy for a man with demons and depression. The mental illness never truly goes away. It can be confronted, never conquered. It can, however, be controlled, not just with medicine, but with maturity.

Tyson, rotund in "The Hangover," is now a lean vegan,

slimmer than his prime fighting weight. He is healthy and, while he might not see it, he is giving himself the best possible change for happiness.

It didn't come from the championship belts, from the millions of dollars, the fawning female admirers or the copious amounts of drugs.

It comes from focus on those immediately around you. And it comes from within — a realization that Mike Tyson couldn't live without.

Roy Jones and James Toney: Nostalgia is Getting Old
April 9, 2012

James Toney has won a championship in one division, world titles in two others. Roy Jones Jr. held titles at middleweight, super middleweight, light heavyweight and heavyweight.

They have nearly 130 wins between them. Both will be in the Hall of Fame five years after they retire — if they ever retire.

Both are 43. The greats are no longer. Their names are all they have left.

Even that doesn't mean as much anymore.

Toney fought Saturday night in a bout seen only by those in an arena in Mississippi. There was no television broadcast. There was no independent pay-per-view. There was no online stream. There weren't even any highlights available on the Internet more than 24 hours after Toney beat Bobby Gunn.

Jones, meanwhile, spent one evening last week in Moscow, walking to a boxing ring wearing a robe and gloves while one of his rap songs played. He wasn't there to fight, however, but to lip synch along to what could charitably be called his greatest hits, a musical interlude before the main event.

The feature fight was headlined by Denis Lebedev, a cruiserweight who had knocked Jones out last May and who defeated Toney by decision in November.

It was too fitting that the first song Jones performed was "Y'all Must've Forgot."

"And I won't stop boxing 'til I retire," he says at one

point. Then later: "Y'all must've forgot. This is what I do. We could go on and on."

The most recent bout mentioned in that song is Jones' decision win over David Telesco in 2000. The album was released in 2002. Two years later Jones was knocked out by Antonio Tarver. He's fought 12 times in the eight years since then, winning six and losing six.

Toney won a heavyweight title from John Ruiz in 2005, only to have that win invalidated because he tested positive for a performance-enhancing drug. In the seven years since he's fought 10 times, going 5-3-1 with 1 no contest.

This is a sport where boxers can profit on their past when they're past their primes. Like aging rock bands making repeated reunion tours, they don't look the same or perform with the same energy, but they still can send the fans home happy.

These faded fighters face opponents who never would have deserved to share the ring with them before. Those are the harmless wins. Then there are the painful defeats, the struggles and sacrificial showings against the younger, fresher and better who benefit from whatever remains of their victims' name value.

Nearly nobody can avoid the allure of the spotlight and the paycheck and the pipe dream of one last run at greatness.

George Foreman's success has produced a series of failures since.

Nobody retires or stays retired. There are more name heavyweights remaining from the '80s, '90s and "the aughts" than there ought to be. Jameel McCline left the sport in 2009 but has fought three times since December. Monte Barrett's retirement lasted as long as the next contract offer. David Tua finally gave up the ghost more than a decade after his one and only title shot.

Evander Holyfield is turning 50 this year.

This isn't the parade down Canastota for the International Boxing Hall of Fame. This is closer to baseball's Old Timer's Game. They're still trying to perform, in limited form.

Rare is the harmless return — Henry Maske coming back at 43 after a decade away to get revenge on a similarly ancient Virgil Hill, Jeff Fenech and Azumah Nelson returning to face each other again years after they had been inducted.

It's easier to turn back the clock when your opponent is of the same vintage. Everything else is either careful — or gutsy — matchmaking.

Erik Morales nearly topped Marcos Maidana last year, his skill and experience carrying him oh so close to taking a win against a man who took him lightly. A year later and Morales looked brave but old and slow against Danny Garcia.

For every Morales-Maidana, there are far many more like Sugar Ray Leonard vs. Hector Camacho.

Morales would have been eligible for induction into the Hall of Fame next year had he not come back. Tommy Hearns' repeated returns mean he won't be enshrined until this year, at 53 years old, about six years after his last fight, about 35 years after his first.

Lennox Lewis wrote this message on Twitter just earlier this month: "I've enjoyed retirement, but there is unfinished business at hand and 125 million reasons to finish." He finished by referencing Sept. 29 and a rematch with Vitali Klitschko.

It was an April Fool's Day joke. It was perfect, as in this

sport most retirements aren't like those of Lewis and Joe Calzaghe.

Lewis left in 2003 after winning an entertaining war over Klitschko, turning down lucrative offers to return. Joe Calzaghe departed after 2008 and a virtuoso performance against Roy Jones Jr., of all people.

It is better to go out at the right time, to know when to hang 'em up rather than hang on.

Nostalgia gets old. Name value lessens. Star power loses luster.

Those rock band reunions still play to sold-out arenas. That's not the case for fighters like James Toney and Roy Jones Jr. Their stages are getting smaller. Their last act is dragging on.

Their curtain calls await.

Kaliesha West:
Far From Daddy's Little Girl
April 14, 2012

This was no place for a woman, he thought. They couldn't do what men can do. They shouldn't do what men can do. They weren't as able. They weren't as tough. This was no place for a woman, he thought, and definitely no place for his preteen daughter.

But she asked, and he relented. She trained, and he trained her. She sparred and fought and won and lost and turned pro and won a world title, and he had long since come to believe, not just in her, but also in others.

There were many like her, many who are more warrior than princess, who are competitive and courageous and skilled in battle.

Kaliesha West has Juan West in her corner, as does the nascent sport of women's boxing. And all of this came to be because a 10-year-old ultimately showed herself to be far from daddy's little girl.

* * *

Juan West was a Navy boxer first, a teenager who started with smokers and local bouts and fighting for his fleet. He left the service but continued to fight, though the knees of a former high school track athlete weren't made for moving around a boxing ring. He retired after six months and six fights in the pro ranks, winning four and losing two. Unable to do but still able to teach, West began to train fighters in the talent-rich Southern California of the 1990s.

Kaliesha watched and admired and wanted to be a part of it.

272

"He didn't take me serious," said Kaliesha, now 24. He had his reasons.

"I knew what I was like being in that ring, and I knew the toughness that she had to have," he says. "I didn't think women had that toughness."

Either she convinced him or he gave in. Either way, Juan West's 10-year-old child laced up the gloves and went through the drills. Within weeks, she was sparring another little boy, chasing him around the ring relentlessly.

She had her first fight at 11. Juan was in her corner, but he wasn't fully behind her.

"I kind of set my daughter up for failure," Juan says. "I really didn't prepare her and I wanted her to take a beating pretty much and just give it up. She got in there with a girl, Cindy Ramos, who was like a little heavier, a year older, and I'm sitting back chuckling like we're going to see what happens, see if she still wants to box after this."

Everyone else at the amateur card had already been paired up when a man had approached Juan to say there was another girl the same size as Kaliesha who could fight her.

"And we're standing back to back," Kaliesha says. "She's taller than me. She's thicker than me. She's fatter than me. And my dad was like 'Okay, we can do it.' We didn't even go on the scale. It was one of those rough match-ups. Supposedly she was six pounds heavier than me. Two weeks later, she was three weight divisions heavier than me. I was at 90, 95, and she was at 106."

Ramos knocked Kaliesha around the ring.

"Cindy Ramos — I'll never forget that name," Kaliesha says. She was knocking me around the ring and my balance was so horrible. I was flying across the ring, I was so frail and small. As soon as I got knocked over, the referee would jump in my face and give me an eight count.

Kaliesha, in turn, would argue that she wasn't hurt.

"After that, Kaliesha was over there saying something to the girl, and the girl is laughing," Juan says. "I'm like, 'What were you saying to the girl, Kaliesha?' She said, 'I want a rematch, of course.' And I said 'What?!'

"Then I knew Kaliesha was the real deal, because that's what's exactly in my heart when I was a fighter. I didn't feel no human in the same ring with me could beat me. If I ever lost, I immediately wanted a rematch, and that's how Kaliesha is."

Juan West had set his daughter up for failure in her first fight. Now he'd spend years preparing her to succeed.

*   *   *

Kaliesha West never pictured herself as successful as she is now — not while she was still an amateur, at least.

"I never really got the decisions," she says. "The judges will tell you the same thing: 'Kaliesha was always hanging tough and it was always a close fight, but she never squeaked out the decision in the end.' Being in junior high and high school and losing decisions, you get discouraged. I felt like 'Man, I suck. I'm never winning. Why am I boxing? I'm not good.' But there's always something deep down inside of me saying 'Just keep doing it. Next time you'll win.'

"I never envisioned being a world champion or even going as far as I did as a pro. All I envisioned was being a better fighter the next time I fought."

Juan believes the judges tended to favor the more amateur style of winning on points, rather than the professional style he preferred to impart. Kaliesha won 68 amateur bouts and lost 10. One of those victories was a rematch over Cindy Ramos, six years after they first fought.

"I had stayed active and she had stopped for about a year," Kaliesha says. "She disappeared. She came back. I think she had some time in juvenile hall. She had tattoos. She was still a roughneck. And we still happened to be the same weight again. In this fight, I had her in the corner and I was beating her down, and they gave her an eight count, and then I gave her another eight count."

Juan puts it much more simply: "Oh, boy, she destroyed that girl."

Kaliesha turned pro in 2006 at the age of 18, going undefeated in her first two years in the sport, winning her first 10 fights. Then she got in the ring in November 2008 with Ava Knight, who was 4-0-2 at the time. Knight won the unanimous decision, five rounds to three, and would go on to challenge for a super flyweight title in her next bout and now holds a belt at 112 pounds.

Kaliesha, meanwhile, wouldn't return until about nine months later, scoring a six-round win over Rolanda Andrews and then, in January 2010, fighting to a draw with Ada Velez. She then went on the road, going to Denmark in March 2010 to challenge Anita Christensen in what ended as another draw. Three months later, she traveled to Peru and stopped Vannessa Guimaraes.

That run, going 3-0-2 in the year and a half after her first pro defeat, landed Kaliesha a shot at the World Boxing Organization's vacant bantamweight belt. In September 2010, Kaliesha, fighting at the Staples Center in Los Angeles on the non-televised undercard of Shane Mosley vs. Sergio Mora, knocked out Angel Gladney to win her first title.

"My goal and dream was to develop a world champion," Juan says. "And my daughter became a world champion."

"I wasn't satisfied," Kaliesha says. "It wasn't exactly where I want to be. A world title was just like one stepping stone out of the way."

But then she nearly lost everything.

*   *   *

The shots that hurt the most are the ones you don't see coming. It is as true in life as it is in boxing.

Kaliesha was driving on a highway in January 2011. Her vehicle was in another driver's blind spot. That person switched lanes, causing Kaliesha to jerk her steering wheel to avoid a collision. She lost control, however, and crashed.

"I've endured a lot of pain in boxing, but I've never had as much pain as in that accident," Kaliesha says. "For the first time in my career, I lied to my dad. I told him I was going to be all right. All I was thinking was I ruined his career, too. I had just won the world title. I was on my way to a meeting with a photographer to work on a promo video."

She recovered from her injuries but remained in excruciating pain. But she had to defend her title or it would be taken away from her.

"I not only defended my world title in a small arena near my hometown, but it was against the only girl who ever defeated me. For no money. I fought for free," Kaliesha says. "It wasn't the purse that I was fighting for.

It was just because I knew it was what I had to do if I wanted to remain the world titlist. No other female wanted to fight me."

Kaliesha and Ava Knight had their rematch in June 2011. Once again, Kaliesha didn't come out with the win. But neither did Knight — the judges had a split draw, the scores reading 96-94 for Kaliesha, 96-94 for Knight, and an even 95-95.

Kaliesha retained the belt against a woman who is a rival in the ring but also a friend outside of it. The possibility of a third bout is unlikely, though. After the draw, Knight dropped two weight classes, from 118 pounds to 112, and won a world title. Kaliesha defended her belt in August of last year against Jessica Villafranca, will face Claudia Andrea Lopez tonight, and is considering a move to the junior featherweight division.

*   *   *

Never mind that women's boxing once had Laila Ali. Kaliesha West wants to be like Ali — Muhammad Ali.

"I want to be known as one of the greatest female fighters who ever lived," she says. "I want little girls to go to the library and look at my autobiography and say 'I want to be a boxer.' That's what I did when I was little. I looked up Muhammad Ali. There were no women. I want little girls to be able to see a book about a female boxer and say 'She was great. She was just as great as Ali was.'"

Juan West long ago learned that women are just as tough and just as able as men can be in the ring. The sport still needs much more recognition, particularly in the United States, where Kaliesha still needs much more exposure before she can become a household name. Her fight tonight is in Mexico, making it four out of her last six bouts to occur outside of her home country.

Kaliesha and Juan talk about how to increase both her popularity and that of women's boxing as a whole. They talk about why promoters and networks need to give female fighters a chance. They see popular female boxers in other countries, and they see the attention given to women in mixed martial arts promotions in America.

This is a sport for women, too. Kaliesha has trained and sparred and fought and won and lost. Juan has been there with her throughout. More than a decade after seeing if he could get his daughter to give up on boxing with her first fight, he is now trying to guide her to what he thinks will be the next phase of her career — and he is trying get her and other women the acclaim that goes along with their ability.

"I'm very proud of her, and we're on a new mission: to be pound-for-pound in the world and to go down in history as one of the greatest female boxers in history. I've been trying to prepare her for those great fights that she has to win to become great," he said.

"She's been televised in South America, and everybody over there knows her. She's been televised in Europe. Everyone over there knows her. She's been televised in Mexico, and everybody knows her. But the United States, nobody knows Kaliesha West. That's a shame."

For Floyd Mayweather, Not All Work is Easy

May 7, 2012

Not all work is easy work, no matter what one of Floyd Mayweather Jr.'s motivational credos insists, not when your nose and mouth are bloodied and your left hand is sore, and not when your opponent makes you fight through all this, all while battling against him, for the 12-round distance.

It wasn't easy work for Floyd Mayweather against Miguel Cotto, despite the clear win in the eyes of nearly all of the unofficial observers watching in the arena and on television, and the even clearer win, a wide decision, from the official tallies of the three judges scoring at ringside.

Perhaps it was because of his bloodied nose. Perhaps it was the injured hand. Perhaps it was the weight difference or the bigger gloves or age finally beginning to catch up with a 35-year-old man. Perhaps it was just a rare off night for a fighter not accustomed to having them when it matters most. Perhaps it was a combination of all of these, or perhaps it was none of that. Maybe Cotto had much to do with it, too.

Miguel Cotto wasn't easy work for Floyd Mayweather, but Mayweather made it through, made it past Cotto because of his talent and because of his tenets, those two characteristics from another credo — hard work and dedication.

Mayweather had been the betting favorite, the former Olympian, future Hall of Fame inductee and, some suggest, one of the greatest fighters of all time. He'd never been defeated as a pro; as he was fond of saying, 42 had tried and 42 had failed. Granted, he'd faced one opponent twice, but the sentiment remained the same.

Cotto, meanwhile, was the clear underdog, a talented three-division titleholder yet not as talented as the superlative superstar who would be standing across the ring from him. He'd suffered devastating damage in his two defeats, losses to Antonio Margarito in 2008 and to Manny Pacquiao in 2009 in which he sustained punishment for a combined 23 rounds. And even when not beaten, he'd been beaten up, winning wars over other opponents.

Mayweather had the skills to hit a fighter who had been hit often and hurt often. Cotto, meanwhile, had to find a way to defeat a fighter who'd yet to be defeated.

This was a different Cotto, though. He wouldn't be as vulnerable, and so Mayweather wouldn't be as able. Yet while Cotto found a way to make Mayweather less effective, Cotto himself still wouldn't be able to do enough to win.

Mayweather is always good, but he's even better at certain distances and against certain styles. From afar, Cotto maintained a high guard and a patient approach, rarely overextended himself, not giving Mayweather as much to work with, neither with potshots nor counter shots. Mayweather was less mobile than usual, too, either because of age or because of a resolution to stand and trade and entertain more than he had in years past. Perhaps it was both.

Cotto, then, was able to push Mayweather to the ropes, where he would put his head on Mayweather's shoulder or chest and dig to the body or aim upstairs for the head, not going overboard with his output as others had done on the ropes against Mayweather, other opponents who felt their offensive opportunities to be few and therefore expended themselves excessively yet not effectively.

Mayweather, as usual, moved and rolled and blocked, limiting the accuracy of most of those shots but failing to avoid them all.

Mayweather began to adjust to what was being presented to him. At one point against the ropes he set a trap, leaning his head forward and inviting Cotto to throw a right uppercut, then dodging it when Cotto bit and countering with a left hook. The high guard of Cotto, meanwhile, could block straight shots better than targeted looping punches, which became one of Mayweather's go-to weapons.

"The right hook and the uppercut were working for me tonight," Mayweather said afterward. "I had watched tapes of Shane Mosley [who fought Cotto in November 2007], and I saw that the right hook was working. And I also watched Zab Judah [who fought Cotto in June 2007] use the uppercut against him, too, so I knew I was going to use those shots tonight."

Mayweather's signature shots came less than they had against other foes: the lead right hand and move to his right out of harm's way, and the counter right hand over a jab. Cotto's jab didn't land much, but it caught Mayweather cleanly when it did, a well-timed, off-rhythm punch with what is actually Cotto's power hand.

Mayweather is neither a pressure fighter along the lines of Antonio Margarito nor a whirling dervish of activity like Manny Pacquiao. He is calculated and clinical, and so he would not have the style to break down this disciplined Cotto with quantity, but would rather aim for quality.

He sent out eight looping right hands over one section of the fourth round, many of them landing in what was one of Mayweather's best rounds of the fight and one of Cotto's worst. Mayweather went 19 of 58 in that round, according to CompuBox statistics, including 17 of 32 power shots, a fight-high 53 percent connect rate. Cotto, meanwhile, was just 4 of 30, with three of those being power punches and the other being a jab.

Through four, Mayweather had landed 66 punches, including 40 power shots, an average of 10 power shots a round. Cotto was limited to 30 landed punches total through four, of which 19 were power shots, an average of five per round. At least one of those punches had brought blood from Mayweather's nose.

Cotto remained undeterred despite how little he was hitting Mayweather, continuing to press forward in the fifth, forcing Mayweather to the ropes and strafing him with shots. Mayweather was willing to oblige but was forced to work, weaving to try to make Cotto miss and countering to try to make him pay.

It was one of Cotto's best rounds of the night, with 11 landed power shots, one of just two rounds in which he was in double figures. It was also one of Mayweather's best rounds, with him landing 24 punches, more in that round than in any other, including a fight-high 23 power punches.

It seemed as if the fight was about to kick into a higher gear.

It didn't happen.

This was more war game than blitzkrieg, with each fighter considering his own tactical maneuvers while being all too respectful of what his enemy might do in response. The sixth and seven rounds got off the ropes and returned to the center of the ring, where Cotto sent out sporadic jabs and body shots, while Mayweather sought openings for occasional two-, three- and four-punch combinations.

It had often been said that will was what would make Mayweather uncomfortable. In this fight, though, it was Cotto's skill that had Mayweather reading his opponent and then recalibrating his offense.

Mayweather landed a three-punch combination in the eighth. Cotto stood up to it, stayed in front of Mayweather and shouldered him back to the ropes, where he went back down to the body and then back up to the head. Mayweather adjusted, seeing Cotto leaning on him and sensing that the left uppercut would land. That punch came once, then again, and one more time, bringing the bout back to the center of the ring.

Cotto kept the distance close there, and Mayweather moved back to the ropes, taking more shots, then shaking his head as some landed, some glanced, and others missed. It was the last round that Cotto would win on the judges' scorecards, the sole round in which Cotto out-landed Mayweather, 20 to 13 in total punches, 16 to 11 in power shots.

The blood from Mayweather's nose was splattered on his face, the crimson shown on-screen as he sat on the corner between rounds, drawing cheers from the crowd. Mayweather smiled; he could only acknowledge what had happened, then try to do something about it.

The most versatile boxer in the sport varied his approach in the ninth, putting together a right hand followed by a left and then another right, sending out a one-two combination later. There were single right and left uppercuts, a looping right hand, a right counter as

Cotto came forward, left hook body shots and a pair of left uppercuts.

As for Cotto, his strong round in the eighth proved to be his last gasp, his output fading in the final four rounds. He kept coming, but he was throwing and landing less, going 10 of 41 in the ninth, 7 of 33 in the 10th, 6 of 36 in the 11th, and 5 of 28 in the 12th.

Mayweather was still picking his spots, and he had more spots than Cotto, including setting him up for a counter left hook in the 11th, and leading him into a right hook and left uppercut that staggered Cotto with a minute to go in the 12th. Mayweather finished stronger, following a 10 for 49 effort in the 10th with 15 of 53 in the 11th and 18 of 59 in the 12th, nearly all of those connected shots in the championship rounds coming from power punches.

The fight went the distance. Mayweather was still bleeding. Cotto was still standing.

Not all work is easy work.

Cotto made Mayweather throw more than he normally does, but he also made Mayweather land less. In his previous five fights, Mayweather averaged about 40 total punches thrown per round and 18 landed, a 45 percent connect rate, and an average of about 10 of 21 on power shots, for a nearly 50 percent connect rate.

Against Cotto, Mayweather averaged 57 punches thrown per round and 15 landed, a 26 percent connect rate, and an average of 11 of 32 on power shots, for a 34 percent connect rate.

Mayweather historically excels both on offense and defense, limiting his opponents to a 16 percent connect rate over the nine fights prior to the Cotto bout. Cotto did better on average, landing 21 percent of what he threw, including 23 percent of his power shots. Still, that only amounted to 105 landed punches in total, or less than nine per round, of which 75 were power punches, or about six per round.

It wasn't enough to win. Two of the judges scored it 117-111 for Mayweather, while the third had it 118-110.

It was enough to make Mayweather work.

It wasn't just the nose or the hand or the weight difference or the gloves or age or an off night. It was Cotto who made Mayweather think and adjust, who made Mayweather show what he is capable of doing even when he isn't able to do everything that has made him one of the best boxers in this generation, and, some would suggest, of all time.

Mayweather won clearly and decisively, though it's doubtful that he'd say it came easily.

Forget what Mayweather has said before: Not all work is easy work.

It takes hard work to do hard work. "Money" Mayweather might be a gambling man in the sports book, but he's not a betting man in the sweet science. He's invested his life in boxing, an investment that once again paid off for him.

Lamont Peterson's New Biggest Fight
May 14, 2012

He and his brother overcame homelessness and poverty, battling through a tougher life than most ever have to experience, all while still a child. They found an opening to a better life through an unforgiving sport where other men not only stood between them and victory, but opportunity, too.

He spent years fighting into contention, only to lose in his first big bout and have to work his way back up. Yet after fighting past setbacks and through obstacles for nearly his entire life, he had another chance at the title, performing in front of his hometown crowd, coming off the canvas to defeat Amir Khan and win two world titles.

Lamont Peterson's story was a compelling one. And now it is being overwritten as a disappointing tale — one of a man who earned so much respect for how he fought so hard to get to the top, only to lose that respect and be toppled without a fight.

Now Peterson has a new biggest fight: the battle to save his reputation.

That is not how the 28-year-old from Southeast Washington, D.C., expected to spend last week and this, when he was supposed to be wrapping up readying himself to defend those two world title belts and all that they meant for him, preparing himself for a rematch with Amir Khan, the man to whom those belts had belonged.

Last week, though, the news broke that Peterson had tested positive for a banned substance. Then more came out: The substance was synthetic testosterone. Peterson had been taking it since before the first fight with Khan.

Now the second bout was being canceled and the result of the first was being called into question.

Peterson and his team are trying to provide answers.

"Lamont Peterson did nothing wrong," said Peterson's spokesman, Andre Johnson, via Twitter last week. "He had a private medical matter that is now public. We will fight to the end to clear his name."

That medical matter is hypogonadism, a condition in which people do not produce enough natural testosterone. Peterson had a "severe deficiency" of the hormone and told a Las Vegas-based doctor that he was fatigued and had difficulty focusing, according to a letter that the doctor, John A. Thompson, sent last week to Nevada State Athletic Commission officials and which was obtained by Lem Satterfield of RingTV.com.

Peterson had testosterone pellets inserted into his hip, allowing the hormone to be released over months, Thompson wrote.

That was in November, about a month prior to the first Khan fight. The hormone remained in his system on March 19, when both Peterson and Khan underwent a drug test while both were in Los Angeles for a press conference for their rematch.

Peterson had requested more stringent drug testing for this fight, and Khan had agreed, both signing on to have the tests done by the Voluntary Anti Doping Association, or VADA, an organization run by the respected former chief ringside physician in Nevada, Margaret Goodman.

Peterson's testosterone ratio, 3.77 to 1, was short of the 4 to 1 benchmark that some agencies and athletic commissions use to flag the use of banned substances, and much less than the 6 to 1 ratio in Nevada's regulations. Yet VADA also uses what is called a carbon isotope ratio test, which can detect whether the testosterone in a sample is synthetic, not produced by the person's body.

Peterson had synthetic testosterone in him, and he and his team admitted as much to the commission and to all who asked. But they had never disclosed it beforehand, had never sought a therapeutic-use exemption that, if granted, would allow him to use a banned substance. They couldn't rewrite history. Peterson had failed a drug test, and the fight with Khan had been canceled.

Peterson was not going to be able to get a hearing in front of the athletic commission to get his fight license until just days before the bout was to take place. Golden Boy Promotions, which promotes Khan and was putting on the card, was not willing to go forward and put more money toward a show that might not have its main event.

The next, biggest fight for Peterson began immediately. This fight, as life has so often been for Peterson, is incredibly tough.

The sporting world has long since transitioned away from being incredibly naïve or blissfully ignorant about the use of performance-enhancing drugs by its athletes, becoming incredibly skeptical of those whose feats are phenomenal and also of those who fail drug tests and then try to explain those results away.

Those explanations have transformed themselves, from the athletes who said they did not intentionally take performance-enhancing drugs (Rafael Palmeiro), to those who said they took tainted supplements (Sean Sherk), to those who said they had taken steroids to help heal from injuries (James Toney), and to those who say they are undergoing testosterone replacement therapy (Chael

Sonnen).

Pro sports has its share of shady characters, the fitness gurus and nutritionists like Victor Conte and Angel Heredia who had been involved in supplying performance enhancing drugs in the past and now say they have cleaned up their acts. It's not just athletic trainers with connections.

There's even more shadiness beyond those operating publicly under the microscope of suspicion — there is doctor shopping, with many in the medical field willing to supply, and finding willing customers with pro athletes and pro wrestlers, such as the anti-aging clinic in Florida whose clients included wrestler Kurt Angle, baseball player Gary Matthews Jr., and a man named "Evan Fields" whose birthday and phone number matched those of former heavyweight champion Evander Holyfield.

And so the cause for skepticism continues, despite the public face that everyone from Peterson down to his trainer and the doctor in question have provided in speaking about the case. There will be questions over whether Peterson's condition is legitimate, and, if so, over whether his low testosterone levels were themselves natural or the consequence of previous performance enhancing drug use.

There will be questions about the testosterone level itself, 3.77. Although Peterson's doctor said the pellets "would not produce a significant enhancement of athletic performance," the fighter's testosterone was high enough that it was just a little less than the level at which many drug tests would be considered as failed. There will also be questions about how Peterson could have forgotten this procedure when first seeking to provide an explanation for his failed drug test, not recalling a procedure in which pellets were placed in his body.

Peterson's team points to the fact that subsequent VADA testing after the March 19 test came up negative for any performance enhancing drugs. They point to the fact that he had asked for and volunteered to undergo better drug testing. Peterson told Satterfield that he has been seeing Dr. Thompson for years, that he had been receiving supplements but had only had the testosterone pellets just this once.

"He was showing me that it was not a steroid, and that it wasn't a performance enhancement drug or anything like that," Peterson told Satterfield last week. "It's not going to make me feel like a super hero. He said it's just going to bring my levels up and that's all, and that my overall health would be better. He told me all of this before he went through with the procedure.

"I even went online to watch videos of them doing the procedure, because I was kind of cautious about it. So I went online, did the research, found out that it was considered an all-natural substance and supplement," he said.

Peterson and his team are continuing to fight the ruling, fighting to clear a name that has since been tarnished with the taint of the years of athletes who failed drug tests and then fought to save their reputations despite the overwhelming cases against them.

There are those who will question everything said in support of Peterson's case, and there are those who will believe him. It's still very early in Peterson's case, and there's still so much more that will be said and reported.

That's because Peterson's team is battling, seeking to overturn the specter of a failed drug test and the shadow that casts over an athlete, reaching back to the time before he was known to be using and reaching into the future, as people will stay skeptical and suspicious.

This is yet another fight for a man whose whole life has been spent fighting — for a man who needs to win this fight because he has so much to lose.

In Defense of Victor Ortiz
June 25, 2012

If our greatest heroes are those whose surplus of heart makes up for their deficiencies in talent, then it makes sense that our greatest villains shouldn't be their opponents, but rather those whose surplus of talent can't make up for their deficiencies in heart.

It would make sense, then, to celebrate the failings of Victor Ortiz.

It would make sense to look at his latest loss, to watch a fighter decide he no longer wanted to fight, to see him quit on his stool, to know that he had given up both on this fight and the fight that would have followed — a return to a pay-per-view main event, a shot at redemption and a guaranteed payday.

Nothing is guaranteed when it comes to Victor Ortiz.

It would make sense that he would falter again, to be his own worst enemy in an enterprise where the man standing across from him should be enemy enough.

His first loss, in 2005 against Corey Alarcon, came in a fight he was clearly winning before the opening round was over, only for him to hit Alarcon illegally on a break and lose by disqualification.

His second loss, in 2009 against Marcos Maidana, came in a fight in which he had put his opponent down three times in the first two rounds, but also went down twice himself — once in the opening round and once in the sixth. He quit, then, too, rising from the canvas but refusing to go on.

"I was hurt," Ortiz said after that fight. He was trying to explain himself but was only able to dig himself deeper. "I'm not going out on my back. I'm not going to lay down for nobody. I'm going to stop while I'm ahead. That way I can speak well when I'm older. May the best man win, and tonight he was the best man.

"I'm young, but I don't deserve to be getting beat up like this," Ortiz had said. "I have a lot of thinking to do."

He'd take even more of a beating because of those comments, assailed for not having a fighter's mentality, for not being tough enough to fight on when a fight got tough.

He'd succumbed under physical pressure against Maidana. He'd succeed under mental pressure two years later against Andre Berto.

With his career on the line, Ortiz found himself in another firefight, trading knockdowns with Berto, each man being sent to the canvas twice. Yet this time Ortiz would rise to the occasion, earning the victory and repairing his reputation.

Five months later, it was again in tatters.

The Berto win had placed Ortiz on the biggest pay-per-view of the year against the best boxer in the world — Floyd Mayweather Jr. From the early rounds, he would dig the top of his head into Mayweather's face. And in the fourth round, as Mayweather began to pull away, Ortiz followed his own flurry with a leaping head butt to Mayweather's mouth.

In a memorable moment afterward, Ortiz apologized to Mayweather with a kiss on the cheek, then soon apologized to Mayweather again with a tap of the gloves, and finally followed up later with one more attempted apology, approaching Mayweather for an embrace, then backing away with his hands down. Mayweather landed a flush left hook and a finishing right hand, sending Ortiz down for the count.

Ortiz smiled at the situation. We seethed.

He was physically skilled but mentally flawed, too prone to fouling when adversity brought anxiety, too tolerable of defeat when a fight got too difficult.

It would make sense, then, that it would happen again against Josesito Lopez.

Ortiz hadn't fought since the Mayweather loss, but circumstance had landed him another chance at a pay-per-view main event, this one this fall against Saul "Canelo" Alvarez. That opportunity had presented itself when other fights had been canceled; Ortiz was supposed to have fought a rematch with Berto this past Saturday, and Alvarez was to have fought Paul Williams this coming September.

Yet Berto tested positive for a performance-enhancing drug, and Williams was paralyzed in a motorcycle accident. That ultimately led to Ortiz being named Alvarez's next opponent.

But he'd already signed for this fight with Lopez. He simply needed to win and not get hurt.

Nothing is simple when it comes to Victor Ortiz.

Lopez, thrown in to be the fall guy, wasn't an easy out, fighting up to his level of opposition and proving to be a stiffer challenge than Ortiz's promoter must have expected.

Ortiz went to war, as he'd done with Maidana and as he'd done with Berto. It'd prove to be his undoing.

He was winning the fight on the official scorecards, though he might not have known that. The bout had been a give-and-take battle, and so it seemed a smart strategy when Ortiz began to box in the ninth. Lopez tagged him a few times toward the round's close, though, and Ortiz began to retreat.

The round ended — and suddenly the fight did, too.

"My jaw is broken," he told the referee.

Some seethed. Perhaps, they felt, his will had been broken as well.

It would make sense that he would falter again. Ortiz had fouled Lopez in the fifth round, hitting his ducking foe with a blatant shot to the back of his head. Now he'd quit, finding a way out of the fight, as had happened before.

Some began to exalt Lopez for the way he won while excoriating Ortiz for the way he lost. That made sense. If our greatest heroes are those whose surplus of heart makes up for their deficiencies in talent, then our greatest villains are those whose surplus of talent can't make up for their deficiencies in heart.

Yet for all the criticism deserved when a fighter won't fight through adversity, that standard shouldn't be the same when it comes to battling through injury.

Not everybody is Arturo Gatti fighting Micky Ward with a broken hand, Muhammad Ali fighting Ken Norton with a broken jaw, Timothy Bradley going the distance on injured feet or even Eddie Chambers battling 12 heavyweight rounds with one good arm. The injuries, the pain and the rush of adrenaline all differ, and how fighters cope with those consequences all depends.

Not everybody is Diego Corrales spewing blood from his mouth and begging the ringside physician for one more round. It's an unfair standard, and one that's only applied depending on the fighter. No one questions Israel Vazquez's fighter mentality anymore, even though he quit with a broken nose in his first battle with Rafael Marquez. Sometimes it's the right choice.

Ortiz's mouth was as agape as those who watched the stunning conclusion to his fight. He dropped his head and spat out blood. He'd be in a hospital the next day, undergoing surgery.

There will be those who say his reputation needs to be repaired again, too. While it's true that he'll need to rebuild once more, he need not be reviled even more. There were already reasons to criticize Ortiz, to root against him and celebrate his failings. This loss to Lopez shouldn't be another reason. Some fighters will be warriors. Some fighters will be quitters. And some will be both.

Adrien, We Have A 'Problem'
July 23, 2012

Adrien Broner's greater sin wasn't so much the one he committed as what it represented.

Broner is far from the first high-profile fighter to fail to make weight. He won't be the last, either, not when the status quo of those competing in combat sports is to boil their bodies down as low as they can go, step on the scales and then rehydrate in the hopes of gaining an advantage over a foe who might not be as big or as powerful.

Yet the outrage directed at Adrien Broner after he came in overweight for his junior lightweight bout against Vicente Escobedo — and then came in heavy again after agreeing that he would have to weigh-in under a certain number the following day — was the sort of anger and annoyance brought out by the serial offenders.

Broner is not Joan Guzman or Jose Luis Castillo, two fighters now known as much for their failures at the scales as they are for their fights. Guzman and Castillo have had bouts called off because of being overweight. Broner nearly did, too, until money triumphed over principle.

This is prizefighting, after all. And Escobedo and his team were able to take advantage of the situation, negotiating for more money and coming to terms that must have been so good for them — and so bad for those at the other end of the bargaining table — that their agreement is being kept confidential.

It must have been worth it for them to take a fighter who already was outclassed and to put him in with an opponent who already had more speed, more skills and more size, but now also would potentially be coming in even heavier while still retaining his other natural advantages.

Broner, after all, had weighed in at 133 and a half pounds, then refused to lose any more, despite being closer to the lightweight limit than he was to junior lightweight. He added 13 and a half more pounds by the night of the fight, while Escobedo had gone through the sacrifices of making 130 before adding a dozen pounds himself, coming in at 142.

It might still have been worth it to Escobedo and his team after five rounds with a fighter who wasn't just bigger, but better, who moved Escobedo with so many clean shots, who made Escobedo look to his corner after one barrage in the final round, and who brought Escobedo's corner ascending the ring steps with towel in hand shortly thereafter.

"I was away from my family and my wife," Escobedo said, the father of a newborn daughter choking back tears in his post-fight interview. "And just to come here and not get a fair, fair, fair fight ... but I'm here to fight. I came to fight."

He escaped an extended beating, but not the damage he'd already taken and the disappointment of defeat. That was his own doing, the price he'd paid — or, rather, been paid — to face Broner despite Broner's not making weight on Friday and then again on Saturday.

But that he was put into that situation to begin with was because of Broner.

Broner is far from the first high-profile fighter to miss weight. That wasn't his greater sin. His greater sin was the way he shrugged off his own failure at the scales not as a fault of self, but rather as a fact of life, as something that he didn't control — and that didn't matter.

"I'm 22, and it's obvious I grew out of the weight class," Broner said to HBO's Max Kellerman in a pre-fight interview.

Kellerman then confronted him about the pictures of junk food Broner had posted on Twitter in the lead-up to the fight. Kellerman only mentioned Twinkies and ice cream sundaes, but Broner in the weeks before the fight had also put up photos of an ice cream bar, a McDonald's parking lot, a bag of Skittles, a bowl of cereal alongside a bottle of caramel syrup and a jug of milk, and a hot dog alongside an Icee cup and more ice cream.

"Um, I don't think ice cream sundaes make you grow out of a weight class, you know," Broner responded. "My body's growing. I'm 22, like I said, you know. I grew out of the weight class, and that's that."

Broner had previously said that the Escobedo fight would be his last at junior lightweight. Then he made sure that wouldn't be the case — his last fight at junior lightweight would instead be the one that came before — paying little heed to making weight, and then paying a fifth of his purse, $60,000, to be split between the Ohio athletic commission and Escobedo.

That was the Friday before the bout. The day of the fight, Broner was supposed to weigh in at no more than 10 pounds over the junior lightweight limit, according to members of Escobedo's team, while those affiliated with Broner argued that the agreement had been that Broner could gain 10 pounds from what he'd been.

The latter is what Broner did, coming in for his second weigh-in at 143.5. Reports over the next several hours were that the fight was teetering between being on and being called off, and the bout was finally set only after even more money went to Escobedo.

Broner is far from the first high-profile fighter to miss weight. But a fighter who misses weight and causes the fight to be canceled is a problem. Adrien Broner is not Joan Guzman or Jose Luis Castillo, but he came close enough to draw the same kind of ire as had been directed at those serial offenders.

Judging by his diet, Broner had intentionally not made weight. And as evident by his inaction after coming in heavy, he intentionally didn't try to make 130 after coming in three and a half pounds over.

Not trying to drop those pounds in just two hours wasn't just practical — but tactical.

Broner had no problem dropping his title at the scales in a division that he was already looking to leave behind. And he knew that he could afford to pay $60,000 to Escobedo and the commission. He is a hyped prospect who has now been featured on HBO for five straight fights, who is headlining Golden Boy Promotions cards and who is managed by influential powerbroker Al Haymon.

Broner likely didn't have to personally fork over whatever additional money sweetened the pot to get Escobedo to agree to fight after Broner missed weight on Saturday, not when Haymon and Golden Boy can get him on HBO, which is always in search of the next great star, and who in Broner has a talented American molding himself both personally and professionally as an imitation of Floyd Mayweather Jr.

And Broner knew that Escobedo probably would agree to fight no matter the bad hand dealt him. Escobedo had seemed too small at lightweight and had found more success one division below, but he'd also not been featured on a major boxing broadcast — or received the major payday that comes with one — since November 2010. Broner had been spotlighted more in his previous four fights than Escobedo had in his entire career.

Broner was unabashed at failing to make weight, and unapologetic when confronted with controversy. He'd taken advantage of a system that enabled him, like so many other 22-year-old athletes who have been given the world and do not hear the word "no."

"The critics will always have something to say, but at the end of the day as long as I get the 'W,' that's all that matters," Broner had told Kellerman before the fight.

None of this was necessary, though, not with an athlete who has been gifted enough to be good and who is being given the opportunity to show whether he can be great.

None of this was necessary in a sport that appreciates accomplishment — that recognizes that Floyd Mayweather Jr. can be wholly unlikable personally but whose professional accomplishments are remarkable, a product not just of his talent but of his mantra of hard work and dedication.

We expect our fighters to approach the sport with professionalism, respecting its rules and traditions, not just seeing it as a business in which you can be cutthroat and can cut corners so long as you come out on top.

We expect our fights to be won with skill, strategy and ability, attributes that are then augmented in training camp and applied in the ring.

Broner won't be punished or penalized any further. He'll be back in the spotlight, back in the main event, back for another major payday from a promoter and a network that sees him as a big talent with a big personality. Like his idol, he'll use controversy to draw more attention to him. His increasing flamboyancy will bring him an increasing following, and his turn toward villainy will be just as valuable. Those who want to see him lose still want to see him.

Broner's greater sin wasn't so much the one he committed as what it represented: The young man nicknamed "The Problem" has no problem with what he did, and will face none despite that.

Erik Morales: Another Sad Goodbye
October 22, 2012

There were worse ways to go out of the sport they love, and the sport that loved them back, than to lose to whom they did — and how they did.

They were not beaten off of television and in a remote location, stubbornly lingering long past their shelf lives and far removed from the spotlight.

There was still sorrow in the final fights of Arturo Gatti and Diego Corrales, the same sadness that came in seeing Erik Morales felled in what truly must be his last stand. Morales spoke Saturday night with a mix of dejection and acceptance. The end is near, he said, and his career will end after he says goodbye with a fight in his native Tijuana.

There are worse ways to go out.

Morales lost to the top-rated fighter in the 140-pound division, a well-rounded boxer named Danny Garcia who, at 24, is a dozen years Morales' junior. Garcia had turned pro nearly five years ago, when Morales had already begun his initial sabbatical, hanging up his gloves for two and a half years.

It had been the right choice for Morales to leave then, too.

He had lost four in a row, and five of his last six. The sole victory had come in the first episode of his trilogy with Manny Pacquiao. But then he came in out of shape and out of his element against a slick boxer named Zahir Raheem, was stopped by Pacquiao in their rematch, and stopped even sooner by Pacquiao in their rubber match. His last hurrah was a valiant yet unsuccessful challenge of lightweight titleholder David Diaz.

He said afterward that he was being hurt by punches more than before. We welcomed his retirement, even if it meant we would lose the warrior who had thrilled us so. We celebrated the punishment he had delivered and recognized that which he had taken. And so we worried when he announced his comeback.

He would be facing opponents who were naturally bigger, who would have less trouble hitting an aging veteran with declining reflexes, who would be hurt less by his offense, and who would not be as slowed by the burdens of time and additional weight.

He never truly found great success, but he never truly embarrassed himself either.

Morales ticked off three wins against lower-tier opposition before stepping in the ring against Marcos Maidana in April 2011. Maidana was the kind of opponent that had made us worry. Morales put on the kind of performance that made us smile. He turned back the clock for one evening, giving Maidana trouble but ultimately not doing enough to score the upset, losing a majority decision.

Later in the year, he stopped an undefeated but unheralded prospect named Pablo Cano to take a vacant alphabet title. That set him up for a bout in early 2012 against Garcia, another undefeated younger foe whose toughest opposition to date had come against an over-the-hill Nate Campbell and an on-the-decline Kendall Holt.

Garcia, however, had shown signs of true talent. Against Morales, though, he also showed too much respect. The bout went the distance, Garcia holding back at times in deference to Morales' experience. Garcia did put Morales down toward the end of the fight, a sign of the disadvantages Morales would have against younger, faster and stronger. And then there was Morales' weight. He had come in over the limit, one more sign that his conditioning wasn't there, that his body no longer belonged in boxing.

Garcia and Morales fought again seven months later. Little had changed for Morales. Lots had changed for Garcia.

Morales had admittedly struggled once again to make 140, though this time he came in below the limit. That might have been helped by the banned substance, clenbuterol, that he had tested positive for in the weeks before the bout. Garcia, meanwhile, was no longer a mere kid titleholder testing himself against a wily veteran, but had since become a confident and capable champion. He had bested the best fighter in his division, Amir Khan, and now was seeking to make the statement against Morales that he'd failed to make earlier in the year.

He wasn't as gun shy against this old gun. He'd always had superior firepower, and now he was even better at using it. Morales, meanwhile, couldn't take it. Not the right hand that buckled his knee toward the end of the third round and left him stumbling back to the wrong corner. And not the left hook that nearly spun his body all the way around before sending him to the canvas — in about the same position he had been at the end of the third Pacquiao bout — and sending his trainer into the ring to keep him from being hurt further.

There are worse ways to go, but it was nonetheless sad to see a warrior who could no longer bear the brunt of battle, who could always call on his surplus of experience and courage and heart but no longer could rely on his chin, legs and reflexes.

It was as sad to see Diego Corrales at welterweight against Joshua Clottey, no longer able to make the lightweight limit and competing two weight divisions above where he had been at his best. Corrales no longer had as much of a size advantage from boiling down his lanky frame. He was slower now, and even more susceptible to getting hit and hurt. Clottey was a very good welterweight. Corrales, clearly, was nowhere near as good.

And it was sad to see Arturo Gatti's final fight, against Alfonso Gomez, a decent welterweight but never top tier. Gatti, like Corrales and Morales, had gone up to a heavier division class after his body no longer could take cutting so much weight. It was one thing for Gatti to be demolished to Floyd Mayweather Jr. It was respectable for him to be stopped by Carlos Baldomir. But the Gomez defeat was the end, and Gatti recognized it.

Gatti retired and was found dead two years after the Gomez loss. Corrales died tragically in a motorcycle crash a month after losing to Clottey. Morales plans to call it a career after one final hometown show.

Their fights had become dances with danger. They were never capable of winning, but instead were doing all they could just to stay competitive in defeat. There are worse ways to go. They weren't fighting on non-televised shows, weren't having their last grasps at significance playing out before a smaller audience.

But they were no longer great at the sport they loved, and no longer able to put forth the performances that made us love them.

Mike Tyson sat in a curtained-off section of an arena in Washington, D.C., in June 2005, barely an hour removed from being stopped in six rounds by an unexceptional opponent named Kevin McBride.

"I just don't have this in my gut anymore. It's just not in my heart anymore," Tyson said during the post-fight press conference. "I'm not trying to take anything away from Kevin McBride. We know his record. We know his credentials. And if I can't beat him, I can't beat Junior Jones."

There was a sense of catharsis in this. However sad it was to see Tyson lose to McBride, to see Gatti bloodied and beaten by Gomez, to see Corrales downed and defeated by Clottey, and to see Morales knocked around the ring by Garcia, it would've been worse to see them continue — for us to know that it was over for them before they had realized the same.

Only One (Decision For) Ricky Hatton

November 26, 2012

Rare is the fighter who retires while on top of a profession so brutal that it can break a man in the span of one night. So rare is this, that champions such as Lennox Lewis and Joe Calzaghe were called out for comeback collisions for years after they hung up their gloves for good, seen as if they were but on sabbatical, as if their final bell had yet to be rung.

Life does not incentivize quitting while you're ahead, not in a culture founded on a belief that there is always another reward around the corner. An actor can always make another movie. A musician can record another album. An athlete can play another season. And a boxer can have another fight.

Except in every industry but that of the Sweet Science, the ability for someone at the top to return for more is dependent on demand — on production studios and record labels and sports franchises. We do not see aging A-list actors taking roles at the community theatre, rock stars headlining Thursday nights at the neighborhood pub, or Hall of Fame shortstops taking to the field in a rec league.

Yet all too often, we see, or sometimes just hear of, pugilists in their futile final fights, acquiescing to the reality that their best days are gone without accepting the true consequences of that conclusion. Rather than retire, they become the faded former champion, the once-acclaimed name now being sacrificed to someone younger, someone who is still relevant.

That's the best-case scenario. Others, such as Antwun Echols and Vivian Harris, lose to opponents who previously never would have shared a ring with them.

There is shame. But there also must be sympathy.

Boxing is nearly all they have known, beginning with the amateur tournaments of their youth and continuing into the paid ranks. It can be difficult to adjust to a life out of the spotlight and without the disciplined structure of training camps. There is no off-season in boxing in which fighters can acclimate themselves to time away from the rigors, and vigor, of competition.

And for those who never saved — after all, there are no pensions or 401k plans in boxing — or for those who never earned much, there is no paycheck more honest than one earned by getting punched in your vital organs.

*   *   *

Ricky Hatton was as honest as a fighter could come.

He was an everyman in temperament who turned that trait into an extraordinary feature. He never looked the part of an elite athlete, not when he was between fights and ballooning in weight, and not even when he was in the ring, his pale body temporarily thinned out. He fought like Rocky in a bar fight, his chin perpetually exposed, alternating between brutal mauling and comical haymakers.

He became a franchise in Manchester, one of the guys done well — 'Let's go see Ricky fight,' they would say collectively, whether it was in the U.K. or the U.S.A., turning up in droves, chanting Hatton's name, singing his praises and drinking throughout, celebrating him with the now-famous anthem, "Walking in a Hatton Wonderland." The variation of the holiday standard led with a chant: "There's only one Ricky Hatton," they'd say, though in reality he was one of them, and they would live through him.

He remained approachable throughout.

That is what made his defeats so difficult. He wasn't just letting himself down, but, in his mind, everyone else as well. A hometown hero will be paraded in victory. Perhaps that meant he would be pitied in defeat.

There was no shame in being knocked out by Floyd Mayweather Jr., as he was in December 2007. The arena in Las Vegas, filled to the brims with Brits, continued to sing his song. There also was no shame in being knocked out by Manny Pacquiao, as he was in May 2009. Mayweather and Pacquiao were two of the best fighters of this era. Hatton, clearly, was not.

But it was the way that he went out — flat on his back, rendered momentarily immobile in a highlight that would be played over and over for months to come — that led to Hatton withdrawing into depression and addiction.

"I was always a very proud fighter," Hatton said last week, speaking on a media conference call days before he was to step into the ring to face Vyacheslav Senchenko for what would be Hatton's first fight since that last knockout defeat.

"I was always a very hard fighter, always fought with a lot of heart and was able to dictate fights," he said. "So you can imagine, when I got destroyed in two rounds by Manny Pacquiao, it was very hard for someone who takes so much pride in themselves, even though it was someone like Manny Pacquiao."

Nearly every fighter hits his ceiling. Once that happens, he either must be satisfied with staying at a certain level — a level lower than he had strived for, or a level at which he can no longer remain — or he must choose not to stay at all.

Hatton didn't fight for more than three and a half years since losing to Pacquiao, but he also didn't officially retire until July 2011, more than two years after he'd last stepped into the ring. His retirement barely lasted a year; he officially announced his comeback this past September.

Rare is the fighter who remains retired. The sport becomes too ingrained in him; his self-worth is defined by what he does between those ropes.

Hatton had withdrawn post-Pacquiao. After all, every time people saw him, they would recall his greatest failings. He again went up in weight, though this time it wasn't coming off temporarily on fight nights. He abused alcohol — no surprise, given his well-chronicled love of a good pint or several — but also turned to cocaine. Anything to fill a void, to bring vigor to a life now lacking in rigor.

It proved to be a greater embarrassment than what had happened on either of those two nights at the MGM Grand in America's Sin City.

"As soon as Manny beat me, I went into depression, and that led to problems that were well-documented in the tabloids, with suicide attempts and nervous breakdowns and panic attacks," Hatton said last week. "Not speaking to my parents for two years, and I'm still not speaking to my parents, which has been very, very hard. Losing my longtime trainer, Billy Graham, tending to a court case.

"My life for the past three years has really turned to mush," he said. "So I'm now returning to my boxing career not just because I got knocked out in two rounds by Manny Pacquiao, but I think I let a lot of people down in that period of time, and I'm here to put a lot of ghosts and demons to rest."

He had officially announced his comeback in September. Nearly all of the tickets were sold within two days, well before an opponent had even been named.

He was an everyman in Manchester, flawed just like the rest of them. It did not matter that he had lost, or how, nor did it matter that he had struggled in times of mental weakness. They would still be there to give him strength.

*　　*　　*

"Win, lose or draw on Nov. 24, if it's not there and if I'm not up to it, I'll walk away," Hatton was quoted as saying by The Daily Telegraph a month before the Senchenko fight. "I'll have done what I needed to."

Ricky Hatton is still as honest as a fighter can come, but he had deluded himself.

He could speak about how this comeback was about putting ghosts and demons to rest, about picking up the pieces of his life and his career. Yet he was no different than any other fighter who cannot stay retired. The sport is ingrained in him; his self-worth was still defined by what would happen in the ring.

This comeback wasn't just about exerting self-control, but also about self-esteem.

"I don't want to be fighting at four- or six-round levels," he was quoted as saying by BoxingScene.com in September. "I want to fight for world titles."

He had lost to Mayweather, the best fighter at the time in the welterweight division. He had lost to Pacquiao, who became the best fighter at the time in the junior welterweight division. He would never be able to beat them, but there were other boxers with world titles, other names that could help him prove he still had a place in the sport.

One name mentioned was Paulie Malignaggi. Hatton had defeated Malignaggi by technical knockout in 2008, back when both were fighting at 140 pounds. Now Malignaggi had a title belt in the 147-pound division. They had history with each other, which would help sell the fight beyond the level that Hatton's fame already could. And Malignaggi, with just seven knockouts in 32 wins, does not have anything approaching the kind of power that Mayweather and Pacquiao had floored Hatton with.

Senchenko was the man Malignaggi had beaten for the belt.

Hatton was deluding himself.

He had hit his ceiling against Mayweather and Pacquiao, and that was when he was still an active fighter. Now he was 34, coming off three and a half years away from the sport, compounded by the fact that his style is the kind that only allows fighters to have a short shelf life. He also was coming back as a welterweight. The years away to heal could only do so much to help; he would still be slowed by the additional pounds as well as the ravages of time.

The jump from 140 to 147 pounds has been difficult for some naturally smaller boxers; Zab Judah, Arturo Gatti and Hatton himself found themselves less effective at welterweight, where their power didn't necessarily carry and where naturally bigger men — even those without significant power — could hurt them.

Hatton hadn't changed his style. He still fought like

Rocky in a bar fight. His chin was still perpetually exposed. He still alternated between brutal mauling and comical haymakers.

He found some success against Senchenko and was winning on all three scorecards through eight rounds. Yet even had he won, the fight was showing that Hatton was setting himself up for failure. A victory would give him false bravado, false hope that he could contend. His face was being badly marked up by Senchenko. His chin would eventually be tested, too, not necessarily by Malignaggi, but by whomever might come next after that.

Hatton never got the chance to find out. This time it wasn't his chin that failed him, but his body.

In the ninth round, Senchenko landed a well-placed left hook to the liver, putting Hatton down on one knee. He never rose back up to beat the count, and instead lay himself on the canvas, suffering from the blow, succumbing to his fate.

He eventually got up. Tears welled in his eyes. Disappointment pooled within. He said he wasn't going to make any rash decisions about his career.

Before the night was over, he had once again retired.

"I know it isn't there anymore," Hatton was quoted as saying afterward by BoxingScene.com. "It's too many hard fights. I've burned the candle at both ends. I've put my body through the mire in and out of the ring. But it doesn't matter how hard I train. I couldn't have done any better.

"I'm a happy man tonight," he said. "I don't feel like putting a knife to my wrists. I have got the answers I needed. I got the opportunity and I got the answers and no matter how upsetting it is, I have got to be a man and say it is the end of Ricky Hatton."

He is as honest as a fighter can come, but he's still deluding himself. This is only the end of his boxing career.

This is a profession so brutal that it can break a person in the span of one night. It is a pursuit that has taken the measure of him as a warrior, but it is what Hatton does outside of the ring that will take the measure of him as a man.

Pacquiao-Marquez 4:
Eight Years, Four Fights, One Punch
December 10, 2012

The measure of a fighter rests not just in what he is capable of, but also in how he applies his abilities against those who oppose him. The greatest boxers can examine what his opponent is, and then exploit what he is not.

Manny Pacquiao and Juan Manuel Marquez were two very different fighters, Pacquiao a whirling dervish of speed and power, Marquez a wizard with skill and precision. But when faced with the other, they were as close as two very different fighters could be.

One point separated them in their first fight, which ended a draw, one point on one scorecard keeping Pacquiao from victory.

One point separated them in their second fight, which ended a split decision for Pacquiao, one point on one scorecard keeping the result from being a draw.

One punch separated Pacquiao from his senses in the fourth fight.

The scorecards didn't matter. The only number that mattered was the 10 count that Pacquiao would not be able to beat. He was unconscious, face down, flat on his stomach. Marquez stood on the second rope, raising his fists exultantly from a blue cord less than 20 feet from where his fallen rival lay prone. He was celebrating a triumph that had long eluded him.

Their first fight was in 2004. Their second fight was in 2008. Their third fight was in 2011. Their fourth fight was Dec. 8.

The greatest boxers can examine what his opponent is,

and then exploit what he is not. It took eight years and four fights for Juan Manuel Marquez and his Hall of Fame trainer, Nacho Beristain, to successfully exploit Manny Pacquiao — with one punch.

With one punch, Marquez caught Pacquiao coming forward, defenseless, led deliberately into a trap.

With one punch, Marquez landed the perfect shot at the perfect time, ending what had been yet another competitive contest, and ending any possibility of controversy on the scorecards.

And with one punch, Marquez showed that this skilled scientist had momentarily turned alchemist, exploiting Pacquiao not in the form of what he had become, but by transforming him into what he once was.

It was Pacquiao's aggression that had posed problems for so many. His speed was faster and his punches harder than expected. He would knock Marquez down three times in their first fight, forcing him to adjust on the fly and down the stretch, initially just to survive, eventually so he could vie for victory.

Marquez was long lauded for his ability to adjust, to dissect and then to defeat. His combinations and counters often were placed and timed perfectly, their trajectories sometimes switching along the way. He had not been able to beat Pacquiao despite this — at least, not officially — but he had earned his respect.

Perhaps Marquez had earned too much of Pacquiao's respect.

Pacquiao's earlier successes in his career, founded upon unrestrained aggression, had been redirected and refined by his own Hall of Fame trainer, Freddie Roach, accentuating evasive movement and an expanded arsenal. Yet that killer instinct that had nearly stopped

Marquez in a single round, that had broken down bigger, stronger and slower men, had seemingly disappeared.

Manny Pacquiao had grown increasingly cautious around Juan Manuel Marquez, and that had nearly been to his detriment. Their first two fights were pitched battles. Their third, however, had been more of a tactical affair, and despite what two of the three judges ringside had ruled, many felt that Pacquiao had not done enough, that Marquez had done more and done better.

If only Pacquiao had known that abandoning this caution would be even worse for him.

His return to aggression would bring him as close to beating Marquez convincingly as he had been since the first round of the first of their four fights. And it would bring him to unquestionable defeat in what is, for the moment at least, the final round of an extended, outstanding rivalry.

"He's a good counter-puncher," Pacquiao told Joe Tessitore of ESPN more than two months before this fourth fight. "If I'm fighting with a good counter-puncher, I have to be a counter-puncher also. If I do that, then the fight will be boring, because both of us [are] waiting for somebody to come inside and be aggressive. So if we're fighting, it has to be that one of us will be aggressive."

Pacquiao had to be directed back toward his corner by the referee before the opening bell even rang. He then beat Marquez to the center of the ring, ready for action. It would be Pacquiao that would bring the fight to Marquez, though without reverting to the careless attacker that had been out-boxed in their first fight. Instead, he stood in front of Marquez, using feints and head movement to set up his shots and to try to throw off

Marquez's timing.

Pacquiao was still wary of Marquez's counters, though not rendered inactive because of them. Instead, when Marquez would counter with a straight right, or even when Marquez would feint with that shot, Pacquiao would move slightly backward. Sometimes that left Pacquiao's body exposed. Marquez, ever able to change trajectories, would land there instead.

Marquez may have appeared cautious, but there is a difference between tentative and tactical.

Those counters, as well as his jabs and left hook leads both upstairs and to the body, were setting Pacquiao up for a thunderous shot. About halfway through the third round, Marquez led with a half-jab that stopped short of Pacquiao's gloves. He then stepped in and bent his body forward, as if to throw another hooking right to the body. Instead, as Pacquiao brought his left elbow downward and leaned his body slightly back, Marquez looped his right hand high and landed it flush to the left side of Pacquiao's face.

Pacquiao crumpled to his back, as suddenly and surprisingly as had happened to Marquez eight and a half years ago.

Now Pacquiao would have all the more reason to be cautious of Marquez, who wasn't just seeking to counter, but was loading up those counters with well-placed, well-timed power. Or perhaps Pacquiao would become even more aggressive, would seek to retaliate, to regain control.

Either idea could play Pacquiao right into Marquez's hands. Except Marquez still had to deal with what Pacquiao's hands could do.

After a cautious fourth round, Pacquiao got the

knockdown back about a minute into the fifth, landing a straight left hand from his southpaw stance that sent Marquez teetering to his side. Marquez righted himself with his left glove, listened to referee Kenny Bayless issue his mandatory eight count, and then set a trap. He feinted forward, then moved back, inviting Pacquiao to come at him. Pacquiao led with a right hook, and Marquez countered with a hard, flush right hand to Pacquiao's head.

It was the same punch that would knock Pacquiao out one round later.

Once again, Pacquiao retaliated. Pacquiao had long ago learned the lessons imparted in boxing, some of which are the same lessons revealed in his newfound religious observance: an eye for an eye, a knockdown for a knockdown, a big punch for a big punch. With 45 seconds to go in the fifth round, he threw a left hand lead that fell short, but followed with a short right hook that caught Marquez on the nose and put him on unsteady legs.

Marquez remained standing and withstood the barrage, firing back amid Pacquiao's flurries, sustaining a cut on the bridge of his nose but surviving the round.

They exchanged combinations in the sixth, standing and trading. And with 10 seconds to go in that round, one point, fittingly, separated Manny Pacquiao and Juan Manuel Marquez on all three judges' scorecards.

And with one second to go in that round, one punch separated Pacquiao from his senses.

Pacquiao and Marquez had exchanged what were largely missed combinations in the final 10 seconds, spurred on by the stick clapping that signals that the round will soon end, each wanting to land the last emphatic shot to steal the round. Pacquiao then feinted with a jab, his gloves down toward his waist. Marquez took a slight step back, then another, and then a third.

Pacquiao charged forward to close the gap, first feinting with a jab, and then beginning to throw it in earnest. Marquez stepped forward with his left leg and looped a short right hand to Pacquiao's head.

Pacquiao had begun to throw the same combination that had long ago been his signature — jab, jab, left cross — with the same reckless abandon. He had fallen into Marquez's trap, just as Paul Williams had fallen into Sergio Martinez's trap two years ago, when Martinez had used the same technique, the same counter, and gotten the same result.

It was the greatest win yet for one of the greatest fighters ever, who long ago had been measured against Marco Antonio Barrera and Erik Morales, Mexican counterparts whose fame had long eluded Marquez.

It was Marquez's first fight with Pacquiao that brought him, deservingly, into the same spotlight, and it was his pursuit of Pacquiao through the years that brought him from being respected as skilled to being recognized as sensational.

It was his wins over fighters such as Barrera, Joel Casamayor, Juan Diaz and Michael Katsidis that kept him in the ranks, and kept him in the running for a rematch with Pacquiao, and then for another sequel.

And it was his ability to give Pacquiao a close, competitive fight that brought him back for one more match.

The measure of a fighter rests not just in what he is capable of, but also in how he applies his abilities against those who oppose him. Marquez had come close, but he had never come out victorious, at least, not officially. It took eight years, four fights — and one punch.

The Heartbreak of Steve Cunningham
December 24, 2012

He thanked every fan and reporter who approached him, each saying that they thought he had won the fight. He spent the next morning and afternoon reposting and replying to others' sentiments on Twitter, all in support of a boxer they believed had deserved the victory.

It all served as cold comfort to Steve Cunningham.

Every voice, every message only added to the outrage. Rather than soothe him, they only underlined the painful reality of what he, and they, could only see as a robbery.

"What more can I do, other than knock a dude out?" Cunningham said afterward. "What more can I do?"

He had done all he could for 12 rounds against Tomasz Adamek.

He had not been knocked down, as had happened three times four years ago, when they had first fought.

He had not been badly hurt, had not been drawn into a war he could not win, had not strayed too far from a strategy of discipline, of using speed and movement to offset his stronger but slower pursuer.

He had not been awarded the decision.

One judge gave Adamek seven rounds to Cunningham's five. Another judge scored it even wider for the Polish heavyweight, at eight rounds to four. Only one official observer had Cunningham ahead, seeing it seven to five.

That single dissenting vote joined a larger chorus. Yet it was just those other two sets of numbers that truly counted.

This is the heartbreak of being a boxer, of being

involved in a sport where the scores are not accumulated via baskets, goals, runs or touchdowns, but instead are decided by a trio of people seated feet away from the action. There is the cliché of a fighter taking his fate into his own hands, of taking his opponent out and making certain that the result is not left to those three observers positioned along the ring apron.

That is not always possible. Sometimes a fighter can only hope to do his job as well as he desires, and then he can only hope that the judges do their jobs as well as the boxers deserve for them to do.

This is the heartbreak of Steve Cunningham. He deserved better than this.

Sports teams have extended seasons over which they can attempt to make up for bad breaks. The athletes often are guaranteed millions of dollars each year no matter the team's performance.

A single fight can change the course of a boxer's career. One bad call can cost him a win — and the windfall that could come with it.

"It saddens me, man. It saddens me because, like I said before, I'm not a superstar," Cunningham said afterward. "I'm a two-time champ. I'm a former two-time world champ, and yet unlike other former champs, like, let's say, a Bernard Hopkins. He can lose to a Jermain Taylor, fight for a million some odd dollars, and then go back and fight [Antonio] Tarver for a million after a loss.

"I can't do that," he said. "I haven't fought for that much money, accumulated, in my career. So my next pay is going to be low, of course. I need these wins, you know what I mean? I need these wins."

He laughed, the kind of gallows humor that comes from a man stunned from disbelief.

"I can't be getting cheated like this," he said. "It's ridiculous."

He had shed tears in the beginning of the post-fight press conference, telling those looking toward him in the conference room at the Sands Casino Resort in Bethlehem, Pa., that "real men cry," then brushing off a reporter asking if he would be taking questions by responding that he had something he needed to say.

He would put forth an emotional extemporaneous monologue for five minutes before turning over the conversation to those seeking to hear even more.

"It's sad and it's disappointing," he had said at the outset. "I go to Europe. This happens in Europe. I come back to America and this happens in America."

Cunningham is a Philadelphia fighter, yet this had been only his second fight in Pennsylvania, and his first bout in the state in nearly a decade, dating back to when he was but a young prospect with just a dozen wins underneath his belt.

But then he became a contender in the cruiserweight division. That meant little in a country where American fight fans historically are more likely to follow the two weight classes that sandwich his: heavyweight and light heavyweight.

And so he went to Poland in 2006 for his first shot at a world title, only to lose a split decision to a fighter named Krzystof Wlodarczyk, losing despite one judge scoring the bout 11 rounds to 1 for Cunningham, with the other two arbiters finding it for the Polish boxer.

Cunningham got a rematch, though, and got the win. He stayed in Europe and stopped Marco Huck, then eventually returned to the United States to defend his belt for the second time.

That was when Cunningham first met Adamek, in a venue called the Prudential Center in the New Jersey city of Newark, which had become Adamek's adopted hometown, where he could attract thousands of people of Polish heritage to see and support him. The two fighters had one of the best brawls of 2008, a fight in which Cunningham threw everything he had at Adamek, yet a fight in which it was Adamek's single-punch power that made the difference. Three times, Adamek knocked Cunningham down, which in turn helped give Adamek the margin of victory.

Cunningham was also knocked down the rungs of the ladder. He had to fight his way back to another title shot, winning a decision over Wayne Braithwaite in Florida in July 2009. Nearly a year later, he was back in Europe, beating Troy Ross for a belt in Germany, then returning to that country three more times, outpointing Enad Licina and then losing both a six-round technical decision and a 12-round unanimous decision to Yoan Pablo Hernandez.

Europe was where cruiserweights could thrive. He was done with both, though, and came back this year to fighting in the United States, fighting as a heavyweight, fighting in September in the Prudential Center and winning his debut in that division with a decision over lower-tier opponent Jason Gavern.

That ultimately helped earn him a rematch with Adamek, whose promoter, Main Events, had been airing cards on cable on the NBC Sports Network and was to be broadcasting a show in front of a potentially significantly larger audience on NBC.

It was an audience that saw Cunningham win, and then saw him lose.

It was far from the first boxing match to end

controversially. He was far from the first fighter to feel he was robbed.

That means little to a man who just experienced it.

"This ain't just a sport. This is a way of life," he said afterward. "I got dented bones from fights. You know what I'm saying? Fighters get hurt. Fighters get killed. Fighters get put in comas, to be out here to perform for you guys and then get cheated."

This is the heartbreak of Steve Cunningham. He was not knocked down. He was not badly hurt. But he was not the winner. And no matter how much others tell him that he should have been, no matter how much or how well he pleads for the sport to do him right, he knows that it will not.

After all the punches, the most damage just might be that done to his career.

In 2012, Performance Enhancing Drug Speculation Became Suspicion
December 31, 2012

Manny Pacquiao had not yet even been resuscitated from unconsciousness before boxing fans and observers began to speculate about what put him there.

And in their minds, it wasn't just Juan Manuel Marquez.

To them, it was a Marquez who looked better at 143 pounds than his body had ever appeared in three other fights at or slightly above the junior welterweight limit. It was also a Marquez who not only knocked Pacquiao out with a perfect punch, but also had knocked him down earlier in the fight with a single shot.

It was the fact that Marquez's strength and conditioning coach had admittedly been involved with distributing steroids and other performance enhancing drugs.

It was the fact that this had been a year in which several notable fighters had tested positive for performance enhancing drugs. People questioned Marquez even though he passed the tests he took — not just because of the Pacquiao knockout and not just because of his strength and conditioning coach — but also because the testing done in boxing still lags behind where it should be in order to ensure that others aren't also using banned substances.

This was the year that speculation became suspicion.

This is because of Lamont Peterson and Andre Berto, because of Antonio Tarver and Erik Morales. Other noteworthy fighters either had tested positive for or been implicated in using performance enhancing substances in the past, including Evander Holyfield, Jameel McCline, Shane Mosley, James Toney and Fernando Vargas. But these four positive tests in particular in 2012 were highly publicized, with two of them leading to major bouts being canceled.

Peterson's team has argued that the boxer's use of synthetic testosterone was for legitimate medical reasons. Berto's camp has claimed that the fighter took a tainted supplement. Morales, meanwhile, blamed tainted beef. But a decade after the window into baseball's steroid problem was first cracked open — and with the countless positive tests that have come since in various sports, and the countless explanations and excuses that have been given for them — the sporting world has become understandably skeptical.

In this post-BALCO, post-Lance Armstrong world, we are long past the days in which someone can claim that they are clean solely because they have passed drug tests.

But we still cannot conclude, without a doubt, that an athlete is dirty unless he has been caught cheating — or named, as with Holyfield, Mosley and McCline, as being clients of companies that distributed these drugs.

That leaves us speculating about the depth of the problem.

That leaves us suspicious about our sport.

It is difficult enough to get Major League Baseball to properly police itself. Though players are still being caught under the league's testing program, it can easily be argued that those caught are the ones who do not know how to beat a system that still is nowhere near as stringent as it could be and should be.

It is even harder to get those who regulate the Sweet

Science to get better policies in place regarding a more shadowy science.

There is no single league — no one body that oversees all of the fights and all of the fighters, no single body that takes in all of the revenue. We are left with athletic commissions in every state, and even tribal commissions with different rules. We are left with various promoters, who are more interested in cleaning up at the box office than they are in cleaning up the sport.

It will take a lot to clean up boxing.

Regulating combat sports can be like regulating business. Promoters, like companies, will go to where it is easier and more profitable to put on a fight. State athletic commissions are left in a conflicted position of striving to oversee that which goes on within their jurisdictions, while also needing big boxing cards to go on in order to support their operations.

Money is the answer. Money is also the problem.

For athletic commissions to expand the scope of their testing — more fighters tested, more testing done, more substances tested for — they will need more money from the boxers and promoters.

Only a small handful of boxing matches have gone on with the stringent testing seen by many as the standard by which the sport should follow. And even that agency — the Voluntary Anti-Doping Association — absorbed the price of testing earlier this year for the canceled Andre Berto-Victor Ortiz rematch and for year-round testing for Nonito Donaire. Those costs were covered through donations to the nonprofit.

The U.S. Anti-Doping Agency also has been involved with drug testing for recent boxing matches, particularly for Golden Boy Promotions in the wake of a pair of

Golden Boy fights being canceled after Peterson and Berto tested positive under VADA.

In lieu of sanctioning bodies being willing or being able to do better drug testing, we are left with outside agencies that are brought in only when the boxers can afford it (sometimes with assistance) or when the promoters pay for it. Yet that leaves large gaps, and not just with the sheer number of major matches that still go on without stringent drug testing.

The nature of drug testing becomes something discussed in — and delayed due to —prolonged negotiations.

And state athletic commissions have not shown the best track record for dealing with the terms of testing done by these independent agencies.

California relicensed Berto, who failed a VADA test, but suspended Tarver, who failed a state test. And the New York State Athletic Commission allowed the rematch between Danny Garcia and Erik Morales to go forward despite the late revelation that Morales had been positive for clenbuterol under USADA's testing. That bout should have been called off, or held up, until the commission had held a full hearing — Morales may have deserved a chance to explain his case, but he should not have been licensed to fight until the commission had issued a ruling.

Promoters, meanwhile, are not going to invest in something that not only would cost them for testing, but also could cost them if they cancel an entire card should a main event boxer come up positive.

Nor will they be forced to adapt. Major League Baseball's executives were called before Congress years ago, told either to clean up their own sport or have the federal government do it for them.

That won't happen in boxing.

That leaves us uncertain about our fighters. There aren't always going to be telling statistical surges that can only be explained by illicit measures — a fighter using performance enhancing drugs isn't necessarily going to score more knockouts the way that a batter might hit more home runs.

But we're also not naïve. We know that athletes in all sports are finding ways to cheat the system. And we know that boxing is no different.

We just don't know how bad boxing has it.

We do know that we won't know until boxing fixes itself.